JOURNALISM
ETHICS

4th Edition

JOURNALISM
ETHICS

A Casebook of Professional
Conduct for News Media

Revised by Fred Brown and other
members of the SPJ Ethics Committee

Marion Street Press
Portland, Oregon

Published by Marion Street Press
4207 SE Woodstock Blvd # 168
Portland, OR 97206-6267
USA
http://www.marionstreetpress.com/

Orders and desk copies: (800) 888-4741

Printed in the United States of America

ISBN 978-1-933338-80-4

Cover art direction by Nicky Ip

"Reporting by TV Docs in Haiti Raises Ethical Issues " Dr. Tom Linden, *Electronic News* (Volume 4 and Issue 2) p. 5, copyright © 2010 by SAGE Publications. Reprinted by Permission of SAGE Publications.

Library of Congress Cataloging-in-Publication Data

Journalism ethics : a casebook of professional conduct for news media / edited by Fred Brown and the SPJ Ethics Committee. -- 4th ed.
        p. cm.
   Rev. ed. of : Doing ethics in journalism / Jay Black, Bob Steele, Ralph Barney, 3rd ed. c1999.
    ISBN 978-1-933338-80-4 (pbk.)
    1. Journalistic ethics--United States--Handbooks, manuals, etc. 2. Journalistic ethics-- United States--Case studies--Handbooks, manuals, etc. I. Brown, Fred, 1940- II. Black, Jay Doing ethics in journalism. III. Society of Professional Journalists (U.S.)
    PN4888.E8J675 2011
    174'.9097--dc22
                                        2011000985

Acknowledgments

This handbook on journalism ethics was first proposed in 1987 by Carolyn Carlson, past president of the Society of Professional Journalists and chair of the SPJ Ethics Committee. The committee's vice chair, Dan Bolton, coordinated fund-raising and publishing efforts of the project. The book first appeared in 1993 as a Society of Professional Journalists publication.

The original authors, whose work still comprises the largest part of this fourth edition, are Jay Black, professor emeritus at the University of South Florida; Bob Steele of the Poynter Institute and DePauw University; and Ralph Barney, professor emeritus at Brigham Young University. Their checklists of ethical questions, for example, are included for all of the major categories of ethical scenarios. The revisions and additions to this fourth edition would not have been possible without the foundations laid by these three outstanding media ethicists and their continuing support.

Originally intended primarily as a handbook for newsrooms, the book was revised for publication as a textbook by Allyn & Bacon in 1995. The Society of Professional Journalists reclaimed the copyright in 2006 and soon thereafter, Howard Dubin, longtime treasurer of the Sigma Delta Chi Foundation, and Gordon "Mac" McKerral, former president of SPJ, proposed that it was time to revise the book.

Fred Brown, a former SPJ president and former chair of its ethics committee, led the editing and proofreading team. Other editors included McKerral, who teaches at Western Kentucky University; Elizabeth K. Hansen, Eastern Kentucky University; Jerry Dunklee, Southern Connecticut State University; Mike Farrell, University of Kentucky; Sara Stone, Baylor University; and Nerissa Young, Marshall University. Jane Kirtley, Silha Professor of Media Ethics and Law at the University of Minnesota, generously contributed the chapter on ethics and the law.

Financial and logistical support for this project was provided by the Sigma Delta Chi Foundation, Indianapolis. Michael Bugeja of Iowa State University helped prepare a prospectus for the book and provided guidance about what makes it stand out from the field.

More than half the case studies in this book are new, researched and written by members of the SPJ Ethics Committee. Sara Stone recruited a number of her Baylor University students to work on scenarios; they included Laura Barth, Brittainy Daniels, Amber Orand, Robbie Rogers and Elizabeth Suggs. Other ethics committee members who contributed case studies are Fred Brown, adjunct instructor in ethics at the University of Denver; Casey Bukro, recently retired from the *Chicago Tribune*; Irwin Gratz of Maine Public Radio, Portland, Maine; Elizabeth K. Hansen of Eastern Kentucky University, Richmond, Kentucky; Jim Pumarlo, media consultant and former editor of *The Red Wing Republican Eagle* in Minnesota; Adrian Uribarri of the *Orlando* (Florida) *Sentinel*; and Nerissa Young of Marshall University, Huntington, West Virginia. Contributors to Appendix A, a discussion of the sections of the SPJ Code of Ethics, were Peter Sussman, a freelance writer and author from Berkeley, Calif.; Paul LaRocque, a veteran newspaper editor and journalism educator from Arlington, Texas; and the previously mentioned Bukro, Dunklee and Brown. Former ethics committee chair, Andy Schotz of the *Herald-Mail*, Hagerstown, Maryland, assigned and coordinated case studies.

The editors also wish to thank the journalism organizations that gave specific permission to quote from their codes of ethics and principles, including: the Association of Food Journalists, American Society of News Editors, Associated Press Managing Editors, *Denver Post, Detroit Free Press*, KHON-TV (Honolulu), *Montreal Gazette, Norfolk Virginian-Pilot, Philadelphia Inquirer*, Public Broadcasting Service, *Racine (*Wisconsin*) Journal-Times, San Jose Mercury News, Sarasota Herald-Tribune*, Society of American Travel Writers and *Washington Post*.

The editors would also like to thank Jim Schuette and Kel Winter of Marion Street Press for the editing, publishing and marketing work for this new edition.

Contents

Introduction

This ethics primer for journalism students and practicing journalists went through three editions with the name *Doing Ethics*. Its authors, Jay Black, Bob Steele and Ralph Barney, used that technique — teaching ethics as a craft and a skill — in their classrooms and at the Poynter Institute in Fort Lauderdale, Florida, a media center where all three also taught. That philosophy still infuses all of this book, a testament to their hard work. This new edition has a new name because it is now broader in scope, incorporating a brief history of ethical thinking and language, a discussion of what differentiates legal from ethical issues, as well as a new tool for analyzing ethical dilemmas.

This fourth edition comes at a time when serious journalism is challenged by heightened technologies and relaxed standards. Technology has brought us round-the-clock news on cable television, cell phones with cameras and an overwhelming number of individualized websites where seekers of information — or affirmation — can find virtually anything they want.

With so many media outlets competing for attention, there's a tendency to emphasize quantity over quality, to not be quite so strict about what meets long-established standards for broadcast or publication. Managers at news outlets say they will no longer "lecture" to their audiences; now it's time to have a "conversation."

Journalists may be trying too hard to be accommodating, and this can only diminish the traditional media's voice of authority. It may also allow the media to become less aggressive and more passive. Let the readers and viewers decide. We'll do what they want.

This is not a good outcome.

Mainstream media will survive only if they insist on providing accurate, reliable and fair information. Let others give readers what they want to see. The ethical journalist's duty is to give them information they need to make sound decisions — information that may challenge assumptions rather than simply affirm prejudices. That sense of responsibility is what divides an ethical journalist from a careless polemicist.

This handbook will help journalists reinforce that sense of responsibility, and students to develop that sense. About half of the case studies in the book are from the past three or four years. Others are older, but the lessons they provide are timeless.

The book contains a new template for analyzing ethics cases. Some of the new cases are outlined in that format. Others are left for students and their instructors, especially, to parse into the various components of the new format, if they choose. This fourth edition also contains a new chapter explaining how ethical obligations may differ from legal obligations.

The book is organized around the Society of Professional Journalists' code of ethics, an industry standard last updated in 1996. It has held up remarkably well over the years, because it's a set of guiding principles, not a rule book of particulars.

Unlike media employers' codes of ethics, the SPJ code is entirely voluntary. It has no enforcement provisions. It provides a framework for evaluating ethical behavior, emphasizing the need to ask the right questions. Most ethical questions do not have a single, simple answer. Different people evaluating the same situation may very well arrive at different decisions.

There are inevitable conflicts in the code: The overriding need to "Seek Truth and Report It" is often at odds with the desire to "Minimize Harm." The need to "Act Independently," rejecting favors and obligations that might compromise impartiality, seems to be at odds with the directive to "Be Accountable." And yet, the conflicts in fact establish a framework for creative argument and resolution of ethics disputes.

The code urges that journalists understand and take responsibility for the consequences of their actions. But, as a voluntary compact, it has no enforcement provision. Accountability for journalists, we believe, is best regulated through other journalists' sensitivity to, and disclosure of, unethical behavior. Disclosure, not sanction, is the journalists' enforcement tool.

And accuracy, reliability and fairness are the keys to ethical journalism in an environment where this poor, battered profession is increasingly seen as unethical or, worse, irrelevant.

Additional Resources:

The Society of Professional Journalists, through its very active and geographically widespread ethics committee, continually offers new ethics-related educational materials, including case studies, through its website (www.spj.org). Related content on the Web also includes a weblog, "Code Words," that students, their professors and working journalists can access for online discussions.

PART ONE

JOURNALISM ETHICS

1

Ethical Thinking: History and Definitions

I t is indeed quite possible to be an ethical person without knowing any of the history or terminology of moral reasoning. The most exemplary ethical people are, after all, those who have excellent instincts about what's right and wrong. But it can be useful to have at least some grounding in the evolution of thought that has led us to where we are today.

And where we are is not a particularly good place to be. As communicators, we may not always practice the best ethics. Journalism, in fact, finds itself spending an increasing and regrettable amount of time identifying and apologizing for its ethical lapses. This increased sensitivity and attention to ethics is a hopeful sign. At least all of this self-criticism serves to illustrate that responsible journalists, and other communicators, do have standards and moral codes, and that they find deviation from those standards unacceptable.

Ethical questions surround us on all sides. Consider: Do I have an ethical obligation to report my roommate's marijuana use to campus authorities? What is the proper relationship between a reporter and a source? When is it permissible to use deception in collecting information for a story? Should I cross a striking clerical union's picket line to attend class? When does a woman's right to control her own destiny trump her unborn child's right to life? What do I do if I think a colleague is fabricating information in his reporting?

Some of these ethical dilemmas are easier to answer than others. Most of us probably know what we would do, and maybe even could explain *why* we would do what we do. But it helps to know the fundamentals of moral theory so that we can compare our thinking with others who have established long-lasting ethical principles.

In the most basic terms, the best way to arrive at an ethical decision is to **ask the right questions**. If you can do that, and if your answers to those questions make sense to you — and if you can then explain your reasoning sensibly to other people — you've done what you need to do to reach a sound, defensible ethical decision. That's true even if someone else, given the same set of circumstances, may arrive at the opposite decision and consider it just as defensible.

Along the way to reasoning through a problem, it helps to know the terminology. For instance, there is a subtle but significant difference between morals and ethics. Morals comprise a system of *beliefs*. Ethics is a way to employ those beliefs in the process of *reasoning*. One *acts* ethically from a moral *foundation*.

Jay Black and Jennings Bryant described the difference concisely in their *Introduction to Media Communications* (from the Fourth Edition, Brown and Benchmark, 1995, pp. 540–541):

> Ask a layperson what he or she means by ethics or morality, and you're likely to hear that these subjects deal with the nature of human values and moral conscience, of choosing and following the "right" rather than the "wrong," and of understanding and applying standards that have been set down by a group, association or community. These definitions are useful for openers, but our fuller understanding of the issues … might be better based on some of the insights and definitions posed by philosophers over the ages.
>
> *Ethics* is based on the Greek word *ethos*, meaning character, or what a good person is or does in order to have a good character. In general, ethics deals with the philosophical foundations of decision making, of choosing among the good and bad options that one faces. *Morality*, on the other hand, comes from the Latin *mores*, and refers to the way or manner in which people behave. Thus *morality* has come to mean socially approved customs, or the *practice* or application of ethics. (One easy way to remember the distinction, according to a philosopher with a sense of humor, is to think of ethics as behavior that occurs about the neck, and morality as behavior that occurs below the neck!)
>
> Ethics, in short, may be seen as being concerned with that which holds society together or provides the stability and security essential to the living of human life. Ethics as a branch of philosophy involves thinking about morality, moral problems and moral judgments. It deals with "owes" and "oughts,"

what obligations we owe or to responsibilities we have toward our fellow humans, what we "should do" to make the world a better place. It is unlike law, which is a bottom-line, minimalistic enterprise that tells us what we *can* do or what we *can* get away with.

Understanding the Context of Moral Reasoning

Metaethics is the study of the very nature of ethics. It deals with the meaning of abstractions such as "good" or "justice." It distinguishes between true ethical problems and simple matters of taste, for example. It's nonjudgmental; a field of inquiry, not a decision-making process.

Normative ethics is the next step in this three-part continuum and is concerned with developing rules and principles for moral conduct as well as general theories of ethics. It's based on society's fundamental *norms* for good behavior (thus *normative*) and has a great deal to do with duty. An example of normative ethics: Don't lie even to get a good story.

Applied ethics is the problem-solving step. It provides road maps, using the rules of normative ethics as a guide, that show how to arrive at a defensible solution to an ethical problem. It's what students study in ethics classes.

Why Study Ethics?

The goals of learning ethics are to:

1. Stimulate your moral imagination and awareness of the consequences of your behavior.
2. Recognize ethical issues and anticipate possible dilemmas.
3. Develop your analytical skills through case studies and classroom discussions and role playing.
4. Enhance your sense of moral obligation and personal responsibility.
5. Learn to respect other points of view and tolerate disagreement.

Sources of Our Values

Our innate moral values, the places from which we begin to develop personal standards, come from several sources.

- Our **parents,** or the people who nurtured us in their homes as we were developing into adults, are probably our most important examples. We tend to behave the way they behaved, giving us a sense of right and wrong, offering rewards and punishment.
- **Peer groups** exert enormous pressure to conform. We encounter them at work, in schools, churches, social groups and among our neighbors. Peer groups are particularly influential during the adolescent years. This enormous pressure can drive us away from the best moral choices, but it also can be a force for good.

- **Role models** are like that, too — sometimes good, sometimes not so good. A coach, a teacher or an editor can be a good role model; a Hollywood celebrity with repeated unsuccessful encounters with drug rehabilitation can be the worst sort of example to follow.
- **Institutions** also give us values. Journalism as an institution has a different set of values than, say, religion. Religion is based on faith. Journalists are always questioning, skeptical, often negative.

A Brief History

The study of ethics can be traced back 2,500 years to Socrates, who traveled throughout Greece asking questions. He wanted the people he engaged in these conversations to think about why they were doing what they were doing, and to probe deeper and more broadly about concepts such as goodness and justice. The Socratic method, the constant testing of ideas through a progressive series of questions and answers, is essential to ethical decision-making,

Socrates (circa 470–399 B.C.E.) is not credited with developing any particular philosophical system, but his method, the "Socratic dialogue," is the foundation for the way of thinking that led to everything else. He believed that anyone, given time to think and question, could gain insight into universally accepted rules of moral conduct.

His protégé and disciple, **Plato** (circa 428–348 B.C.E.), expanded on Socrates' delving into the nature of such universal moral values as goodness and justice. He argued that justice is achieved through *wisdom*, consisting of a person's experience and knowledge of the world; *moderation* of thought and behavior in striving to reach sound ethical decisions; and *courage* in living up to and defending those decisions. He believed that "good" was an enduring value and that a moral person may sometimes have to defy current standards of what's moral to achieve a higher good.

Aristotle (384–322 B.C.E.), who studied under Plato for many years, is given credit for developing the clearest articulation of *virtue ethics*, which is the overarching concept and logical evolution of the thinking of the three ancient Greek philosophers. The idea is that a virtuous person will do the right thing primarily because he or she is of good character, someone whose instincts tend toward universal ideas of justice.

Using Moral Theory

In the broadest of terms, moral theories are of three types:

Deontological, or duty-based, in which the moral agent's motives are more important than the outcome.

Teleological, which emphasizes the consequences of one's actions, and

Virtue ethics, focusing more on good character than on moral behavior.

Virtue Ethics

Aristotle's **golden mean** theory holds that virtue, in most cases, is somewhere between the extremes. The ideal falls between doing nothing and doing too much, between overachieving and underachieving, between excess and deficiency. In contemporary journalism, the golden mean most often comes down to finding a balance between telling the truth and minimizing harm. Telling the truth can cause great discomfort to some people, adding to the grief of the bereaved, even ruining the careers of public officials or business executives.

Minimizing harm doesn't mean avoiding the truth because it may hurt, but it does at least require that a moral person understand what the consequences of his or her actions may be. The "golden mean" may also be defined as the middle path that achieves the best balance among possible outcomes. It's rarely a 50-50 balance, though, and some things are always wrong. "The very names of some things imply evil," Aristotle himself wrote, "for example, the emotions of spite, shamelessness and envy, and such actions as adultery, theft and murder."

The golden mean is rather like the *golden rule*, which is a fundamental creed of the **Judeo-Christian** ethic. "Love thy neighbor as thyself," it says. Remember that everyone — rich or poor, famous or forgotten — is as deserving of respect and fair treatment as you are. Treat them all the way you would want to be treated. Historically, it's the next significant development of moral theory after Aristotle's enduring work. It is equally as enduring and perhaps even easier to comprehend.

Deontology — Duty-Based Ethics

Perhaps a harsher version of the golden rule is Immanuel Kant's **categorical imperative**. Kant (1724–1804) was one of the most important figures of the 18th century intellectual movement known as the Enlightenment. His imperative holds that an ethical person should never do anything that he or she would not want to see applied as a universal standard of behavior. It's less forgiving in nature than the basic concept of the golden rule.

While the Judeo-Christian ethic elevates the dignity of all as an end in itself, Kant believed in following standards of behavior simply because they are good standards, not because of the consequences. He puts duty above all. A thinker more attuned to *teleology*, believing the ends justify the means, would argue that Robin Hood was good because he stole from the rich only to give to the poor. A deontologist like Kant would say Robin Hood was wrong to steal, never mind what he did with the loot.

Several Teleological Theories

Utilitarianism holds that the best ethical decision is that which produces the greatest good for the greatest number. It is one of the major systems of ethics and is important to journalists, who often argue that what they have reported is for the greater good of society. Kant would ask if your intentions were good; if you were pursuing a cause that is just. The proponents of utilitarianism, chief among them John Stuart Mill (1806–1873) and Jeremy Bentham (1748–1832), would ask how many people are going to benefit from your actions. Today's practitioners would add that you should not forget the animals, either, or the planet.

Relativism is the anti-Kant school of thought that arose in the late 19th and early 20th centuries. If Kant was an absolutist, obsessed with duty, thinkers such as Bertrand Russell (1872–1970) and John Dewey (1859–1952) were moral libertarians. Essentially, they said the moral thing to do depends on one's point of view. "You decide what's right for you; I'll decide what's right for me." They will not pass judgment on the decisions of others. Critics say it can lead to anarchy, a way to justify whatever you feel like doing.

Egalitarianism embodies the idea that all individuals deserve equal treatment; minorities, and minority viewpoints, should be given exactly the same consideration as the majority — at least at the beginning of one's consideration of an ethical dilemma. Philosopher John Rawls (1921–2002) said this "original position" should occur behind a "veil of ignorance" in which one sets aside any preconceptions he or she may have established from parents, peer groups or institutions.

Ideally, everyone affected by the decision would enjoy an equal outcome; there should be no double standards. Rawls does concede, however, that there can be morally defensible reasons for an outcome that hurts some more than others. This is something journalists have to think about all the time — yes, minimize the harm that may come from your news coverage, but recognize that you can't totally avoid it.

— Fred Brown, SPJ Ethics Committee

Professional Journalism Organizations' Codes of Ethics

Society of Professional Journalists (adopted 1996)

Preamble

Members of the Society of Professional Journalists believe that public enlightenment is the forerunner of justice and the foundation of democracy. The duty of the journalist is to further those ends by seeking truth and providing a fair and comprehensive account of events and issues. Conscientious journalists from all media and specialties strive to serve the public with thoroughness and honesty. Professional integrity is the cornerstone of a journalist's credibility. Members of the Society share a dedication to ethical behavior and adopt this code to declare the Society's principles and standards of practice.

Seek Truth and Report It

Journalists should be honest, fair and courageous in gathering, reporting and interpreting information.

Journalists should:

- Test the accuracy of information from all sources and exercise care to avoid inadvertent error. Deliberate distortion is never permissible.
- Diligently seek out subjects of news stories to give them the opportunity to respond to allegations of wrongdoing.
- Identify sources whenever feasible. The public is entitled to as much information as possible on sources' reliability.
- Always question sources' motives before promising anonymity. Clarify conditions attached to any promise made in exchange for information. Keep promises.
- Make certain that headlines, news teases and promotional material, photos, video, audio, graphics, sound bites and quotations do not misrepresent. They should not oversimplify or highlight incidents out of context.
- Never distort the content of news photos or video. Image enhancement for technical clarity is always permissible. Label montages and photo illustrations.
- Avoid misleading re-enactments or staged news events. If re-enactment is necessary to tell a story, label it.
- Avoid undercover or other surreptitious methods of gathering information except when traditional open methods will not yield information vital to the public.

- Use of such methods should be explained as part of the story.
- Never plagiarize.
- Tell the story of the diversity and magnitude of the human experience boldly, even when it is unpopular to do so.
- Examine their own cultural values and avoid imposing those values on others.
- Avoid stereotyping by race, gender, age, religion, ethnicity, geography, sexual orientation, disability, physical appearance or social status.
- Support the open exchange of views, even views they find repugnant.
- Give voice to the voiceless; official and unofficial sources of information can be equally valid.
- Distinguish between advocacy and news reporting. Analysis and commentary should be labeled and not misrepresent fact or context.
- Distinguish news from advertising and shun hybrids that blur the lines between the two.
- Recognize a special obligation to ensure that the public's business is conducted in the open and that government records are open to inspection.

Minimize Harm

Ethical journalists treat sources, subjects and colleagues as human beings deserving of respect.

Journalists should:

- Show compassion for those who may be affected adversely by news coverage. Use special sensitivity when dealing with children and inexperienced sources or subjects.
- Be sensitive when seeking or using interviews or photographs of those affected by tragedy or grief.
- Recognize that gathering and reporting information may cause harm or discomfort. Pursuit of the news is not a license for arrogance.
- Recognize that private people have a greater right to control information about themselves than do public officials and others who seek power, influence or attention.
- Only an overriding public need can justify intrusion into anyone's privacy.
- Show good taste. Avoid pandering to lurid curiosity.
- Be cautious about identifying juvenile suspects or victims of sex crimes.
- Be judicious about naming criminal suspects before the formal filing of charges.
- Balance a criminal suspect's fair trial rights with the public's right to be informed.

Act Independently

Journalists should be free of obligation to any interest other than the public's right to know.

Journalists should:

- Avoid conflicts of interest, real or perceived.
- Remain free of associations and activities that may compromise integrity or damage credibility.
- Refuse gifts, favors, fees, free travel and special treatment, and shun secondary employment, political involvement, public office and service in community organizations if they compromise journalistic integrity.
- Disclose unavoidable conflicts.
- Be vigilant and courageous about holding those with power accountable.
- Deny favored treatment to advertisers and special interests and resist their pressure to influence news coverage.
- Be wary of sources offering information for favors or money; avoid bidding for news.

Be Accountable

Journalists are accountable to their readers, listeners, viewers and each other.

Journalists should:

- Clarify and explain news coverage and invite dialogue with the public over journalistic conduct.
- Encourage the public to voice grievances against the news media.
- Admit mistakes and correct them promptly.
- Expose unethical practices of journalists and the news media.
- Abide by the same high standards to which they hold others.

Radio Television Digital News Association *(adopted 2000)*

PREAMBLE

Professional electronic journalists should operate as trustees of the public, seek the truth, report it fairly and with integrity and independence, and stand accountable for their actions.

PUBLIC TRUST: Professional electronic journalists should recognize that their first obligation is to the public.

Professional electronic journalists should:

- Understand that any commitment other than service to the public undermines trust and credibility.

- Recognize that service in the public interest creates an obligation to reflect the diversity of the community and guard against oversimplification of issues or events.
- Provide a full range of information to enable the public to make enlightened decisions.
- Fight to ensure that the public's business is conducted in public.

TRUTH: Professional electronic journalists should pursue truth aggressively and present the news accurately, in context, and as completely as possible.
Professional electronic journalists should:

- Continuously seek the truth.
- Resist distortions that obscure the importance of events.
- Clearly disclose the origin of information and label all material provided by outsiders.

Professional electronic journalists should not:

- Report anything known to be false.
- Manipulate images or sounds in any way that is misleading.
- Plagiarize.
- Present images or sounds that are re-enacted without informing the public.

FAIRNESS: Professional electronic journalists should present the news fairly and impartially, placing primary value on significance and relevance.
Professional electronic journalists should:

- Treat all subjects of news coverage with respect and dignity, showing particular compassion to victims of crime or tragedy.
- Exercise special care when children are involved in a story and give children greater privacy protection than adults.
- Seek to understand the diversity of their community and inform the public without bias or stereotype.
- Present a diversity of expressions, opinions, and ideas in context.
- Present analytical reporting based on professional perspective, not personal bias.
- Respect the right to a fair trial.

INTEGRITY: Professional electronic journalists should present the news with integrity and decency, avoiding real or perceived conflicts of interest, and respect the dignity and intelligence of the audience as well as the subjects of news.

Professional electronic journalists should:

- Identify sources whenever possible. Confidential sources should be used only when it is clearly in the public interest to gather or convey important information or when a person providing information might be harmed. Journalists should keep all commitments to protect a confidential source.
- Clearly label opinion and commentary.
- Guard against extended coverage of events or individuals that fails to significantly advance a story, place the event in context, or add to the public knowledge.
- Refrain from contacting participants in violent situations while the situation is in progress.
- Use technological tools with skill and thoughtfulness, avoiding techniques that skew facts, distort reality, or sensationalize events.
- Use surreptitious newsgathering techniques, including hidden cameras or microphones, only if there is no other way to obtain stories of significant public importance and only if the technique is explained to the audience.
- Disseminate the private transmissions of other news organizations only with permission.

Professional electronic journalists should not:

- Pay news sources who have a vested interest in a story.
- Accept gifts, favors, or compensation from those who might seek to influence coverage.
- Engage in activities that may compromise their integrity or independence.

INDEPENDENCE: Professional electronic journalists should defend the independence of all journalists from those seeking influence or control over news content.

Professional electronic journalists should:

- Gather and report news without fear or favor, and vigorously resist undue influence from any outside forces, including advertisers, sources, story subjects, powerful individuals, and special interest groups.
- Resist those who would seek to buy or politically influence news content or who would seek to intimidate those who gather and disseminate the news.
- Determine news content solely through editorial judgment and not as the result of outside influence.
- Resist any self-interest or peer pressure that might erode journalistic duty and service to the public.

- Recognize that sponsorship of the news will not be used in any way to determine, restrict, or manipulate content.
- Refuse to allow the interests of ownership or management to influence news judgment and content inappropriately.
- Defend the rights of the free press for all journalists, recognizing that any professional or government licensing of journalists is a violation of that freedom.

ACCOUNTABILITY: Professional electronic journalists should recognize that they are accountable for their actions to the public, the profession, and themselves.

Professional electronic journalists should:

- Actively encourage adherence to these standards by all journalists and their employers.
- Respond to public concerns. Investigate complaints and correct errors promptly and with as much prominence as the original report.
- Explain journalistic processes to the public, especially when practices spark questions or controversy.
- Recognize that professional electronic journalists are duty-bound to conduct themselves ethically.
- Refrain from ordering or encouraging courses of action that would force employees to commit an unethical act.
- Carefully listen to employees who raise ethical objections and create environments in which such objections and discussions are encouraged.
- Seek support for and provide opportunities to train employees in ethical decision-making.

In meeting its responsibility to the profession of electronic journalism, RTD-NA has created this code to identify important issues, to serve as a guide for its members, to facilitate self-scrutiny, and to shape future debate.

National Press Photographers Association *(as of January 2011)*

Preamble

The National Press Photographers Association, a professional society that promotes the highest standards in visual journalism, acknowledges concern for every person's need both to be fully informed about public events and to be recognized as part of the world in which we live.

Visual journalists operate as trustees of the public. Our primary role is to report visually on the significant events and varied viewpoints in our common world. Our primary goal is the faithful and comprehensive depiction of the subject at hand. As visual journalists, we have the responsibility to document society and to preserve its history through images.

Photographic and video images can reveal great truths, expose wrongdoing and neglect, inspire hope and understanding and connect people around the globe through the language of visual understanding. Photographs can also cause great harm if they are callously intrusive or are manipulated.

This code is intended to promote the highest quality in all forms of visual journalism and to strengthen public confidence in the profession. It is also meant to serve as an educational tool both for those who practice and for those who appreciate photojournalism. To that end, The National Press Photographers Association sets forth the following.

Code of Ethics

Visual journalists and those who manage visual news productions are accountable for upholding the following standards in their daily work:

1. Be accurate and comprehensive in the representation of subjects.
2. Resist being manipulated by staged photo opportunities.
3. Be complete and provide context when photographing or recording subjects. Avoid stereotyping individuals and groups. Recognize and work to avoid presenting one's own biases in the work.
4. Treat all subjects with respect and dignity. Give special consideration to vulnerable subjects and compassion to victims of crime or tragedy. Intrude on private moments of grief only when the public has an overriding and justifiable need to see.
5. While photographing subjects do not intentionally contribute to, alter, or seek to alter or influence events.
6. Editing should maintain the integrity of the photographic images' content and context. Do not manipulate images or add or alter sound in any way that can mislead viewers or misrepresent subjects.
7. Do not pay sources or subjects or reward them materially for information or participation.
8. Do not accept gifts, favors, or compensation from those who might seek to influence coverage.
9. Do not intentionally sabotage the efforts of other journalists.

Ideally, visual journalists should:

1. Strive to ensure that the public's business is conducted in public. Defend the rights of access for all journalists.
2. Think proactively, as a student of psychology, sociology, politics and art to develop a unique vision and presentation. Work with a voracious appetite for current events and contemporary visual media.

3. Strive for total and unrestricted access to subjects, recommend alternatives to shallow or rushed opportunities, seek a diversity of viewpoints, and work to show unpopular or unnoticed points of view.

4. Avoid political, civic and business involvements or other employment that compromise or give the appearance of compromising one's own journalistic independence.

5. Strive to be unobtrusive and humble in dealing with subjects.

6. Respect the integrity of the photographic moment.

7. Strive by example and influence to maintain the spirit and high standards expressed in this code. When confronted with situations in which the proper action is not clear, seek the counsel of those who exhibit the highest standards of the profession. Visual journalists should continuously study their craft and the ethics that guide it.

Online News Association

OUR VISION

ONA is a leader in the rapidly changing world of journalism; a catalyst for innovation in story-telling across all platforms; a resource for journalists seeking guidance and growth, and a champion of best practices through training, awards and community outreach.

OUR VALUES

We believe that the Internet is the most powerful communications medium to arise since the dawn of television. As digital delivery systems become the primary source of news for a growing segment of the world's population, it presents complex challenges and opportunities for journalists as well as the news audience.

Editorial Integrity: The unique permeability of digital publications allows for the linking and joining of information resources of all kinds as intimately as if they were published by a single organization. Responsible journalism through this medium means that the distinction between news and other information must always be clear, so that individuals can readily distinguish independent editorial information from paid promotional information and other non-news.

Editorial Independence: Online journalists should maintain the highest principles of fairness, accuracy, objectivity and responsible independent reporting.

Journalistic Excellence: Online journalists should uphold traditional high principles in reporting original news for the Internet and in reviewing and corroborating information from other sources.

Freedom of Expression: The ubiquity and global reach of information published on the Internet offers new information and educational resources to a worldwide audience, access to which must be unrestricted.

Freedom of Access: News organizations reporting on the Internet must be afforded access to information and events equal to that enjoyed by other news organizations in order to further freedom of information.

Public Radio News Directors Inc.

Code of Ethics

Public Radio News Directors Inc. is committed to the highest standards of journalistic ethics and excellence. We must stand apart from pressures of politics and commerce as we inform and engage our listeners. We seek truth, and report with fairness and integrity.

Independence and integrity are the foundations of our service, which we maintain through these principles:

TRUTH

Journalism is the rigorous pursuit of truth. Its practice requires fairness, accuracy, and balance.

We strive to be comprehensive. We seek diverse points of view and voices to tell the stories of our communities.

FAIRNESS

Fairness is at the core of all good journalism.

We gather and report the news in context, with clarity and compassion.

We treat our sources and the public with decency and respect.

Our reporting is thorough, timely and avoids speculation.

INTEGRITY

The public's faith in our service rests on our integrity as journalists.

Editorial independence is required to ensure the integrity of our work.

We identify the differences between reporting and opinion.

We guard against conflicts of interest — real and perceived — that could compromise the credibility and independence of our reporting.

We are accountable when conflicts occur. We disclose any unavoidable conflicts of interest.

Ethical Decision-Making: Procedures

In today's saturated media environment, with so many technologies competing for information seekers' attention, successful media need a loyal base audience. Credibility is crucial to retaining those readers and viewers, and an ethical decision-making process is key to credibility.

Ideally, ethical questions should be discussed in groups. Much of ethical decision-making involves a back-and-forth testing of ideas. A lot of it is just good instinct. Newsrooms should have more ethical discussions, and those discussions would benefit from some input from outside the newsroom as well.

The process outlined below is based on several models, including those developed by Bernard Gert of Dartmouth College and Louis Alvin Day of Louisiana State University. The important thing is to identify all pertinent facts and then — especially — to ask the right questions.

Most of the case studies in this book use this model. Others do not. Instructors may want to use those scenarios that do not follow this template to test their students' abilities to identify the elements of an ethical dilemma. The exercise that follows is based on a decision that was made by a Danish newspaper in 2006 and the furor that ensued.

WHAT: *Describe the situation. Assemble all relevant facts, list all the angles. In other words, do the reporting. Put the ethical dilemma in the form of a question; write it down to be sure it makes sense.*

For example, considering the furor over publication of caricatures of the Prophet Muhammad, assemble all pertinent facts:

- The original motivation for publication.
- Why it took so long after their initial appearance for the images to cause such a violent reaction.
- Differences of opinion in the Islamic community, including over whether any depiction of the Prophet is considered blasphemy.

Think of all the questions you can, and try to answer them. Boil it down to one basic question. Perhaps this one:

Question: Do we publish the cartoons or not?

WHO: *The principals (people) who will make the decision and those who will be affected by it. First, decide who is responsible for the decision. The managing editor? News director? Does this go all the way to the top? Then list the major stakeholders, ranging from the subjects of the story to the public. Remember that not everyone will be affected to the same degree by what you decide to do.*

The decision-maker here most likely would be at least at the managing editor level at a newspaper, perhaps the news director at a television station.

The stakeholders include the local Islamic community, Muslims around the world, people in places who may be targeted by riots, your newspaper or TV station and its reputation for truth-telling and fairness, and readers and viewers who have an interest in seeing what is driving such outrage. You may be able to think of others whose interest in the outcome of your decision should be considered.

WHY: *These are principles (standards) you will use in deciding what to do. In most cases, it comes down to a balance between telling the truth and minimizing possible harms. Identify these and other moral responsibilities. The best decision is the one that does the greatest good for the greatest number of stakeholders.*

Several principles are at issue in the case of the caricatures. Is it freedom of expression? Is it unnecessary provocation? Is there an acceptable middle ground between showing the blunt truth and minimizing the harm of insult?

Consider the principles that may have motivated the principals, and then consider your options. At the extremes, they could range from publishing all 12 cartoons on the front page or to show them with riot scenes on your newscast, to the other extreme of simply describing a couple of them. Or you could provide a link to a website where they could be viewed.

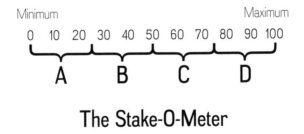

The Stake-O-Meter

HOW: *This is your decision: How do you achieve the outcome you've identified as the best? How do you answer the question you raised in the first step? Again, if you write it down, you will have a better idea of whether it makes sense. Also, write down your rationale, and consider making your decision-making part of your coverage. Articulating your reasoning will help you answer the questions you're bound to get.*

For example, you may begin simply by saying, "We decided to publish only one cartoon because ..." In this case, different media made different decisions. Whatever the decision, it's important to have a serious discussion and a good reason for it.

In attempting to arrive at an ethical decision, it's important to identify as many individuals, groups, businesses and institutions as you can that may be affected by your decision. It's important, too, to realize that not all of them are affected equally.

Think of this "Stake-O-Meter" as a Celsius thermometer. Some individuals with a minimum investment in the outcome will barely be affected by your story; others with a maximum involvement may reach the boiling point of stress.

That concept may run counter to the ideal of Egalitarianism, which holds that all individuals deserve equal treatment. But it runs closer to reality.

The consequences of publishing your story about official misfeasance, for example, will be the most severe for the official implicated — somewhere toward "D" on the scale above. Others in that official's department, as well as contractors, clients, etc., would not be quite as affected by the story, but still may fall at "C" or thereabouts.

In most stories, the public's stake in the outcome — the impact on your readers and viewers — is not all that great. It may be around "B" if the official's misconduct affected a public project or misused large amounts of tax dollars. If the unsavory activity were instead an interoffice exchange of suggestive e-mails, say, the public's investment in the outcome of the story would be very low, down toward "A."

As the publisher or broadcaster of the story, you have a stake, too. If the story has a major impact on improving public policy, for example, your reputation will soar. If it strikes the public as unfair, poorly researched and insufficiently supported by the facts, your reputation can suffer. In either case, your "stake" in the story is a fairly weighty one.

Consider Case Study 2: "A Congressman's Past," on pages 56–59. Three weeks before the 2004 election, *The (Portland) Oregonian* published a story about a sexual assault complaint filed against U.S. Rep. David Wu while he and the complainant were students at Stanford University, 28 years earlier. Neither the woman involved nor Wu wanted to talk about it; the newspaper assembled its 3,000-word story from other sources.

Clearly, Wu is the stakeholder who faces the most severe consequences from the story. And the woman involved, even though she was not named, is at the high end of the scale, too. But in this case, so is the newspaper. As the newspaper's public editor wrote, "Reader after reader raised questions about fairness, relevancy and timing" of the article.

It's important to caution that it's possible to put too much weight on the consequences for one individual. Typically, the number of people affected increases as the impact of the consequences decrease, with the largest number — the public — often the least seriously affected.

Thus, the ethical principle of utilitarianism, that the best decision is that which produces the greatest good for the greatest number, should enter into your reasoning, too.

2

The Role of the Journalist

With startling regularity, journalists and newsrooms find themselves vigorously discussing whether to run stories they know will cause a storm of discussion on talk shows and in the streets.

Debates rage over publishing unproven accusations of sexual improprieties against powerful figures (including several recent examples in the political world), or naming alleged rape complainants (as in the Kobe Bryant case) or juvenile offenders.

Questions swirl around whether public accusations of improprieties or other behavior that invade the privacy of a celebrity or a public figure should be plucked from tabloid newspapers and weblogs and given wider distribution in the "mainstream" press.

The questions may not be whether such stories should be published but how well journalists reason and explain decisions that cause obvious and grievous harm to an individual, even a public official.

Television talk shows inevitably pit defenders of publication against critics of the press. Unfortunately, the critics most often carry the day, correctly pointing to the harm. This happens largely because journalists and their defenders find it difficult to spell out clearly and convincingly why the media often have a moral obligation to publish such stories.

Rights versus Obligations

Defenders tend to speak of the *right* rather than the moral *obligation* to publish such material. It is as if insistent assertions of the right to publish would somehow turn away attacks and public outrage. The *right* to publish, granted by the First Amendment to the U.S. Constitution and confirmed by judicial decisions, is widely documented and discussed in civics classes and history lectures. But the *obligation* to distribute information, which resides in the soul of a journalistic ethic, is rarely discussed. It is the *why* of this process that demands articulation, so the public can understand and appreciate the journalist's motives for telling so much.

Journalists are often denounced and ridiculed for invoking First Amendment rights in their demands for access to sensitive information. They are bitterly criticized as they invade privacy in pursuit of information. The citizens' sense of justice often demands that journalists act differently. Journalists are accused of selfishly claiming special privileges for themselves while victimizing others, particularly in privacy invasions. Later in this book we explore cases in which journalists published the name of the benefactor of a city destroyed by floods who did not want to be identified publicly, published gory photographs of shooting and accident victims, and carried racist and homophobic language. Often, the strongest critics in such cases are those who feel threatened by media disclosures or practices, those who have a vested interest in passive media. These public people often try to convince the rest of the public, often successfully, that journalists are jackals. The grieving families of the victims and a brief FBI suspect in the Atlanta Olympics bombing, as well as many others, would agree.

The force and durability of the accusations cause the industry to smart. Journalists are jostled into introspection, asking whether traditional rules still apply and, in a complex world, what they *should* do to serve a critical society.

- Does ethics require publication or temporary withholding of names of suspects or other public figures named in police reports?
- Is it obligatory or optional to expose extramarital escapades and drug experimentation of political candidates, or are other issues more important and useful in the election process?
- What moral obligation requires a reporter to keep sources confidential, and when may those sources ethically be "burned"?
- Is it a moral obligation of journalists to detect and warn about impending disasters, and when is it acceptable to declare a consensus on such matters as the causes and effects of global warming?
- How can journalists balance their obligations to tell the truth, remain independent and minimize harm during — and after — such extraordinary crises as the September 11, 2001, terrorist attacks in New York City and Washington, D.C.?

News people increasingly are perplexed about how to handle problems that until recently seemed black and white.

Until the first Gulf War, combat had never been viewed live by both sides on a single commercial television outlet. Cable News Network kept the world informed, blow by blow. In other wars, the military generally has controlled the communications systems. Direct portable satellite transmission and cellular telephones allowed many journalists to bypass that control in the Gulf.

When rape and sexual attacks never got to court without evidence of a brutal assault, torn clothing, bruises, and evidence of resistance, the procedures for news coverage were clearly prescribed. In today's more sensitive society, ambiguities between accused and accuser make old coverage policies seem inadequate.

What moral burden rested on *The Seattle Times*, for example, to find provable truths before it published allegations of sexual harassment against a sitting U.S. senator, Brock Adams, particularly when a similar accusation had been investigated and dismissed by a government agency? By the same token, what allowed Oregon media, when confronted with repeated complaints about Sen. Robert Packwood's sexual harassment, to keep silent as he ran for re-election and largely deprived the state of his representation for two years while he tried to defend himself?

Can journalists argue that they ought not be expected to be so expert in finance that they could detect approaching financial disaster, such as the collapse of the dot-com boom or the 2009 recession, months or years before disaster struck?

When thousands of Los Angeles buildings were torched during riots that erupted after the controversial Rodney King verdict in 1992, what moral rules directed helicopter-borne camera operators to broadcast live picture showing where dangers lay or where there were no police? Such coverage provided sensitive information to two disparate groups — frightened citizens and marauders.

Complicating the journalist's mission are the public relations experts who make favorable information abundantly available while obscuring the trail to unfavorable information.

As these dilemmas arise, often requiring decisions on deadline, journalists must search beyond the dogma of news values and tradition for help. A critical tool in the search is a greater understanding of the ethical role a journalist plays in making the wheels of society turn and in keeping those wheels on.

Journalism is Different

The journalist's social role is critical, but often is not understood by the public and poorly explained by the profession. While most journalists talk about protections the Constitution and the courts offer them, few explain to critics and the public **why** society protects journalists. What are the foundations of the First Amendment and favorable court interpretations? *Seattle Times* executive editor Michael Fancher described the painstaking procedures *Times* staffers followed in assuring fairness in the case of former Sen. Brock Adams, accused of sexual improprieties by several women, yet Fancher still cited "traditional standards" to be met for publication. Recall for a moment the traditional standards for deciding what is news, standards you first learned in journalism school or on the job: conflict, novelty, prominence, proximity, impact, timeliness, etc. These traditional standards may be suitable for defining routine news coverage, but they have no ethical or philosophical foundation. In short, these definitions of newsworthiness are amoral. Relying upon them to defend yourself against an accusation of questionable ethics can't satisfy an intelligent critic. In fairness to *The Seattle Times*, we must add that its editorial staff did go beyond these minimalistic standards; many other journalists, however, never get that far.

Unlike other professionals who have institutionally defined social roles and ethics, journalists have been left to their own devices in working out their social roles and in determining their ethics and then in justifying those roles and ethics to the public.

> Journalists are not licensed, as are surgeons, nor are they hired, legitimized and controlled by government, as are generals.

Surgeons, in contrast, enjoy a clear mandate. It is unthinkable that most of us would pick up a knife and cut on a friend. Yet the surgeon has that specific moral charge: Inflict some pain and shed some blood, but be sure to bring more benefit than trauma to the patients. Thus, the surgeon has a role bestowed and protected by society: Shed blood for a greater good. Likewise, a military commander has a role that morally justifies sending people to their deaths and inflicting death on an enemy, presumably for a greater good.

While it is generally accepted that surgeons have a moral right to shed blood, and generals in certain circumstances may morally end the lives of human beings they do not know, it is more difficult to define the journalist's role.

Journalists are not licensed, as are surgeons, nor are they hired, legitimized and controlled by government, as are generals. Thus, individual journalists and the profession as a whole must work out their own role definitions according to (1) their perceptions of what society needs, and (2) an ethical recognition that Constitutional protection must not knowingly be socially destructive. Because it would be silly for society to protect a class of people who are hastening its destruction, it must be assumed that journalists bear a strong moral obligation to avoid conscious social damage.

A substantial amount of unjustifiable social damage can be avoided if journalists satisfy themselves that what they publish, however controversial it may be, has a high probability of being the truth. While truth is sometimes difficult to identify, the journalist nevertheless should generally err in favor of disclosure, rather than withhold information in cases in which probability of truth is high.

In a society that protects people who speak or write, any person (literate or illiterate, learned or ignorant, socialized or rebellious, passive or outraged) may become a journalist without standards imposed either by government or professional groups. Even regulation by society at large in the form of intimidating public opinion, while often formidable, are difficult to enforce because of the Bill of Rights. First Amendment protection slows suppression, even by the compelling power of public opinion, until society considers and discusses restrictions.

A big problem for journalists as they compare their duties with those of the surgeon and the general is that their discussions all too often begin by citing law rather than explaining the moral obligations that journalists are attempting to fulfill. Defenders talk of the *right* to publish, rather than the *reason* they publish. There is a tendency by journalists to wrongly assume the public understands the rationale behind First Amendment protections. Just as the public now questions basic assumptions about the environment and natural resources, so journalists are being pressed to answer basic questions about their function.

Journalists distribute information, a traditional role that often puts the journalist at odds with individuals and power brokers who want to keep power by controlling information.

The democratic principle supporting quality journalism has been expressed by philosopher Carl Friedrich. He wrote that since everyone is fallible in making decisions, society needs the collective judgments of many fallible people to produce valid social decisions and solve social problems. The journalist is the central figure in improving the odds that good decisions will be made. He or she provides key information that will assist the populace in giving informed consent to public proposals. Constantly opposing the journalists, for good reasons of their own, are those with competing, strong ideas about how the world should turn out and a corresponding commitment to promote their own agendas. Discouraging journalists from distributing contrary information is a common way true believers attempt to advance causes.

Because information helps ensure informed consent, the principle of open communication has a unique standing in American society. In that context, ethical reasoning requires a considerably different approach than is common in professional ethics. The First Amendment and subsequent court rulings give journalists unparalleled freedom to inform the fallible without government interference.

The conscientious journalist needs to deal with the moral question of social contract. In this case, it is a question of a journalist's contracts with an audience: What contract is created between me and my reader or viewer when that person buys my newspaper or spends time watching a newscast to which I contribute?

In a democratic society, the audience is expected to process a much broader range of information than in other cultures.

So, when we speak of journalism ethics, then, we speak not of regulated behavior, the phenomenon most familiar to us as we look at the activities of doctors, lawyers, plumbers and others who follow professional codes. In journalism, we speak of the far more important concepts of "reasoned" and "principled" behavior. Journalists must decide for themselves, rather than having others decide for them, what information they will distribute and what form that information will take. Even professional groups, without authority to keep journalists from practicing their craft, may not tell the journalist how to perform.

Most discussions of professional ethics imply the existence of documented restrictions on ethical behavior as a means to protect society. Such restrictions are expected to be universally accepted and mandatory. A free society, however, specifically rejects most speech and press restrictions. Therefore, mandatory standards for journalism are rightly unenforceable and unworkable. Judicial interpretations of the First Amendment consistently resist pressure to insist that journalists be licensed. Thus, anybody can be a journalist without fear of being prohibited from practicing the craft (or being de-pressed or excommunicated, if you would).

This absence of professional discipline makes journalistic codes, including the SPJ Code of Ethics, more advisory than mandatory. That is in sharp contrast to the enforceable codes of the legal and medical professions and a source of concern to those who see a need to "control" anyone who possesses the kind of power the media are perceived to have. But it also means that journalists, individually and collectively, have a greater need for an articulated sense of ethics than do the more regulated professions.

Into the Arena of Principle and Reason

Journalists should be aware of several propositions as they participate in principled and reasoned decision making. These propositions, abbreviated here, are expanded in other ethics publications, but they provide a starting place for someone working to understand the journalistic role.

First, society is committed to the possibility of the free flow of information as a means of (a) informing the population so its members may (b) make informed decisions, which (c) combine with thousands or millions of other decisions to (d) contribute to the strength of society or determine how society will treat its individual members.

Second, the journalistic mission is often obscured because information control is related to power. Distribution of information is a redistribution of power.

Thus, because the traditional function of the journalist is the distribution of information, the journalist is often at odds with individuals and entities wishing to retain power by controlling or withholding information.

Distribution of information can be a mixed bag. All information may help someone while at the same time harming others. Disclosure about nursing home abuses may benefit patients by improving care. It also reduces the power of nursing home operators, placed in a public spotlight, to control their own operations. Nursing home disclosures may also cause anxiety and even guilt feelings in families who comfortably assume family members in *all* nursing homes are receiving competent, caring treatment.

Surgeons cut people open, and generals commit lives to combat. Both life-and-death or pain-inflicting functions have strong public support. Journalists do their job by taking power from groups bent on retaining or accumulating it. They then redistribute power to the public by disseminating information. Brock Adams had the power to run again

> A society that trusts the media to keep it informed has mixed feelings about those media.

for the Senate, but *The Seattle Times* story gave the public information that diminished his power. The citizens of Washington, with more information, gained the power to decide whether Brock Adams should continue to hold public office.

The journalist is likely to be immersed in a variety of differing loyalties and ties that affect the pure gathering and distribution of information: the desire to win fame and fortune; biases for or against social institutions or individuals; conceptions about what a journalist or investigative reporter is, or does, etc. Such pressures may blunt the journalist's moral judgment, producing faulty journalistic decisions. The public then suffers from distorted information. Despite journalists' service to audiences, those largely defenseless and unorganized groups seldom express themselves. They contrast with special interest groups which, because they tend to be extremely vocal, create an impression of a public opinion outpouring. This book is concerned with giving voice to the voiceless, those who have minimal leverage or position in society. The voiceless can then air their views, along with the views of more vocal special interests, to produce legitimate public opinion, which in turn can be understood and enhanced by the news media. Communications media thus fulfill their basic functions of communicating — making experiences common or sharing information — and mediating — coming between and pulling together various interest groups.

A society that trusts the media to keep it informed has mixed feelings about those media. Minimizing harm while trying to keep audiences fully informed requires that journalists formulate justification mechanisms to defend publishing decisions. Those defenses must go beyond mere restatements of traditional journalistic rights or unquestioned institutional norms. They need to be articulated journalistic obligations.

Conclusion

In using this handbook, then, one must recognize the paramount importance of distributing information to a democratic society. Once that role is understood as a primary obligation, journalists can use moral reasoning and can follow principles, rather than routine and tradition, in making ethical decisions. Those decisions should support journalists' obligation to distribute necessary information fully — to tell the truth — while avoiding unnecessary harm and holding themselves accountable.

The remainder of this book is devoted to guiding journalists through a decision-making process that will protect society by supporting the full disclosure of information and giving voice to the voiceless, while protecting innocent people from needless harm.

— Jay Black, Professor Emeritus,
University of South Florida, St. Petersburg,
adapted from the Third Edition

3

Codes of Ethics and Beyond

Ever since the first journalist began assembling the first information for the first news story, people have been concerned about journalism ethics. Millions of words have been spoken, and thousands of pages written, about identifying and resolving the tough calls journalists face while gathering and reporting the news.

For all the work that has been put into ethics through the years, however, the job is nowhere near finished. In the words of Philip Meyer, author of *Ethical Journalism*, journalists are still ethically confused. As a profession, journalism has come a long way in its ability to identify ethical issues and dilemmas. Journalists, however, have a long way to go before knowing how to resolve those problems carefully and systematically. They have heightened their sensitivity far more than they have expanded their decision-making skills.

Much of the credit and a fair share of the blame for this confusing state of affairs can be laid at the feet of those who invoke codes of ethics as the panacea. At best, the codes have helped define many of the problems and have kept the profession alert to its responsibilities to gather and report news thoroughly and accurately and to remain vigilant toward governmental and other forces that would usurp the media's independence. At worst, codes have short-circuited journalists' ability to act as independent decision-makers.

Pros and Cons of Codes

One of the prerequisites of a profession is to have its own code of ethics. Codes of ethics are supposed to act as the conscience of the professional, of the organization, of the enterprise. A code of ethics falls somewhere between societal and personal values on the one hand and law on the other. A code is neither as subjective as personal beliefs and opinions nor as rigid and enforceable as the law.

The strength of an ethics code is a function not only of its various principles and mandates, but also of its legitimacy and power in the eyes of those for whom it is written. The code will be obeyed because individuals willingly subject themselves to ethical standards above and beyond their own personal beliefs or because the code has specific provisions for enforcement, which they fear should they violate it.

Even the best codes have built-in limitations. Codes of ethics identify useful lists of sins and to some extent outline truly noble behavior. They are of some use to newcomers who need a road map that points out troublesome ethical intersections, sharp corners and the biggest potholes. They also have some public relations value to an industry that tries to convince the public of its seriousness about ethics. But codes cannot delineate all the territory likely to be encountered, and they aren't much help when negotiating the vast foggy terrain through which journalists travel daily. As a result of these natural limitations to codes, many journalists erroneously conclude that there are no useful guidelines, that each ethical decision is made *ad hoc* or independently of all other decisions.

The goal of this book is like the goals of moral philosophers throughout history: to help individuals and groups make ethical decisions that are morally defensible and to base those decisions on justification processes that hold true from situation to situation, person to person, time to time. The authors of *Journalism Ethics* hope to help journalism students and practitioners systematically work through ethical dilemmas because of an articulated ethical mission, a dedication to *doing the right thing for the right reasons*. To accomplish such a complex goal requires more than a code.

Bruce W. Sanford, counsel to the nation's oldest and largest journalism organization, the Society of Professional Journalists, writes, "History teaches that the most effective way to promote ethical behavior is through discussion and information, not enforcement."

In an article in the Associated Press Managing Editors publication *Ethics Codes: Sunrise or Sunset?* Sanford quotes Geoffrey Hazard, who makes a good case for relying on a deliberative process rather than a list of dos and don'ts:

> Ethical principles can be established only as a result of deliberation and argumentation. These principles are not the kind of thing that can be settled by fiat, agreement or by authority. To assume that they can is to confuse ethics with lawmaking, rule-making, policy-making and other kinds of decision-making.

For years, SPJ members have been debating the pros and cons of enforcement procedures for their code. Some maintained that a professional organization without the means and willingness to censure code violations is undeserving of the public trust. Others insisted that the constitutionally protected enterprise of journalism had fought too hard and long for freedom from outside control and journalism should not impose any more control over itself than absolutely necessary. Still others argued that to enforce the code would invite litigation financially devastating to the Society and establish precedents that would serve the purposes of those seeking a universal standard of conduct enforceable in court. And others claimed that the wording of the Society's code combines lofty idealistic statements and minimal standards of performance in such a way as to render the code unenforceable in the first place.

In 1987, SPJ deleted from its code of ethics a clause requiring journalists to "actively censure" code violators (see Appendix B). In its place, the Society promised a strong education program that stressed ethics and encouraged journalists to adhere to the code's honorable ideals. Preeminent among these ideals was the desire "to preserve and strengthen the bond of mutual trust and respect among American journalists and the American people." That bond is based on both credibility and ethics, the former being the profession's image, the latter its substance.

The code as revised in 1987 also called on journalists in print and broadcasting to frame individual and institutional codes of ethics. In their fear that having clearly articulated standards would play into the hands of lawyers, however, some journalists appeared to back away from the hard but necessary work of spelling out precisely what they believe is ethically proper. As time has gone on, however, and as journalists have become more sensitive to ethical problems, more and more journalists have been drafting or revising their newsrooms' codes or policy manuals.

— from the Third Edition, Black, Steele and Barney

The 1996 SPJ Code

Codes of ethics, like muscles, brains and old house pets, wither and atrophy unless they are exercised occasionally. The SPJ code is no exception.

SPJ has had a written code since 1926, very early in its history. (It had been founded in 1909 as Sigma Delta Chi, a fraternity also known as SDX.) It borrowed the American Society of Newspaper Editors' canons of journalism, which served SDX until it drafted its own code in 1973, in the aftermath of Watergate. The 1973 code, unanimously approved by delegates to the national convention, was amended several times in the ensuing years. The 1987 amendment, as noted earlier, dropped the "censure" clause and replaced it with an "education" clause.

A decade of changing technologies, changing managements, changing marketplaces, changing roles, changing reputations and changing dilemmas suggested to the nation's largest organization of journalists that it was time once again to change its code of ethics. A two-year effort that involved thousands of SPJ members from hundreds of chapters, and the work of the several committees and subcommittees, resulted in adoption of a totally new code in 1996. It was framed around a set of three guiding principles proposed in earlier editions of *Doing Ethics in Journalism*: to seek truth, to minimize harm and to remain independent. A fourth principle was added in light of numerous discussions, and an increasingly apparent public concern, that journalists should hold themselves publicly accountable. The fourth principle is not an enforcement clause *per se*, but it is as close to one as SPJ has had since 1987.

The debate over enforcement continues, as do discussions about updating the code. Some members of SPJ's ethics committee believe the language should reflect the challenges presented by a growing Internet presence and the emergence of "citizen journalists." Others maintain that the principles remain the same; only the technology of delivering information changes. Some want a longer, more specific code. Others say if anything is changed, those changes should make the code simpler and shorter. As it is with so many ethical issues, the discussion is ongoing.

The Preamble

The five sentences constituting the preamble to the SPJ Code of Ethics claim, in lofty language, what it is that professional journalists stand for:

> Members of the Society of Professional Journalists believe that public enlightenment is the forerunner of justice and the foundation of democracy. The duty of the journalist is to further those ends by seeking truth and providing a fair and comprehensive account of events and issues. Conscientious

journalists from all media and specialties strive to serve the
public with thoroughness and honesty. Professional integrity
is the cornerstone of a journalist's credibility.

Members of the Society share a dedication to ethical behavior and adopt
this code to declare the Society's principles and standards of practice.

This preamble sets the stage for the set of four fundamental guiding principles (truth, harm, independence and accountability) and more specific lists
of the profession's generally accepted standards of practice. It is significant to
notice that the guiding principles are abstract and idealistic, whereas the standards of practice are much more specific. Unlike many codes, however, both
components tend to be framed in the affirmative ("Thou shalt") rather than the
negative ("Thou shalt not"). This was a conscientious choice on the part of the
code writers, believing as they did that more professional, ethical behavior will
result from conscientious application of principles than from blind obedience
to minimalist rules.

Principles and Questions

Members of the SPJ Ethics Committee, bolstered by thoughtful observers of
journalism and by work across the spectrum of ethical decision-making, believe
it is possible to help journalists weigh the ingredients of a good ethical decision
without compromising deadlines. The following four principles (and subsequent checklists of 10 questions, plus a decision-making template) are intended
to help journalists work their way through an ethical dilemma.

These are not "fault" standards that can be trotted out by libel lawyers
seeking to discover some bottom line of propriety below which journalists may
have fallen. Rather, they are proactive models for clear thinking, drawn from
interviews with several hundred working journalists, the contents of more than
100 news media codes of ethics and policy statements, and the insights of many
philosophers and news media critics. The object is to help journalists recognize
ethical dilemmas when they arise, to explore the complexities of decision-
making, to resist moralizing and to recognize the limits of blind obedience to
customs and codes. Throughout this book, we will see how these principles and
questions play out in the decision-making process.

Guiding Principles for the Journalist

- **Seek Truth and Report It**. Journalists should be honest, fair and courageous
  in gathering, reporting and interpreting information.
- **Minimize Harm**. Ethical journalists treat sources, subjects and colleagues as
  human beings deserving of respect.
- **Act Independently**. Journalists should be free of obligation to any interest
  other than the public's right to know.

- **Be Accountable**. Journalists are accountable to their readers, listeners, viewers and each other.

This book explores how each of these four principles plays out in the world of journalism. It is important to note, at this early juncture in the discussion, that the four guiding principles are intended to work in tandem and not alone. That is, a given ethical dilemma entails a balancing act between or among two or more of the principles.

For instance, how can journalists seek and report truth without disrupting the status quo and causing a certain amount of harm? And how can journalists act independently while being held accountable? The tendency to polarize these two sets of principles is very tempting indeed. But there is a better way.

Journalists frequently maintain that they are justified in causing harm during the gathering and reporting of information the public needs to know about. Be that as it may, the choice should not be either/or. A good choice probably rests somewhere along a continuum: How much harm is necessary to tell how much important truth? Do you name a rape victim or identify a sexual predator, citing community interest? Is it necessary to photograph a badly disfigured youth who happens to be in the midst of an unpleasant lawsuit?

All else being equal, journalism's first objective is to seek and report truth. Ethical journalists do not revert to minimizing harm as the first step when doing journalism but as a second step. The harm principle is not invoked as a means of blunting criticism, or currying favor, or avoiding having to do substantial truth-telling. All too often journalists "wimp out" when better journalism — and more civic good — would have resulted from putting truth-telling and minimizing harm in their proper contexts.

Likewise, a balance between independence and accountability must be sought. Journalists, bolstered by the First Amendment and a history of favorable court rulings, are cantankerously independent. Traditionalists in the craft worry about face-licking journalism. They don't think the recent public

SEEK TRUTH AND REPORT IT

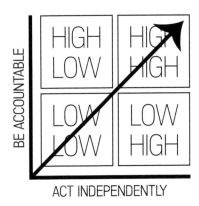

ACT INDEPENDENTLY

journalism movement is healthy because they see it as a lessening of journalism's hard-fought independence. Sharing trade secrets and airing dirty laundry (the ombudsman movement, news councils, etc.) could chip away at the nascent profession's mystique because such exercises in public accountability allow the barbarians to cross the moat.

Upon closer examination, it is perfectly reasonable for journalists to maintain enough independence to remain free from external and internal pressures that dilute the truth-telling enterprise, while simultaneously recognizing that as professional journalists we are accountable to our readers, listeners, viewers and each other.

It's time to reframe the thought process. We can accomplish this by avoiding the either/or polarization of ethical decision-making. Instead, picture journalism on a set of horizontal and vertical axes.

"Bad" journalism occurs when we do a lousy job of truth-telling and when sources or subjects are harmed for no good reason. ("Low/Low" on the horizontal and vertical axes.) "Better" journalism may occur when we cause a lot of harm (disrupting people's comfort zones) during the process of telling highly significant truths ("High/Low") or when we cause only a small amount of harm while telling an insignificant story ("Low/High"). Ethical and excellent journalism, of course, maximizes the amount of truth and minimizes harm.

The same goes for the principles of independence and accountability.

The bulk of this book shows how journalists in some four dozen case studies attempted to deal with these four principles, consciously or not, when making decisions on deadline.

Codes of Ethics

General Introductory Material

Society of Professional Journalists

Members of the Society of Professional Journalists believe that public enlightenment is the forerunner of justice and the foundation of democracy. The duty of the journalist is to further those ends by seeking truth and providing a fair and comprehensive account of events and issues. Conscientious journalists from all media and specialties strive to serve the public with thoroughness and honesty. Professional integrity is the cornerstone of a journalist's credibility.

Members of the Society share a dedication to ethical behavior and adopt this code to declare the Society's principles and standards of practice.

Detroit Free Press

We are committed to fairness and balance in all aspects of our coverage and presentation. These principles are foremost in building trust with readers. To that end, we strive for journalism free of favoritism or prejudice. Our general rules are to tell the truth, correct our mistakes, pay our own way, protect the integrity and independence of the Free Press and never abuse our positions as free press employees...

CyberJournalist.net

Some bloggers recently have been debating what, if any, ethics the weblog community should follow. Since not all bloggers are journalists and the weblog form is more casual, they argue they shouldn't be expected to follow the same ethics codes journalists are. But responsible bloggers should recognize that they are publishing words publicly, and therefore have certain ethical obligations to their readers, the people they write about, and society in general.

CyberJournalist.net has created a model Bloggers' Code of Ethics, by modifying the Society of Professional Journalists Code of Ethics for the weblog world. These are just guidelines — in the end it is up to individual bloggers to choose their own best practices. CyberJournalist.net follows this code and urges other weblogs to adopt this one or similar practices.

Integrity is the cornerstone of credibility. Bloggers who adopt this code of principles and these standards of practice not only practice ethical publishing, but convey to their readers that they can be trusted.

San Jose Mercury News

The *San Jose Mercury News* is committed to the highest ethical standards. To take pride in the work we do, we must do our work honestly.

Fairness and accuracy are among our core values. But perhaps nothing stands above the need for the newspaper to maintain and preserve its integrity. We cannot hold the people we cover to standards we do not meet ourselves. The public's trust in our work — our most important asset — depends on our meeting these high standards. ...

No policy can forecast every possible conflict of interest or ethical quandary that an employee of the *Mercury News* might confront. But this policy is an attempt to provide boundaries and encourage employees to be aware that, as journalists, we must adhere to a code of conduct that is equal parts ethics and common sense.

National Public Radio

NPR is primarily a news organization. We are always testing and questioning the credibility of others. We have to stand that test ourselves, whether we are functioning as reporters, hosts, newscasters, writers, editors, directors, photographers or producers of news, music or other content. Our news content must meet the highest standards of credibility.

The purpose of this code is to protect the credibility of NPR's programming by ensuring high standards of honesty, integrity, impartiality and staff conduct. We accomplish this by (a) articulating the ethical standards we observe in pursuing and presenting material through our various distribution channels, (b) setting rules and policies that prevent conflicts of interest, (c) establishing guidelines for outside work and activities that may reflect on NPR, and (d) establishing policies and procedures to ensure that the activities of NPR that fall outside journalism and daily production — corporate underwriting, foundation funding, marketing and promotional activities — do not jeopardize our journalistic independence or involve NPR journalists in activities inappropriate to their roles.

The Denver Post

What follows is *The Denver Post* ethics policy. It is the product of months of work by reporters and editors on the staff to develop shared guidelines and principles by which we conduct ourselves. We believe it is important to share this policy with the public, so that you better understand the standards we live by. At the end of the day we want to be able to say we did our jobs honestly and fairly and are beholden to no one in the process. I know you will do your part to hold us accountable. — *Greg Moore, Editor*

Montreal (Quebec, Canada) Gazette

A newspaper's greatest asset is its integrity. Respect for that integrity is painfully won and easily lost. It is maintained by constant attention to a host of minor details on a day-to-day basis.

The Philadelphia Inquirer

A vigorous and courageous press is one of the guarantors of a democratic community. Therefore, the *Inquirer* has both the right and the obligation to pursue the truth, without bias or favor, in all matters of public interest and importance, believing that a fully informed populace is the best guarantee of freedom and justice.

The *Inquirer* is responsible to its readers for the accuracy and fairness of its work. We should, therefore, be as accessible to those readers as humanly possible. In all our contacts with members of the public, we should strive to let them know that we are seeking the truth, that we are open-minded, and that we want to listen to what they have to say.

The New York Times Co.

In keeping with its solemn responsibilities under the First Amendment, our company strives to maintain the highest standard of journalistic ethics. It is confident that its staff members share that goal. The company and its units also recognize that staff members should be free to do creative, civic and personal work and to earn extra income in ways separate from their work in our organization. Before engaging in such outside activities, though, staff members should exercise mature professional judgment and consider the stake we all have in the irreplaceable good name of our company and its newsrooms.

American Society of News Editors

The First Amendment, protecting freedom of expression from abridgment by any law, guarantees to the people through their press a constitutional right, and thereby places on newspaper people a particular responsibility. Thus journalism demands of its practitioners not only industry and knowledge but also the pursuit of a standard of integrity proportionate to the journalist's singular obligation. To this end the American Society of Newspaper Editors sets forth this Statement of Principles as a standard encouraging the highest ethical and professional performance (adopted 1922; revised 1975).

Associated Press Managing Editors

These principles are a model against which news and editorial staff members can measure their performance. They have been formulated in the belief that newspapers and the people who produce them should adhere to the highest standards of ethical and professional conduct.

The public's right to know about matters of importance is paramount. The newspaper has a special responsibility as surrogate of its readers to be a vigilant watchdog of their legitimate public interests.

No statement of principles can prescribe decisions governing every situation. Common sense and good judgment are required in applying ethical principles to newspaper realities. As new technologies evolve, these principles can help guide editors to ensure the credibility of the news and information they provide. Individual newspapers are encouraged to augment these APME guidelines more specifically to their own situations.

4

The Right to Be Wrong: Law and Ethics

Journalists in the United States have long been considered to be the freest in the world. The First Amendment to the Constitution prohibits government interference with the press, declaring that "Congress shall make no law ... abridging the freedom of speech, or of the press." Notice that this absolute language — which has been interpreted by the courts to apply to the legislative and judicial branches and to state and local government authorities, as well — does not say that this guarantee of freedom from government interference depends on journalists being "responsible" or "objective."

This omission was no accident. The founders were very familiar with a cantankerous and highly partisan press. They knew that government would always protect journalists who supported it and try to shut down those that did not. They knew that newspaper columns, pamphlets and monographs critical of the monarchy and of taxation without representation had been instrumental in rallying support for the War of Independence. Accordingly, they repudiated laws imposed on the American colonies by the British Parliament requiring publishers to be licensed by the government and prohibiting criticism of the Crown or its appointed officials. The men who drafted what became the First Amendment subscribed to the philosophy of the Age of Enlightenment, rejected the idea that the State was omnipotent and infallible, and believed that freedom of the press was analogous to freedom of thought and therefore, essential to the functioning of a democratic system.

But is the First Amendment as "absolute" as it appears? To answer that question, we must examine the rulings of the U.S. Supreme Court, which is the final arbiter of what the Constitution means.

Prior Restraints

Most legal scholars agree that at a minimum, the First Amendment means that prior restraints — that is, governmental restrictions on what someone may write or publish — will rarely, if ever, be permitted. In 1931, in a case called *Near v. Minnesota*, the Supreme Court struck down a state statute that permitted government officials to suppress publication of "malicious, scandalous, and defamatory" material. The newspaper called *The Saturday Press* had accused officials in Minneapolis and St. Paul of corruption, claiming that they accepted bribes from and condoned bootlegging and racketeering by "Jewish gangsters" operating in the Twin Cities. The language used in the stories, at least to contemporary readers, was highly inflammatory, anti-Semitic and offensive. Nevertheless, the high court found that because the statute allowed censorship of criticism of the government, it was unconstitutional. It went on to rule that any prior restraint would be presumed to violate the First Amendment. This meant that whenever any branch of the government attempted to prevent someone from publishing, it would not be up to the publisher to explain to a court why he should be allowed to speak. Instead, the government would have to justify why he should be silenced.

To be sure, the Supreme Court never said that all prior restraints are unconstitutional. For example, publication of troop movements during wartime, obscenity or incitement to violence are all examples of speech that the high court has suggested may be suppressed under certain circumstances. But remarkably, in all the years since *Near*, the high court has never upheld a prior restraint on the publication of news.

For example, in the "Pentagon Papers" case decided in 1971, the administration of President Richard Nixon asked two federal courts to stop *The New York Times* and *The Washington Post* from continuing to publish leaked, classified government documents pertaining to the Vietnam War. Despite the government's arguments, the Supreme Court was not persuaded that immediate and irreparable harm to the national interest would result and refused to stop the newspapers from publishing.

Justice Harry Blackmun, was troubled, however, by the potential for serious damage caused by what he considered to be the irresponsible behavior of the newspapers. He observed that if, as the government asserted, soldiers died, diplomatic alliances were broken or the war were prolonged as the result of the publication of the Pentagon Papers, "then the Nation's people will know where the responsibility for these sad consequences rests" — with the press.

Exactly how the press would be "held responsible" is an interesting question. Several of the justices suggested that Congress may enact laws that would permit news organizations to be prosecuted for espionage after the fact if they obtained and disseminated classified information to those not authorized to receive it — including the public. But no such prosecution has taken place to date, despite multiple examples of journalists publicizing leaked government information, often revealing sensitive and controversial government activities, including the existence of secret prisons used to hold suspected terrorists and of programs permitting surveillance of the communications of American citizens. Action has been taken against the leakers — when the government can discover who they are — under the theory that these individuals have obligations to honor promises of secrecy made as a condition of their employments. Journalists who do not work for the government and do not typically have security clearances, however, argue that their loyalties lie not with the state but with their readers and viewers.

But especially in the post-9/11 world, journalists' audiences do not always agree with that premise. Even when the decision to publish is made after consultation with the government, news organizations are often criticized for substituting their own judgment about the need for secrecy for that of intelligence and law enforcement agencies. On the other hand, some have condemned journalists for withholding any information at all, often accusing them of delaying publication for partisan reasons. They argue that access to everything that may be relevant is essential to full participation in the democratic process.

These are difficult calls for the press to make, and the answers are not always easy to find. What is clear is that the law, for the most part, leaves it up to the press, not the government, to decide.

Libel

Libel involves the publication of something about an individual that is both false and defamatory — that is, that harms that person's reputation among right-thinking people. An allegation of libel can lead to a civil lawsuit seeking money damages, or even, in rare cases, criminal prosecution. Until 1964, libelous speech was considered to be outside the protection of the First Amendment. But the landmark case of *New York Times Co. v. Sullivan*, decided amid the turmoil of the civil rights movement, changed all that. The Supreme Court ruled that to promote robust discussion and commentary about the actions of government officials, newspapers must be given protection from crippling libel judgments, even if they publish false information. The high court ruled that, to prevail in a libel suit, the public official must prove that the news organization either knew that what it published was false, or that it acted with reckless disregard for the truth — also known as "actual malice."

This requirement to demonstrate a very high level of fault on the part of the journalist was subsequently extended to include public figures and, in some states, to anyone who wished to sue the press for libel, especially if that individual is involved in matters of public concern. It recognizes that under deadline pressure, it is inevitable that some errors will occur, even when journalists do their utmost to be accurate. It is intended to set the bar for a successful lawsuit particularly high to avoid chilling speech and to encourage the free flow of ideas and information. And in 1974, in *Gertz v. Robert Welch, Inc.*, the Supreme Court recognized that statements of pure opinion, which can neither be proven true nor false, are absolutely protected by the First Amendment as well.

These strong protections were all intended to protect speech about matters of public concern, which is regarded as the most valuable kind of speech in the marketplace of ideas. It is the kind of speech that makes up most of good journalism. But these principles also have consequences that may be less desirable. Some argue that the *Sullivan* standard encourages journalists to be careless and to repeat rumors and gossip, especially about public figures, without taking time to verify them. Others suggest that by making it almost impossible for elected officials to sue successfully for defamatory falsehoods, it discourages qualified people from seeking public office.

> The obligation to seek and tell the truth remains, for the press, primarily an ethical, not a legal, one.

And there are ramifications for journalists as well, which may not always be positive. For example, the plaintiff in a libel case who must prove actual malice has the right to probe newsroom practices and policies to determine whether the reporter knew — or had reason to know — that what she published was false. This may allow the plaintiff to inquire about the existence and identity of confidential sources. Sometimes a plaintiff cites aspirational ethics codes and guidelines as evidence that a journalist failed to follow reasonable practices in gathering the story, essentially arguing that she committed journalistic malpractice. Because there is no single, binding ethics code that applies to all journalists, it is not unusual for each side in a libel case to retain competing expert witnesses to offer their opinions on whether the journalist acted "recklessly."

Libel law, as it has evolved in the United States, grants journalists significant privileges when reporting or commenting on matters of public concern. A libel suit is not a mechanism for determining whether the press "told the truth." Rather, it is a means of providing redress for those whose reputations have been harmed as the result of reckless or knowing publication of false information. The obligation to seek and tell the truth remains, for the press, primarily an ethical, not a legal, one.

Privacy

The Constitution does not explicitly recognize a right to privacy — what some have called "the right to be left alone." The right to privacy also gives individuals the ability to control the dissemination of information about themselves. Although the Fourth Amendment has been interpreted by the Supreme Court to protect individuals from unreasonable intrusion into their private lives by the government, it says nothing about the actions of journalists and others. With the exception of statutes governing electronic surveillance, the federal government does little to regulate the actions of private citizens. But every state has come to recognize at least one of four forms of invasion of privacy: intrusion on seclusion, publication of private facts, portraying someone in a false (but not necessarily defamatory) light and misappropriation of an individual's name or image for commercial purposes.

Here again, however, the Supreme Court has recognized that the Constitution protects some journalistic activities that may be regarded as invasions of privacy. Although journalists are not above the law and therefore are subject to general laws prohibiting trespass or secret tape recording, courts will sometimes recognize that balancing the public interest in obtaining accurate information about matters of public concern may outweigh an individual's desire to be left alone, especially if that individual has voluntarily chosen to enter the public arena.

Similarly, the First Amendment generally protects the publication of truthful private facts, even if the subject would prefer to keep them secret. Such publication cannot be the basis of a libel suit because the facts published are not false. But even if the information is intimate, and its disclosure, at least in the abstract, is regarded as highly offensive to a reasonable person, publication will not be actionable in a court of law as long as it is deemed "newsworthy."

Obviously, reasonable people can disagree about whether lurid details about the sex life of a candidate for public office or of a celebrity are "newsworthy." In deciding the question, courts sometimes make a distinction between a matter of legitimate "public interest" — for example, information that may be relevant to a politician's fitness for office — and something that is merely interesting to the public. Simply because something has appeared in the news media doesn't make it a matter of public interest in the eyes of the law. But as a general rule, courts will defer to the editorial discretion of journalists, erring on the side of upholding their legal right to publish.

As with the doctrines of prior restraint and libel, the broad protections of the First Amendment mean that journalists must give serious consideration to ethical principles when making newsgathering decisions that will implicate an individual's privacy. For example, it may be perfectly legal in a particular state to use a hidden camera to conduct an investigation. But even though the law allows it, news organizations must also consider the probable public reaction to the use of what many regard as a deceptive technique. Or, state law may protect the right of a news organization to obtain and report details of the arrest of a public official's teenage son on shoplifting charges, even though this type of information may not be reported as a matter of course if it concerned another juvenile. Does publication of the information in this case contribute significantly to public oversight of government affairs, or does it needlessly embarrass a young person who never sought the spotlight? Obviously, there are no uniform answers to these questions, depending, as they do, on the specific circumstances of each case. This is where careful analysis and balancing of ethical issues become crucial.

Confidential Sources

Journalists insist that, as a matter of ethics, they have an obligation to refuse to disclose the identity of sources to whom they have promised confidentiality. They insist that unless they can honor these promises, their sources will refuse to speak to them in the future, resulting in less information for the public.

Unfortunately, the Supreme Court has yet to rule that the First Amendment provides a "reporters privilege" guaranteeing this right. When the high court last considered the question in 1972, in *Branzburg v. Hayes*, it explicitly held that there is no constitutional privilege protecting journalists from being compelled to testify before grand juries about their sources if the information is relevant to a criminal investigation. Since that ruling, many state and federal courts have recognized some sort of privilege in other situations, such as in civil cases, and more than 30 states have passed statutory shield laws as well. The scope and extent of these privileges vary, but even when they do not absolutely protect a reporter's right to refuse to disclose a source, they usually at least require that the party seeking the information demonstrate that it is relevant, essential and unobtainable from any other source.

The failure of the Supreme Court to recognize a constitutional privilege has placed journalists in an untenable position. When a reporter has promised a source absolute confidentiality, she will contend that she ethically cannot violate that promise. To a judge, however, the reporter's refusal to testify obstructs the interests of justice. In that situation, the judge may hold her in contempt of court. To encourage the reporter to comply with the order, the judge may resort to a variety of "civil contempt" sanctions, including imposing a daily monetary fine or sending the reporter to jail. Civil contempt is designed to coerce the reporter into cooperating and could theoretically last as long as there is need for the reporter's testimony — even for many months, such as the term of a grand jury, or the duration of a trial. If the reporter agrees to comply, however, the contempt will be "purged," and the reporter will be released. In rare cases, if a reporter's conduct is considered to be particularly defiant or offensive — for example, in a case where a reporter has repeatedly refused to identify someone who is believed to have committed a crime — the judge may impose criminal contempt penalties that cannot be "purged," even if the reporter relents. This means the reporter will have a criminal record.

Clearly, making a promise of confidentiality to a source is a serious matter. Apart from the ethical considerations, which are discussed in greater detail elsewhere in this book, reporters must recognize that, however strongly they believe in their ethical obligation to honor promises to their sources, the First Amendment may not protect them. Some journalists believe that it is unethical to seek statutory protection from state legislatures or from Congress, asserting that seeking a special privilege from the government compromises independence. And inevitably, any shield law that provides a privilege for reporters will have to define who is allowed to claim it. That could lead to the government's defining who is a journalist, raising constitutional questions that some equate with government licensing of the press.

The bottom line, at least until the Supreme Court rules otherwise, is that journalists must recognize that upholding a promise of confidentiality to a source may be tantamount to an act of civil disobedience, for which they must be prepared to face the legal consequences.

Access

The Supreme Court has said that "without some protection for seeking out the news, freedom of the press would be eviscerated." Even so, as a matter of law, journalists have no greater right of access to places — that is, no exemption from laws of trespass, or other criminal laws — than anyone else, even if they claim they are engaged in newsgathering. A reporter who tries to smuggle a firearm through an airport metal detector can be prosecuted for doing so, just as anyone else would be. In practice, though, it is not unusual for officials to refrain from charging a reporter with violation of the law under these circumstances, though this is a matter of prosecutorial discretion, not constitutional mandate. It is also common for officials to grant journalists special rights of access to places ranging from accident scenes to sporting events to war zones. Again, such access rights are not based not on the First Amendment but are derived from long-standing tradition and practice, or, in some limited cases, from specific statutory provisions. As with shield laws for reporters, these access rights may be restricted to individuals who are recognized as credentialed journalists, which is not always an easy, or equitable, determination to make.

The right of access to courtrooms works differently. In 1980, in the case *Richmond Newspapers Inc. v. Virginia*, the Supreme Court recognized the press and the public have a constitutionally guaranteed right of access to criminal court proceedings. This right of access is not absolute, and observers can be excluded under rare circumstances when an overriding interest, such as the right to a fair trial, is implicated. But even so, court proceedings in the United States are presumptively open to journalists, who are regarded as surrogates of the public. As former Chief Justice Warren Burger once wrote, "People in an open society do not demand infallibility from their institutions, but it is difficult for them to accept what they are prohibited from observing."

The right to attend a court proceeding, however, may not extend to a right to bring in cameras or other recording equipment. Cameras are banned from federal trial courts and the U.S. Supreme Court; the various federal circuit courts of appeal have authority to decide for themselves whether they will admit electronic equipment. Most states, at least in theory, allow cameras in some of their courtrooms, but many allow any of the parties or the judge to exclude them, often for no rational, or even articulated, reason. Despite the long tradition of open courtrooms, this disparity of treatment between print and electronic media remains. It is one of the last bastions of control that judges can assert over journalists without implicating the First Amendment, and it is significant that those who continue to resist admission of cameras to courtrooms often cite perceived ethical lapses, such as sensationalism or invasion of privacy, as the justification for these restrictive policies.

> ## We have the legal right to be wrong — sometimes.

This brings us, then, full circle, back to where we began: to the First Amendment. The drafters who wrote in such absolute terms did so because they recognized that, left to their own discretion, government officials would restrict freedom of the press. No matter what they say, often these actions are based on pretexts having little to do with promoting the public interest. Instead, they are designed to conceal misconduct or malfeasance, or to punish the press for vigorous reporting and well-founded criticism.

In the 21st century, many journalists believe that it should not be necessary for them to justify their important role as government watchdogs and as conduits of information to the public. Surely, they think, the First Amendment has already settled all that. We have the legal right to be wrong — sometimes.

But whether we like it or not, the reality is that presidents and governors, legislators and (especially) judges are consumers of news. They pay close attention to what journalists do. To the extent that we deviate from our principles or pander to the lowest common denominator, we give them one more excuse to eviscerate the public's right to know by controlling what we do.

Knowing this should not discourage journalists from doing their jobs. If anything, it should be a mandate to do the best work we possibly can do; to act independently, even courageously, when seeking and pursuing truth. Inevitably, there will be times when our interests will conflict with those of the government. The question is whether our readers and viewers will recognize that we are putting the interests of the public first.

— *Jane E. Kirtley*
Silha Professor of Media Ethics and Law
School of Journalism and Mass Communication
University of Minnesota

5

To Tell the Truth: Accuracy and Fairness

The principles of accuracy and fairness stand at the very heart of journalism's "prime directive" (to borrow from the philosophy followed by notable explorer, Capt. James T. Kirk), and that is to tell the truth.

Indeed, accuracy and fairness speak to the obligation of providing meaningful information to citizens who depend on its quality, authenticity and lack of bias to understand issues and to make important decisions.

Accuracy means getting it right. It is an essential responsibility of individual journalists and news organizations. To provide wrong information is a disservice to the public and a sure way to erode the credibility of journalism.

Audiences deserve, and in most cases still pay for, a reasonably accurate and unbiased picture of the world they live in. Every effort should be made to ensure that statements of fact are correct and that information is presented in context. It is not appropriate to use deadlines, competition, personal excuses, equipment problems, wardrobe malfunctions, staffing shortages, or any other reason to justify inaccuracies or bias.

Fairness means pursuing the truth with both vigor and compassion and reporting information without favoritism, self-interest or prejudice.

Accuracy and fairness mean challenging traditional definitions of news, ensuring coverage of societal issues and groups of people under-reported in the past.

Accuracy and fairness also mean portraying individuals and issues with a basic sense of open-mindedness, avoiding biased reporting, stereotypical portrayals and unsubstantiated allegations.

To be sure, journalism can never tell the full truth in every story because facts compete against each other, and additional facts and more information emerge over time. Many stories must be reported piecemeal, as they develop. But the fuller picture will come only from journalists committed to the fundamental principles of accuracy and fairness.

Accuracy Checklist

Do you have a high level of confidence about the facts in your story and the sources that are providing them? If not, can you tell your story in a more accurate manner? If you have any doubts about your sources, can you delete them or replace them and achieve a higher likelihood of reliability?

- Have you attributed or documented all facts?

- Have you double-checked all facts?

- Can you provide the properly spelled name and accurate telephone number of every source cited?

- Are you highly confident that all the factual statements in your story reflect the truth?

- Are you prepared to defend publicly your fact-checking and whatever other measures were taken to verify your story?

- Are the quotes in your story presented fairly, and in context?

- Are you quoting anonymous sources? Why are you using those sources? Are you prepared to defend publicly the use of those sources?

- Are you using any material, documents or pictures provided by anonymous sources? Why? What is your level of confidence about the validity of this material? Are you prepared to defend publicly the use of that material?

- Have you described people, minority groups, races, cultures, nations or segments of society — e.g. businesspeople, combat veterans, cheerleaders — using stereotypical adjectives? Are such descriptions accurate and meaningful in the context presented?

- Have you used potentially objectionable language or pictures in your story? Is there a compelling reason for using such information? Would the story be **less** accurate if that language or picture was eliminated?

- Do your headlines (or broadcast promos or teases) accurately present the facts and context of the story to which they are referring?

Accuracy and the New Media

The Internet offers many challenges and opportunities for journalists. The challenges include that the Internet is luring away a chunk of mainstream media's readers and viewers, as well as the risk for reporters of using the Web as a resource when much of its content may not be accurate. The opportunities of this electronic environment include almost unlimited research and interviewing possibilities.

The new media, especially the Web, have been widely touted as the source of choice for a new generation of news consumers. But a closer examination of the figures suggests the new media aren't fully replacing the old media. The growth in new media doesn't match the loss of viewers and readers of old media. Perhaps some people simply have decided to live news-free lives.

Then there's the problem that much of this new-media content is not reliable information. A decade ago, as few as a quarter of weblog readers told pollsters they trusted those blogs to be accurate, but more recent surveys show a growing level of faith.

On the Web, it's all supposed to be hammered into something approaching reality as other individuals weigh in with their own version of the truth. But what if you as an information-seeker access the site before the hammering is finished?

> **Accuracy is not the same as truth. Different people have different truths.**

Still, the Web is an important tool for a journalist. But it's important to think about what you can get from the Internet with some sense of confidence and what you have to be careful about.

E-mail interviews are convenient and e-mail provides an easy tool for fact checking. Weblogs are a good source for opinion, even if they're a questionable source for facts.

In this world of multiple choices for information — or affirmation — how can the mainstream media compete? By providing consistently trustworthy information, comprehensive and free of bias. By remembering the importance of accuracy, fairness and reliability in reporting.

Accuracy is not the same as truth. Different people have different truths. Evolution. The age of the Earth. Whether a fetus is the same as a baby, or global warming is caused by humans. Your job is to report those beliefs, those sometimes disparate truths, accurately.

Reliability means that people can trust your accuracy consistently. You don't make mistakes — or you make as few as is humanly possible, and what you report is an accurate reflection of what sources say.

Fairness means you give everyone with a stake in the story a chance to explain his or her version. It's not often a 50-50 balance. You have to use your judgment. Some points of view don't carry as much weight as others.

Traditional media will survive only if they insist on providing accurate, reliable and fair information.

Let others give readers what they want to see. Your responsibility as an ethical journalist is to give them information that they need to make sound decisions. And a sense of responsibility is what divides an ethical journalist from a careless polemicist.

Using the Internet for Accuracy and Fairness

The Internet is a mixed bag. It can't always be relied upon for accuracy and fairness. For some things, though, it's a great tool for traditional reporters. Such as:

1. Internet interviews: A great way to let people think about what they're going to say; a lousy way to get a "gotcha" moment. And you can't be sure, if you're interviewing a famous person, celebrity or politician this way, that it isn't some spokesperson responding — or, worse, an impostor.

2. Fact-checking: When you're uncertain you've got a fact right, you can e-mail your proposed sentence or paragraph or two to the source to see if it's phrased correctly. Make it clear you're not going to change it unless it's inaccurate. But accuracy is more important than independence.

3. Weblogs are a great way to gauge sentiment. They can be a sort of informal poll. But remember that they're best as a source for opinion; be skeptical of accepting them as fact.

PART TWO
TO TELL
THE TRUTH:
CASE STUDIES

CASE STUDY 1:

Cooperating with Government

WHAT: It was the longest prison standoff in recent U.S. history. On January 18, 2005, two inmates at the Arizona prison complex near Buckeye armed themselves with homemade weapons and took over a prison guard tower. They held two correctional officers hostage, releasing one of them, a male, a week into the standoff and the second, a female, before surrendering two weeks later, on February 1. But the public didn't know about any of this until after it was over.

> Media were not allowed within half a mile of the prison; the airspace was closed to helicopters.

The governor's office, explaining that it feared for the safety of the two prison guards, telephoned news executives around the state and urged them not to reveal certain basic information. As the standoff continued, authorities said they were worried that publicity would reach the inmates and foil negotiations.

Television viewers, radio listeners and newspaper readers were not told the names of the hostages or the names, criminal histories or disciplinary records of their captors until after the siege ended. State officials refused to confirm their identities or to release most details about how the standoff began or what happened afterward.

But also, Arizona news organizations agreed to wait until the standoff ended before publishing many details or any names they might learn from other sources. They held off on interviewing relatives of the inmates they suspected might be the captors. Media were not allowed within half a mile of the prison; the airspace was closed to helicopters.

The inmates eventually were charged with kidnapping, aggravated assault, escape and sexual assault, which gives you some idea of what went on during the standoff. The names of the guards weren't made known after they were released.

Question: Should your news organization agree to the information blackout?

WHO: Put yourself in the position of a managing editor at a newspaper or a news director of a television station. You're the one who has to decide.

The stakeholders you must consider include, obviously, the hostages, who have more at stake than anyone else, including possibly the prisoners who took them captive, who also are major stakeholders.

WHY: As is so often the case, the major principles involved here are the reporter's duty to tell the truth and the competing principle of minimizing harm. Did the Arizona media do the right thing in this case? What would you have done? Would you have cooperated with the authorities? Would you have put conditions on your cooperation? How much would you worry about what the competition is doing? How long would you have waited to release information? Should the media have worked together to develop a unified position? Would you change your stance if media outlets outside the state began reporting details the Arizona media agreed not to report?

— by the SPJ Ethics Committee

CASE STUDY 2:

A Congressman's Past

WHAT: Three weeks before the 2004 election, *The (*Portland*) Oregonian* published a sensational story. David Wu, a Democratic congressman seeking a fourth term, had been accused by an ex-girlfriend of a sexual assault some 28 years previously. But criminal charges never were filed, and neither Wu nor the woman involved wanted to discuss the case now.

The Oregonian spent months trying to discover the truth about this persistent rumor. On October 12, 2004, it published an article more than 3,000 words long explaining what it found out.

On that same day, Congressman Wu held a news conference to say he did something regrettable in his youth, but he didn't think it was relevant now. Other media picked up the story, of course, and his Republican opponent used it in her campaign.

Here's a quick summary:

Wu and his ex-girlfriend were science majors at Stanford University. She broke up with him in the spring of 1976. That summer, Wu was questioned by Stanford campus police after his ex-girlfriend said he tried to force her to have sex with him.

Wu told police it was consensual. He was not arrested. The woman declined criminal prosecution and didn't file a formal disciplinary complaint.

Wu refused to be interviewed or to answer written questions about the incident when *The Oregonian* asked him about it 28 years later. Wu's ex-girlfriend also declined to comment, either in person or through a representative. Stanford officials wouldn't discuss it either, citing university policy and student confidentiality laws.

So how did *The Oregonian* get its story? Here are some quotes from the newspaper's initial article:

"Reporters contacted scores of former Stanford students, current and retired university officials and professors, law associates, and former campaign staffers and friends of Wu to determine what occurred. ...

"The account that follows is based on recollections of the Stanford patrol commander, the woman's counselor, two professors who supervised dormitories at the time and several classmates who were on campus that year."

Question: If you are *The Oregonian*, do you publish this story three weeks before the election? If you're a competing news media outlet, do you follow it?

WHO: Wu, obviously, is the major "Who." Almost as equally affected is the unnamed woman who filed the complaint against him. Wu's opponent most likely would benefit from the story. The public is a stakeholder, in that it will go to the polls in less than a month to make a decision about who should represent the district in Congress. The newspaper itself also is putting its reputation on the line, as is often the case in controversial stories.

WHY: Certainly, there is a truth to be told here, and the truth potentially could change the outcome of the election. But is an apparent sexual encounter that remains unclear all that important more than a quarter-century later? The woman who made the complaint doesn't want to rehash the events of the episode. Readers might think that the news side of *The Oregonian* is only furthering the editorial page's agenda, because it endorsed Wu's opponent.

HOW: Clearly, the newspaper decided to run the story. But it may have had second thoughts (see the sidebar by Michael Arrieta-Walden, *The Oregonian*'s public editor, published October 17, 2004). Wu, by the way, won re-election in a landslide.

— *SPJ Ethics Committee*

THE PUBLIC EDITOR:

STORY ON LONG-AGO INCIDENT WORRIES READERS, EDITORS

More than 350 readers called or wrote last week to criticize *The Oregonian*'s publication of a story about an allegation that David Wu sexually attacked a college girlfriend 28 years ago. The newspaper explained its decision in an editor's note and invited comment from readers. They responded.

Reader after reader raised questions about fairness, relevancy and timing. Many of the questions were ones that editors struggled with for weeks leading up to the publication of the story, issues of journalistic judgment that editors, let alone readers, disagree about. Here are several of the major questions readers raised and an attempt to address them:

Timing of the article: Many readers asked why the newspaper published the story only three weeks before the election, especially given that the allegation was 28 years old and Wu already had served three terms in Congress. They argued the timing was unfair to Wu. "I'm insulted by it," said reader Nathan Whittlesey of Newberg. "I don't think you are honorable."

The timing troubled editors, as well. A reporter had heard a rumor about the allegation in 2000 but hit a dead end. When new information emerged earlier this year, editors devoted three reporters to the story and worked for months to confirm it as soon as possible. Critical information did not emerge until September, and then editors' questions and concerns generated the need for even more reporting and editing. The final drafts were edited over the weekend and prepared for publication on Tuesday. Although the story would be published just days before ballots were mailed, editors believed voters still would have enough time to weigh any response and to consider other information about Wu.

Relevancy of the allegation: Many readers questioned whether a 28-year-old allegation involving behavior as a 21-year-old college student is relevant to an election today. Several readers recalled their sexual and drug activities from college days that would be embarrassing or criticized today.

"We all made mistakes when we were in college," says Steve Dimeo of Hillsboro. "I can't believe that you published the article. It's beneath you."

Editors would agree that most of us have events in our pasts we'd prefer to forget. But Editor Sandy Rowe says that the seriousness of the allegation — an attempted sexual assault — demanded investigation by reporters, and that people who seek public office offer themselves for such scrutiny. She also concluded that an allegation that could have generated a criminal charge — even one as old as this one — is especially relevant in Oregon, where sexual scandals involving public officials have heightened Oregonians' awareness and concern.

Second-hand sources: Readers were troubled that the newspaper would print such a serious allegation based on sources, as the story acknowledged, who themselves could not know the whole story. "This article on David Wu is pure hearsay," said Carolyn Landsverk, in deciding to cancel her subscription to the newspaper after 32 years. "It's so uncharacteristic of the paper."

The lack of eyewitnesses was deeply troubling to editors; no one other than Wu and his former girlfriend can know what went on in that dorm room. That's why editors insisted that reporters talk to as many sources as possible and that only named sources be used. Their confidence in the accuracy of the story was bolstered by the fact that they were able to interview university officials involved at the time, including a campus police officer, counselor and professor. Rowe said editors had to accept that precisely what went on in that room was unknowable. And although Wu admitted after publication to "inexcusable behavior" for which he was disciplined by the university and didn't challenge the accuracy of the story, the details of the incident will likely never be known.

No cooperation from the victim: Readers said that if the victim did not want to revisit the issue because of her privacy, the newspaper should have honored that wish.

That also received strong consideration, but it's not unusual for the newspaper to report on criminal incidents in which the victim would prefer there was no publicity. Those incidents are considered newsworthy, often because of the public service the information provides. In this case, Rowe said the newspaper went to lengths to try to shield her identity, including making even more changes at the 11th hour to obscure her identity after talking again with her representative.

Editorial opinion and story: Many readers suspect that the newspaper published the story because it had recently endorsed Wu's opponent, Goli Ameri.

The appearance of the article four days after the endorsement makes that conclusion understandable. But those who made the decision and wrote the editorial endorsing Ameri had no role in the story about Wu, and the reporters on the Wu story had begun pursuing it even before his opponent emerged from the primary in May. The editorial board did not know the full details of the story when it made its decision, or whether a story would be published.

Goldschmidt influence: Many readers charged that the Wu story was an attempt by the newspaper to repair its reputation, which was damaged by its lack of aggressiveness in the original pursuit of the allegations of sex abuse by former Gov. Neil Goldschmidt.

In *The Oregonian* newsroom, the influence of the Goldschmidt story is undeniable. Rowe says the Goldschmidt case made the reporters more persistent in pursuing the allegation over several months, but that it wasn't what pushed her to publish the story. The Wu story had to stand on its own, although the reader reaction to the stories of Goldschmidt and former Sen. Bob Packwood did make it abundantly clear to her that allegations of serious sexual misconduct matter to readers of the newspaper.

On the Wu story, I admire the reporters and their editors for their persistence, diligence and thoroughness. They were not intimidated by the attempts by Wu's camp to undermine the reporting and to keep the newspaper from pursuing the story. All of that serves readers well.

I also admire how the newspaper's editors struggled and deliberated over the decision to publish. Despite the contrary view of many readers last week, reporters and editors dislike these types of stories and knew they would face significant criticism for publishing the story. As with any difficult ethical decision in journalism, there is no clear right or wrong answer. It's a judgment call, a subjective choice that no editor relishes. You must weigh your responsibility to the public against potential harm and make the best decision you can. In this case, while I find the stories reflect exhaustive reporting and editing and are ethically justified, many of the concerns voiced by readers resound with me, causing me to disagree with the judgment of those editors.

With only three days left before the mailing of ballots, the bar for publication of any allegation against a candidate should be exceedingly high to reach. Too many hurdles loom for me and many readers: You must accept that the 28-year-old incident is relevant. If you do so, you still must overcome concerns about not knowing with absolute certainty what happened in that room, no public records or criminal charges, no firsthand accounts from the two people most closely involved and no established pattern of behavior.

I understand and respect how the journalistic duty of never wanting to withhold important information from voters — especially about such a serious allegation — trumped those and other concerns, but I'm not comfortable with it.

My discomfort is aggravated by how I think the newspaper has failed to serve those voters in other ways.

In its pursuit of the story, the newspaper essentially has neglected to cover the race for the 1st Congressional District. Until last week, only one local story of any substance has been written about the tight race between Wu and Ameri.

And until a profile on Friday, the newspaper also failed to deliver a fuller portrait of Wu, with the story on the allegation or in coverage in past months. Wu provided no help by refusing to grant the newspaper an interview on any subject, but the newspaper should have shared more with readers about his public service and character.

That neglect allows the story about Wu's college incident to have a potentially disproportionate effect on voters and readers, and leaves them understandably questioning its fairness.

— *Michael Arrieta-Walden,*
The Oregonian's *public editor*

Reproduced with permission of The Oregonian, *"STORY ON LONG-AGO INCIDENT WORRIES READERS, EDITORS" published October 17, 2004; © 2004* The Oregonian. *Permission conveyed through Copyright Clearance Center, Inc.*

CASE STUDY 3:

A Media-Savvy Killer

WHAT: It started three decades ago. "It has always been part of the paper's lore," Rick Thames, former editor of *The Wichita Eagle* told *Editor & Publisher*'s Joe Strupp. Since his first murder in 1974, the "BTK" killer — his own acronym, for "bind, torture, kill" — has sent *The Eagle* four letters and one poem.

The Eagle's website was subpoenaed in 2004 when investigators thought BTK might be posting items on a discussion board. And in the spring of 2005, the killer sent the paper a letter after 16 years of silence, apparently sparked by a story about the 30th anniversary of the first killing.

BTK killed eight people. The first was January 15, 1974, the last 12 years later, in 1986. The killer's first communication with the newspaper was 10 months after the first killing. A reader found a letter inside a book at a local library and called the newspaper. The last letter arrived in March 2004 and included photos from the 1986 crime scene, as well as a copy of that victim's driver's license. The killer also has sent letters and made phone calls to a local television station, but his main media connection has been *The Eagle*.

> In April 2005, the Sedgwick County District Attorney subpoenaed the identities of six people who had posted items to a BTK bulletin board on *The Eagle*'s website.

The newspaper has involved itself in the in other ways. In 1974, when it was still the *Eagle-Beacon*, it offered a $5,000 award for information leading to an arrest. And editors unknowingly included a 1978 poem from BTK in romantic messages the paper runs on Valentine's Day.

Eagle Reporter Hurst Laviana, who followed the case for more than 20 years, was one of three reporters who were asked to give DNA samples in 2004, in a desperate attempt to find the mysterious killer. "It seemed like a logical thing for them to do," Laviana told *E&P*, adding that police told him they'd received five tips from people urging that he be tested. Apparently he was cleared; he never heard back from investigators.

In April 2005, the Sedgwick County District Attorney subpoenaed the identities of six people who had posted items to a BTK bulletin board on *The Eagle*'s website. *The Eagle* cooperated without a fight but was criticized by the district attorney for running a story about the subpoenas.

All of this puts the newspaper in an awkward position. The killer seems almost to be using it as an agent of communication. It is both a provider of evidence and chronicler of the news. Some employees worried that BTK might target them as attention increases.

Two questions: How should a newspaper, or other media outlet, handle communications from someone who says he's guilty of multiple sensational crimes? And how much should it cooperate with law enforcement authorities?

WHO: Put yourself in the shoes of the editor of *The Eagle*, or of a television station that might have received similar communications.

Consider the stakeholders: The Wichita community, terrorized for years by a mysterious killer, certainly has a stake in finding out who this person is and incarcerating him or her to prevent future potential harm. This is a case where the public's stake is higher than it might be in other cases.

The killer is a prime stakeholder who seems to enjoy tantalizing the media and the public with taunts about his identity. Law enforcement authorities are stakeholders, in that they've been spinning their wheels for years.

WHY: Does cooperating with the killer by publicizing his taunts create more opportunities that he'll be caught? Or does it simply play into the killer's twisted desire for attention? What would happen if you were to stop forwarding every communication from this clearly imbalanced individual? What is the greatest good for the greatest number?

HOW: Decide how to establish the outcome you've identified as best. Explain it to yourself, and write it down to help you articulate it. You might also want to explain your decision, and the decision-making process, to your readers and/or viewers. Prepare for the inevitable questions you'll get from them.

(Epilogue: Dennis Rader, who admitted to being the BTK Killer, was arrested February 25, 2005, by Wichita Police. On June 28, 2005, he pleaded guilty to 10 counts of murder.)

— SPJ Ethics Committee

CASE STUDY 4:

A Suspect 'Confession'

WHAT: John Mark Karr, 41, was arrested on August 16, 2006, in Bangkok, Thailand, at the request of Colorado and U.S. officials. During questioning, he confessed to the murder of JonBenét Ramsey, who had been beaten and strangled to death in the basement of her Boulder, Colorado, home sometime during Christmas night 1996. (The murder was a media obsession for much of 1997, and video clips of the young beauty contestant competing in various costumes ran, it seems, every few hours.)

Karr was arrested after Michael Tracey, a journalism professor at the University of Colorado, alerted authorities to information he had drawn from e-mails Karr had sent him over the past four years. Karr had initiated the correspondence, apparently intrigued by Tracey's argument, in documentaries and elsewhere, that John and Patsy Ramsey had been unfairly implicated in their daughter's death. Karr was returned to Boulder for DNA testing and ultimately cleared. But he wasn't freed; he also faced misdemeanor child pornography charges in California.

WHO: Put yourself in the shoes of a news director or managing editor. Could you resist this story, especially if you were in Colorado? In the first three weeks after Karr's "confession," the *Rocky Mountain News* ran 150 stories about him, including this first-day lead: "The decade-long search for JonBenét Ramsey's killer came to a startling end in Thailand on Wednesday." *The Denver Post* probably ran a similar number, but its website list cuts off after 10 hits. In JonBenét's home town of Boulder, the *Daily Camera* ran 120 stories during the same period.

Or imagine you're Professor Tracey. Do you break a confidence with your source if you think it can solve a murder — or protect children half a world away?

There are many stakeholders in this case, including the media, Tracey and, of course, Karr himself. Add Boulder law enforcement authorities, who had been criticized for bungling the original case 10 years previously, and now for spending $23,656, including two business-class airfares, to bring a delusional man back to face dubious charges. Ramsey family members are major stakeholders. Even the University of Colorado j-school is among many parties with a peripheral interest.

WHY: The principles involved in deciding what to do include the media's obligations to their readers and viewers to present the news in full while maintaining

John Mark Karr

a sense of responsibility and balance. For Professor Tracey, there's a struggle between confidentiality and collaboration. And should the media be critical of authorities who, after all, pulled Karr away from the temptation of children in Thailand, where he was about to begin a teaching job?

HOW: We've seen how the media reacted to this story — at full throttle. Was it overkill? A bit more skepticism and proportionality would have been more professional. Was Professor Tracey's role appropriate? He considers himself an academic, not a journalist. But even if he were a journalist, wrote *Rocky Mountain News* media columnist David Kopel, he should act like an ethical human being. Kopel's argument is worth repeating.

"Some critics claim that if journalists cooperate with the police, they will lose the trust of their audience. But just imagine how much less most readers would trust the newspapers if readers learned that a reporter refused to reveal non-confidential information which could have led to the capture of a notorious murderer."

ANALYSIS: Some principles (from the SPJ Code of Ethics), and comment

• Journalists should be honest, fair and courageous in gathering, reporting and interpreting information. (Quantity, more than quality, is the question.)

- Test the accuracy of information from all sources and exercise care to avoid inadvertent error. (In a highly competitive rush, it's difficult — but still necessary.)
- Show good taste. Avoid pandering to lurid curiosity. (Lurid curiosity is sometimes unavoidable.)
- Be judicious about naming criminal suspects before the formal filing of charges.
- Be vigilant and courageous about holding those with power accountable.
- Clarify and explain news coverage and invite dialogue with the public over journalistic conduct. (There was plenty of explaining where the information came from, and a flood of letters to the editor.)

— SPJ Ethics Committee

CASE STUDY 5:

Pre-publication review

Once upon a time, a reporter would never let a source see what the reporter intended to write. But there has been growing acceptance of the idea that it's more important to be accurate than to be independent.

Actually, both are great ideals, but accuracy takes precedence. That's why attitudes have changed. It's a credibility thing. Some argue that pre-publication review gives a journalist's sources more confidence that the reporter is going to get it right. And, let's face it, there are some very complicated topics where it is probably a good idea to go back to one's source and say something like: "Here's what I understood you to say about cold fusion's potential as a power source. Please tell me if I've got it right."

College texts for reporting students have made note of this change in the acceptance of pre-publication review (or PPR for short). Steve Weinberg, former head of Investigative Reporters and Editors, is quoted in one as saying, "I have practiced PPR as a newspaper staff writer, a magazine free-lancer and a book author. Never have I regretted my practice. What I do regret is failing to do it during the first decade of my mindless adherence to tradition."

Weinberg said the offer of review makes sources more willing to talk on the record. And it doesn't compromise the writers' control over their stories. If a source wants to change a story, remind him or her that the review is only for accuracy, not for interpretation or tone.

This is not about turning over your story to your source. There are rules, after all. And the No. 1 rule is "no editing." You're not going to let a source edit your copy — or change its tone, context or organization, either. You're just checking the facts.

Make that clear to your source. Accuracy is your motivation; not accommodation.

There are other rules, too:

Don't change direct quotes, especially if you have them on tape. Sometimes a source will say that isn't really what he intended to say and will want to rephrase it. You can either play "gotcha" or negotiate — especially if the rephrasing is more accurate or pertinent. After all, the source did say both the old and the new versions.

The best time to double-check is during the initial interview. "I think I understood what you said about bird flu and down pillows, but let me read it back to you from my notes to be sure I have it right."

You might occasionally want a source to review an entire story, but it's better practice simply to go over specific passages. You can do it by phone or by e-mail — or, better yet, e-mail the snippets to the source and then discuss it over the telephone.

A few journalists routinely ask their sources to review entire stories to see if there are any errors. Jay Mathews, a veteran education reporter for *The Washington Post*, made a practice of showing entire stories to sources, even though it made his editors uneasy. He wrote about that in *The Post*'s May 31, 2003, edition.

One Possible Policy on PPR:

Make it clear that your source is not your editor. He or she can't change what you've written.

The review is for accuracy only. Just the facts, not context, tone or organization.

Don't change direct quotes. You should have them on tape. But it's OK to negotiate.

The best time to double-check is during the interview.

It's better to review specific passages with the source than to hand over the entire story for review.

Remember: YOU DON'T HAVE TO CHANGE ANYTHING! But if it's incorrect, you certainly should.

"I have shown every story I have written to all the sources I could find," he said. "... They are welcome to argue about the tone, the analysis or anything else that bothers them, but I change only the things that I am convinced are inaccurate."

Pre-publication review gives sources confidence that the reporter cares about getting it right. Offering to let them check what you've written gets them to open up. It enhances your credibility and reputation.

You won't lose control of your story. You're still the one who has the final say on what goes into your story before it's submitted to an editor — who is, other than you, the only one who can change what you've written.

It's best to have a written newsroom policy on this, something written down that a reporter can refer to when a source asks to check a story before it's published.

And when does fact-checking become excessive? Texas Republicans in 2005 accused an *Austin American-Statesman* writer of collaborating with a Democratic district attorney to criticize the Republican Party. E-mails showed the political reporter/columnist gave the prosecutor advance versions of an article he was writing. The writer said he was only trying to avoid errors. The Republicans claimed the journalist and DA were in cahoots, trying to make their party look bad.

Journalists have mixed reactions, although most of them feel it's not a good idea to be quite so accommodating. But they do want to get it right.

— *Fred Brown, SPJ Ethics Committee*

CASE STUDY 6:

Who's the 'Predator'?

"To Catch a Predator," the ratings-grabbing series on NBC's *Dateline*, appeared to catch on with the public. But it also raised serious ethical questions for journalists.

The television newsmagazine, working with law enforcement, trolled for men to engage in sexually charged online chats with minors, then invited them to a face-to-face meeting, supposedly at the child's home. Armed with liquor, condoms and little common sense, the men arrived at the front door. The kids weren't home, but the suspects don't know that when they walked into a kitchen and came face to face with reporter Chris Hansen.

The conversations were recorded by a bevy of hidden cameras, and the men were met by law enforcement officers once they left the house. The "suspects" were portrayed as sexual predators without any apparent constitutional protections.

Critics questioned this blending of reporters, "watchdog" groups and police, arguing that the men caught in the sting

> Should a journalist buy into the agenda of an advocacy group, even if it's a worthy agenda?

were entrapped at worst and faced public ridicule and humiliation at best. One target of the sting, a Texas district attorney who made contact online, but never ventured out for a personal meeting, committed suicide before facing the cameras. When police, armed with a search warrant — and a *Dateline* camera crew — showed up at prosecutor Louis Conradt Jr.'s home in Terrell, Texas, no one answered the door, according to the police who took part in the attempted arrest. After forcing their way into his home, police found the 56-year-old prosecutor in a hallway holding a semiautomatic handgun. "I'm not going to hurt anybody," he told police before firing a bullet into his own head.

Dateline isn't the only media organization that has been involved in these stings. They date back to at least 2003, and what they have in common is a website called Perverted-Justice.com. It's a highly motivated advocacy group, committed to finding perverts and removing them from circulation.

Perverted-Justice.com scans chat rooms looking for men who can be lured into sexually explicit conversations with correspondents pretending to be underage boys and girls. It works with police and news media to entice the unsuspecting marks to set-up trysting places where the cops — and the cameras — are waiting.

Judging from the ratings, the public loves this. Perverts who would harm children are exposed and made to account for their perversion.

But the media should be more questioning. Is it ethically defensible to take part in the deceit that is a sting? Should a journalist buy into the agenda of an advocacy group, even if it's a worthy agenda? Is it ethical to work with law enforcement authorities in this manner?

Question: If your newspaper or television station were approached by Perverted Justice to participate in a "sting" designed to identify real and potential perverts, should you go along, or say, "No thanks"? Was NBC reporting the news or creating it?

Once Perverted-Justice.com had an alliance with a national network, the smaller local stations that first cooperated with the group probably will no longer face the decision of whether to join forces in similar "stings." NBC aired the last new episode of "To Catch a Predator" in December 2007, but episodes are still available on MSNBC.com.

The biggest stakeholders in this ethical decision clearly were the men lured before the cameras. Their wives and families also faced major consequences from what NBC did. Law enforcement officers provided plenty of "perp walks," arrests and bookings in clear view of cameras for additional video footage of the suspects, in return for coverage of their cleaning up the community of predators. Perverted Justice got airtime for its cause and financial reward for its efforts. NBC had a primetime audience of more than eight million viewers.

The public had a stake, too. There is no question that law-abiding citizens want to bring sexual predators to justice. Even one communication ethics student, a young mother, said she could find no reasonable arguments against using a sting to trap potential perverts.

"I do not see in any way that a news station would be looked down upon for giving society what I would consider this service," she wrote. "... If one child can be saved from this horrific event, then by all means do it. I think if you were to take a poll the majority of society would agree."

That's most likely true. But responsible media shouldn't base their ethical standards on what's popular.

Enticing (the term Hansen prefers to use, as posted on his blog) or entrapping subjects holds many legal and ethical issues. Should reporters seek out criminals? Is this indeed a public service as NBC contends? There is also an evidentiary problem when law enforcement and media join forces to prosecute criminals. Are outtakes, notes and other reporting tools now part of a criminal investigation?

In one case a district attorney's office announced it would not prosecute cases during one of NBC's stings, citing a lack of evidence. The office claimed

Perverted Justice members refused to testify and turn over records (they deny these accusations), and NBC needed to provide additional footage to help build a case. Running the online trolling and sting house in two different counties caused a jurisdictional dispute, creating another legal issue.

Media critics and ethicists question the reporting methods and standards of running this type of "undercover" operation. Al Tompkins, who teaches ethics in television journalism at the Poynter Institute, told rival ABC in a report about the show, "The project, from the very beginning, had lawsuit written all over it."

Critics cite the Society of Professional Journalists Code of Ethics as a guideline for fair and accurate reporting, including:

- Avoid undercover or other surreptitious methods of gathering information except when traditional open methods will not yield information vital to the public. Use of such methods should be explained as part of the story.
- Remain free of associations and activities that may compromise integrity or damage credibility.
- Be wary of sources offering information for favors or money; avoid bidding for news.
- Avoid misleading re-enactments or staged news events. If re-enactment is necessary to tell a story, label it.
- Diligently seek out subjects of news stories to give them the opportunity to respond to allegations of wrongdoing.
- Avoid conflicts of interest, real or perceived.
- Show good taste. Avoid pandering to lurid curiosity.
- Be judicious about naming criminal suspects before the formal filing of charges.

NBC engaged the services of Perverted Justice, inviting scrutiny for creating a news story. By paying actors to pose as minors and engage in sexual chat, did the newsmagazine become the story? NBC surrounded the criminals with law enforcement waiting patiently outside to record the outcome. This was the reverse of most crime scenes. Justice and the media were both perverted throughout this predatory process.

The important thing is to have a discussion and to ask the right questions. Among them: Is this a justifiable, ethically defensible use of deception? Should you buy into the agenda of an advocacy group? How ethical is the group itself? Do you compromise your "watchdog" role by cooperating with law enforcement authorities?

DECISION: Let law enforcement conduct sting operations and the media report on the arrests.

— Robbie Rogers and Sara Stone, Baylor University

CASE STUDY 7:

The Media's Foul Ball

WHAT: The Chicago Cubs in 2003 were five outs from advancing to the World Series for the first time since 1945 when a 26-year-old fan tried to grab a foul ball, preventing outfielder Moises Alou from catching it. The Florida Marlins rallied for an 8–3 victory to tie the National League championship series in game 6, then went on to defeat the Cubs. The man in the left field seats who deflected the ball was escorted by security guards from Wrigley Field after he was threatened and cursed by angry fans and pelted with beer and debris.

The hapless fan's identity was unknown. But he became recognizable through televised replays as the young baby-faced man in glasses, a Cubs baseball cap and earphones who bobbled the ball and was blamed for costing the Cubs a trip to the World Series.

Question: Given the potential danger to the man, should he be identified by the media?

> At least one journalist at the time thought the *Chicago Tribune* might have distinguished itself by continuing to refuse to identify Bartman...

WHO: After working through the night and the next morning, the *Chicago Sun-Times* identified the infamous Cubs fan as Steve Bartman, the Lincolnshire, Ill., consulting firm where he worked and the suburb where he lived. *Sun-Times* reporter Frank Main, who covered the story, explained why the *Sun-Times* editor at the time decided to reveal Bartman's identity. "He was the center of a national news story and there was no legal or moral problem in naming him. We did not think there was a serious possibility of his being assassinated by fans. We decided to go with the story and tell readers what we knew." *Chicago Tribune* editors said they printed Bartman's name after he released a statement saying, "I am truly sorry from the bottom of this Cubs fan's broken heart." James Burke, a member of the Ethics AdviceLine for Journalists team, said identifying Bartman was "an act of irresponsible journalism" and a violation of the SPJ ethics code which urges journalists to minimize harm. Chicago's Mayor Richard Daley chastised the media for identifying Bartman, and was quoted by the *Sun-Times* saying "do you put your CEO's name and address out?... You wouldn't do that. You'd be fired tomorrow...And that is not fair to that young man..."

WHY: One of the highest principles in the SPJ Code of Ethics is to seek truth and report it. But journalists also should balance that principle with others, such as whether revealing Bartman's identity could result in harm. Other than the statement expressing regret for deflecting the ball from Alou's glove, Bartman made no further comment or allowed interviews. He has remained a private figure who has insisted on his privacy and made every attempt to avoid the publicity he was getting. The *Chicago Tribune* justified identifying Bartman by saying other media were doing it.

HOW: Journalists have an obligation to consider the honorable course of action, such as whether Bartman should have been identified and whether his identity was something the public needed to know. This was, after all, a baseball game in which Bartman was a mere spectator. Bartman did not lose the game; the Chicago Cubs lost the game and the series. Each news organization should consider acting independently.

At least one journalist at the time thought the *Chicago Tribune* might have distinguished itself by continuing to refuse to identify Bartman even though he issued a statement and others were identifying him. The SPJ Code of Ethics urges journalists to show compassion and special sensitivity when dealing with inexperienced sources or subjects. That could have applied to Bartman. Journalists could have asked him if he wanted to be identified before doing so. This was not a case where the public needed to know his identity. And in retrospect, Bartman did not surface again from his momentary, unwanted celebrity. It was thrust upon him against his will. He was a victim of fate and happened to be where a foul ball fell from the sky.

In his statement, Bartman said in part: "I had my eyes glued on the approaching ball the entire time and was so caught up in the moment that I did not even see Moises Alou, much less that he may have had a play." The media could have taken pity on the guy.

— Casey Bukro, SPJ Ethics Committee

CASE STUDY 8:

McVeigh's Confession Goes Online

Summary

Seven hours before its newspaper hit print, *The Dallas Morning News* posted a story on its website reporting that Timothy McVeigh, then a suspect in the Oklahoma City bombing, had confessed to the crime to a defense team investigator. It was the first time that a newspaper had broken a major story online before its printed edition was published. For that reason, *The Dallas Morning News* found itself at the epicenter of a controversy almost immediately.

The Web article said McVeigh had told his lawyers that he had driven the truck used in the bombing and decided on a daytime attack to ensure a "body count." The bombing at the Alfred P. Murrah Federal Building killed 168 people and injured 500. The story on *The Dallas Morning News* website appeared on the day prospective jurors were required to turn in court questionnaires.

McVeigh's lead attorney, Stephen Jones, accused *The Dallas Morning News* of jeopardizing his client's right to a fair trial. At a news conference, Jones called the report "irresponsible" and "sensational." He also suggested the newspaper had stolen the information, "hacking" into his computer files. At one point, Jones claimed the defense team had fabricated the documents that *The Dallas Morning News* had used in its story.

After several days of reporting different responses from Jones, *The Dallas Morning News* published a graphic showing how the attorney's positions had changed. Calling Jones' accusations "totally untrue," *Morning News* editor Ralph Langer said the newspaper obtained the information legally — though he did not explain how *The Dallas Morning News* accessed the defense files. "Clearly, we would not publish a story if we weren't confident of the quality of information we have," Langer said in *The Dallas Morning News* article published the morning after the initial Web story appeared.

Langer said *Morning News* editors decided to first publish the confession on the newspaper's website because the newspaper wanted to deliver a "blockbuster" story to readers as soon as possible. The story had been written and edited by mid-afternoon, then quickly posted to the Web. In addition, a *Morning News* reporter had interviewed government officials, prosecutors and Jones — all of whom knew a story was going to be published about McVeigh's confession — and the newspaper feared being scooped by its competitors, Langer said.

Some critics charged that the newspaper wanted to avoid any prior restraint attempts by Jones, but Langer said Jones never threatened to ask a judge to block the story. In *Quill*, Langer wrote that he, other editors and the newspaper's attorney had discussed whether to publish McVeigh's confession over parts of several days before the story appeared on the Web. The decision process, he said, covered basic questions concerning the use of material from defense files and the possible impact on the trial.

"We had concern about the trial but, ultimately, came to believe that the information in that part of the material was of national importance and that we were obligated to publish it," Langer said.

Prosecutors, the judge and McVeigh's defense team later agreed that *The Dallas Morning News* report would have no effect on the trial. McVeigh ultimately was convicted and sentenced to death.

Analysis

The publication in *The Dallas Morning News* of the purported confession of Timothy McVeigh offers a classic case in journalism ethics. Just as important, it offers a significant case study in the process of ethical decision-making.

At its core, this case is about competing principles and conflicting values. It is about the tension between the First and Sixth amendments. It is about duty and responsibility, about consequences and alternatives. It is about fairness to the accused, concern for the families of victims and respect for the judicial process. It is also a case about public service, journalistic independence and competitive instincts.

> At its core, this case is about competing principles and conflicting values.

Clearly there are legal issues, but why, when, what and how to publish are essential ethical decisions. While ethics is about right and wrong, it is prudent to resist the temptation to cast a thumbs-up or thumbs-down on *The Dallas Morning News'* actions. Ethical decision-making is more complex than that.

Additionally, we are missing pieces of the puzzle necessary to evaluate the newspaper's decisions. We have not seen the documents *The Dallas Morning News* used as the basis for its story. Nor were we in the newsroom to observe and hear the deliberations on the decision to publish.

Morning News editor Ralph Langer said the paper had an obligation to publish the story about McVeigh's alleged confession because "the information in that part of the material was of national importance and ... we were obligated to publish it."

Since the public did not have the same access to the documents as *The Dallas Morning News*, Langer is asking us to make a considerable leap of faith in accepting its reasons. It is appropriate, therefore, to be more detailed in explaining how it reached its decision. We want to know why the paper decided to publish the story on that weekend. And it's very important to understand to what degree journalists considered the interest of the victims and victims' families. Until we know more, it is best to hold *The Dallas Morning News* accountable by challenging rather than cheering or condemning.

The case has high stakes on many levels for all of the affected parties. The editors of *The Dallas Morning News* still need to tell us more about their decision-making process. That public accountability will help all of us judge whether the newspaper responsibly fulfilled its journalistic obligation.

— from the Third Edition, Black, Steele and Barney

(In *Quill*, Bob Steele suggests a series of questions that would have informed *The Dallas Morning News'* decision to publish McVeigh's purported confession. The questions deal with issues of news-gathering techniques, sources, authenticity, fairness, consequences, independence, publishing, process and accountability. See "Until we know, let us challenge," *Quill*, April 1997, pp. 28–29.)

Accuracy

What the Codes Say

Detroit Free Press

WE ARE COMMITTED TO:

Seeking and reporting the truth in a truthful way

- We will dedicate ourselves to reporting the news accurately, thoroughly and in context.
- We will be honest in the way we gather, report and present news.
- We will be persistent in the pursuit of the whole story.
- We will keep our word.
- We will hold factual information in opinion columns and editorial to the same standards of accuracy as news stories.
- We will seek to gain sufficient understanding of the communities, individuals and stories we cover to provide an informed account of activities.

San Jose Mercury News

TRUTHFULNESS

It is obvious that we should not knowingly publish falsehoods.

A reporter should not make it sound as if a source made a statement to the reporter if, in fact, it came to us through a third party. Nor should we write about an event we did not attend in a way that gives the impression we did.

In the interest of integrity and fairness, photographers and editors should exercise caution in the use of "set-up" photographs. In the same way that reporters do not make up quotes, photographers do not reconstruct scenes or events with the purpose of making them appear as if they were "found" moments.

However, photographers are often called upon to make environmental portraits or do illustrative photography. In no way should such photographs be approached or treated as anything but what they are. They are either portraits or are demonstrative of a situation. Both should be clearly labeled.

That means that care should be taken in writing captions so they do not suggest the picture is something it is not. For example, is Clark Kent working in his study or is he simply in his study (for purposes of a portrait)? Is Lois Lane actually practicing her technique of boomerang tossing or is she demonstrating her technique of boomerang tossing (for purposes of a photograph)? Such distinctions make a difference.

The Denver Post

Nailing our stories can be as simple as phoning three people — or as grueling as spending months chiseling away the nonessential, the rumor, the red herrings.

Our aim is to deliver the facts with precision and context.

We believe in getting not only both sides, but "all" sides.

The best stories are multi-sourced. Facts are triple-checked. Issues are balanced with diverse views and sources.

They are, simply, as complete as possible.

The New York Times

No one needs to be reminded that falsifying any part of a news report cannot be tolerated and will result automatically in disciplinary action up to and including termination. (Dates from December 2000, three years before the Jayson Blair episode.)

The Washington Post

This newspaper is pledged to minimize the number of errors we make and to correct those that occur. Accuracy is our goal; candor is our defense. Persons who call errors to our attention must be accorded a respectful hearing.

The Virginian-Pilot (Norfolk, Virginia)

A number of techniques commonly used in fiction writing must be avoided. Among them:

- The telescoping of time so that, for example, events that actually happened during several days are reported as happening in a single day.
- Vivid description of scenes that the writer could not have seen or had specific knowledge of.
- Passages conveying that the reporter knew what an individual was thinking or feeling without having been told.

Hearst Newspapers

The deliberate introduction of false information into our newspapers will not be tolerated. Legitimate mistakes do occur, and when they do, we have the responsibility to correct those errors in a timely and complete fashion. While the editor, the managing editor and the reader representative have the final responsibility for corrections, reporters should not hesitate to bring errors in their own work to the attention of their supervisor.

Associated Press Managing Editors

The newspaper should guard against inaccuracies, carelessness, bias or distortion through emphasis, omission or technological manipulation.

It should acknowledge substantive errors and correct them promptly and prominently.

American Society of News Editors

ARTICLE IV — Truth and Accuracy. Good faith with the reader is the foundation of good journalism. Every effort must be made to assure that the news content is accurate, free from bias and in context, and that all sides are presented fairly. Editorials, analytical articles and commentary should be held to the same standards of accuracy with respect to facts as news reports. Significant errors of fact, as well as errors of omission, should be corrected promptly and prominently.

6

Deception

The issue of deception is a significant ethical matter, for it deals with truth, and seeking truth is what journalism is all about. Only recently has the debate over deception reached the stage where media organizations have begun to address the issue head-on in their codes of ethics. The discussion has intensified of late because of the conversion to digital photography and the ease with which reality can be manipulated, along with the disturbing tendency of so many news operations to turn to surreptitious reporting and hidden cameras as a first rather than a last resort when conducting investigations.

Deception in journalism can take many forms, from outright lying, to misleading, or misrepresenting, or merely being less than forthright. All of these actions are intended to cause someone to believe what is not true.

Our society depends on a level of trust, a belief that people will exchange and share information that is true. Without such trust, interaction among people will be stifled, and the functioning of society will be thwarted.

Given the premium value on truth, when, if ever, is it appropriate for a journalist to deceive someone in gathering information or reporting a story?

Journalists disagree. Some subscribe to a rigid rule, saying that any form of deception to obtain information is unacceptable in a profession whose mission is truth-telling. Others would argue that while deception is to be avoided, it may be acceptable in those rare instances in which the value of the information sought is of overwhelming importance, and the information can be obtained in no other way. Others would suggest there is a distinction among forms of deception, between outright lying and merely not revealing everything, between using hidden cameras in a public place and hiding cameras on the person who is at the same time pretending to be someone else.

The issue of deception places a premium on the ability of individual journalists and news organizations to do solid, ethical decision-making. In some cases, deception might allow journalists to come closer to exploring the truth, but those who deceive can cause great harm to the credibility of journalism and may harm individuals who are deceived.

Deception: Checklist

What does it mean to lie? Ethicist Sissela Bok wrote an outstanding book on this subject, called *Lying: Moral Choice in Public and Private Life*. In that book, she says lying is one form of deception. "I shall define as a lie any intentionally deceptive message which is stated." The act of deception, Bok says, can be much broader. "When we undertake to deceive others intentionally, we communicate messages meant to mislead them, meant to make them believe what we ourselves do not believe. We can do so through gesture, through disguise, by means of action or inaction, even through silence."

In an effort to determine when the use of deception at whatever level might be justified by journalists, the participants in an ethical decision-making seminar at The Poynter Institute for Media Studies created the following criteria:

> When is deception by a journalist justified? What are the criteria for a "Just Lie"? To justify a lie or deception one must fulfill all of the criteria.
>
> - When the information sought is of profound importance. It must be of vital public interest, such as revealing great "system failure" at the top levels, or it must prevent profound harm to individuals.
> - When all other alternatives to obtaining the same information have been exhausted.
> - When the journalists involved are willing to fully and openly disclose the nature of the deception and the reason for it to those involved and to the public.
> - When the individuals involved and their news organization apply excellence, through outstanding craftsmanship as well as the commitment of time and funding needed to fully pursue the story.
> - When the harm prevented by the information revealed through deception outweighs any harm caused by the act of deception.
> - When the journalists involved have conducted a meaningful, collaborative and deliberative decision-making process in which they weigh:
>   - the consequences (short- and long-term) of the deception on those being deceived
>   - the impact on journalist credibility
>   - the motivations for their actions
>   - the deceptive act in relation to their editorial mission
>   - the legal implications of the action
>   - the consistency of their reasoning and their action

CASE STUDY 9:

ABC and Food Lion

WHAT: This case has been a classic study in the use of deception since the report first aired more than 15 years ago. ABC News journalists have used hidden cameras on a number of occasions over the years, the reports often airing on the network's *PrimeTime Live* program. Stories revealed dangerous or illegal situations in care homes, child care facilities and veterans' hospitals. In other cases journalists used hidden cameras to help expose insurance scams and racial discrimination by landlords and real estate agents.

Yet, no *PrimeTime Live* story up to that time generated as much public attention and journalistic soul-searching as the reporting on the Food Lion supermarket chain. To investigate allegations of unsanitary food-handling practices at Food Lion, two ABC producers worked briefly in the spring of 1992 at several of the company's supermarkets in the Carolinas. The producers misrepresented themselves on their job applications, and once employed they concealed cameras in wigs and clothing to tape video and sound for their report.

The *PrimeTime Live* exposé aired in November 1992. The hidden camera video revealed rat-gnawed cheese, and spoiled meat and chicken being washed with bleach, repackaged and given a new sell-by date. In interviews, Food Lion employees and former employees attested to being told to take part in such practices, and many former store workers signed affidavits swearing to the same effect.

Food Lion claimed its reputation was severely damaged by the revelations and that it lost $1.7 billion to $2.5 billion in sales and stock value.

Still, Food Lion did not sue for libel, where the truth of the report would be the standard. Instead, Food Lion sued on grounds of fraud and trespass, seeking to show that the ABC employees spent their time on the job at the stores performing their journalistic role instead of performing the work they were hired to do. Food Lion lawyers also said the journalists had made some mistakes in reporting, even helping to create some of the bad conditions they exposed. The plaintiff's lawyers also sought to discredit statements by some people it characterized as union supporters dissatisfied with management at the non-union chain.

So when the case of *Food Lion v. Capital Cities/ABC* went to trial in December 1996, the judge did not allow jurors to view the news report but rather directed them to assume that the facts of the report were true.

The network did not deny that it had used deceptive news-gathering methods, but it did deny committing fraud and trespass. Fraud requires intent to

When do the ends justify the means?

injure, and by performing their supermarket jobs well, the undercover journalists could do no harm as food workers.

The jury found in favor of Food Lion. Although the grocery chain sought as much as $1.9 billion from ABC, the jury awarded it $5.5 million. In August 1997, an appellate judge reduced the award to $315,000. In 1999, a federal appeals court overturned the jury verdict, ruling that ABC News did not commit fraud. The court did find the two producers liable for submitting fake employment applications and trespassing in Food Lion stores and ordered each to pay $1 to Food Lion.

There is a pivotal question. Is it ever appropriate for journalists to lie to get to the truth? Put another way, is it ever justifiable for a journalist to violate the principle of honesty in order to honor the principle upon which journalism is founded, a duty to provide the public with meaningful, accurate and comprehensive information about significant issues?

> Did the quality of reporting measure up to the highest standards required for a case where it lied to get to the truth?

WHO: *PrimeTime Live* must make a convincing argument that the use of deception to get journalists inside Food Lion supermarkets was justifiable. ABC had considerable anecdotal evidence, including dozens of interviews with current and former Food Lion employees, that Food Lion supermarkets were selling tainted meat and fish products and violating other health, safety and employment standards. But ABC News needed firsthand evidence to be sure of the accuracy of those allegations and to document the extent of wrongdoing. While undercover reporting is clearly invasive, the journalist's direct observation can heighten fairness to the accused by minimizing reliance on other sources who might have tainted motives.

ABC must also make a convincing argument that in this case no other reporting methods would provide the same level of verification as undercover reporting. Granted, ABC could have purchased meat and fish products at the counter and tested them, but that approach is not foolproof, nor could it have revealed the behind-the-meat-counter story that would indicate the extent of wrongdoing and the reasons for it.

In a forum on ethics, ABC News must justify the level of expertise it brought to this story. Did the quality of reporting measure up to the highest standards required for a case where it lied to get to the truth? Were the journalists comprehensive and exhaustive in their investigation? Did they offer a contextual as well as factually accurate picture of what was happening at Food Lion? Finally, there is this critical question: If ABC News used the threat to public health as a reason for the extensive undercover investigation and the use of deception, why did it take so long to ring the warning bell? Why did the network wait six months after going undercover before *PrimeTime Live* aired the report?

WHY: Absolutists will argue that a journalist should never lie, no matter what is at stake. That position avoids the essence of ethical decision-making and ignores the unique and essential role journalists play in a democratic society. Ethics involves making difficult choices when faced with competing values, conflicting principles and multiple stakeholders. Ethical decision-making often involves choosing a course of action among several options, each of which carries negative consequences.

Journalists can and do face these agonizing dilemmas when reporting on issues of national security, government corruption or public safety. The consequences can be profound, sometimes involving risk to human life, the ruin of a person's reputation or the downfall of an institution or business enterprise. Even on routine stories about health care, crime, education and government, journalists face hard choices about what to report and what to hold back, about when and how to approach vulnerable people and when to step back.

ABC News encountered such ethical dilemmas in the past in deciding to use deception and hidden cameras to get to the truth. *PrimeTime Live* journalists went undercover to produce reports on abhorrent treatment of patients in VA hospitals and in care homes, spotlighting government regulatory failures that jeopardized the welfare of patients. *PrimeTime Live* used deception and hidden cameras to document the insidious racial discrimination that threatens the fabric of our society.

To be sure, hidden cameras are overused and misused by both network and local television, and journalists too often use forms of deception and misrepresentation as a shortcut in their reporting. These tools have extremely sharp edges, and when improperly used, they harm innocent people and erode journalistic integrity. When these tools are overused, they become dull, losing their impact.

Hidden cameras and any form of deception should be used judiciously and rarely. They should be reserved for those exceptional stories of great public interest involving significant harm to individuals or system failure at the highest levels. Furthermore, deception and hidden cameras should be used only as a reporting tool of last resort, after all other approaches to obtaining the same vital information have been exhausted or appropriately ruled out. And news organizations that choose to use deception and hidden cameras have an obligation to assure their work meets the highest professional standards.

There is no judge or jury to offer a verdict on whether ABC measured up to such high ethical standards in the Food Lion case. The public and other professionals render that verdict. Perhaps more importantly, ABC must scrutinize its own journalism to see if it met the highest standards.

HOW: This case clearly demonstrates how courtroom verdicts are cast in the extremes of black and white while ethical decisions most often emerge from situations painted in multiple shades of gray.

With the law, juries vote on right or wrong after listening to polarizing arguments from two sides of a case. With ethics, there is no defined forum with a witness stand and jury box, and there is no volume of case law. It is the public, and to some degree professional colleagues, who will judge the moral positions of both this major network news organization and this huge supermarket corporation.

In the court of law, a federal jury said ABC News and *PrimeTime Live* journalists trespassed and committed fraud when researching accusations that Food Lion supermarkets sold spoiled meat.

The debate over ethics in this case continues in the court of public opinion, focusing on issues of honesty, accuracy and fairness.

ABC had good reasons to appeal the legal ruling in the Food Lion case. It is equally important that ABC hold its own news reporting to the highest standards. Journalists need considerable freedom to do their work on behalf of the public. They have a responsibility to honor that freedom by being ethical and excellent at what they do.

— from the Third Edition, Black, Steele and Barney

CASE STUDY 10:

The Masquerading Mortician

Summary

Freelance reporter Jonathan Franklin posed as a mortician and entered the mortuary at Dover Air Force Base, the sole Desert Storm casualty processing center, during the Persian Gulf War. He wanted to find out if the military had been underestimating the number of casualties. He found that it had.

On the basis of previous reporting he had done on the war dead after the invasion of Panama, Franklin was convinced the Pentagon was "screwing with the numbers." The Pentagon had forbidden journalists to photograph or witness the unloading of the dead at Dover Air Force Base, and Franklin was stymied in all his above-board efforts to penetrate the cloak of security around the returning dead.

He tried contacting the undertaker who won the government contract to prepare the bodies returning from the Gulf for burial, attempted to get the number of dead from airlines shipping the bodies home, and

> If a journalist uses deception in the news-gathering process, that deception must be disclosed to the public when the story is published.

sought unsuccessfully to locate the officers who were informing the families of the dead. After exhausting those avenues of inquiry, Franklin decided to go undercover.

Craig McLaughlin, then managing editor of the *Bay Guardian,* a weekly newspaper in San Francisco, said he chose to run Franklin's freelanced piece, although he usually turns down story ideas involving undercover work. He said he felt it was his responsibility as an editor to show the public what the war really resulted in: not just flashy graphics on the television, but mangled American sons and daughters.

McLaughlin said the deception perpetuated on the military's mortuary "was not a lie directed at an individual. It wasn't an invasion of privacy. It was directed at a government body failing to uphold the Constitution."

McLaughlin gave Franklin's story the green light because it passed his two requirements for undercover work:

1. There are no other means by which the story can be reported.
2. The information in the story is politically vital to the readers, with important public policy ramifications.

Inside the morgue, Franklin apparently was the only journalist to actually see the Gulf casualties. He found that many of the combat deaths due to friendly fire were being reported inside the morgue as "training accidents," a practice that also occurred after the Panamanian invasion. And Franklin discovered a source who estimated there were "about 200" combat deaths, compared to the official Pentagon figure at the time: 55.

Franklin's one-page story in the *Bay Guardian* prompted at least one letter to the editor, in which the writer complained only about the gruesome descriptions of the bodies Franklin had seen inside the morgue. The story also won second place in the annual Project Censored awards for the most important stories bypassed by the mass media each year.

Analysis

The use of deception to gain access to information is always an ethical concern. The primary principle of journalism, truth-telling, requires reporters **to be honest themselves in their gathering, reporting and interpreting of information.**

At the same time, there can be rare cases in which the only way to inform the public fully about significant events necessitates misrepresentation or deception. Craig McLaughlin's two criteria outlined in the case above provide the base of a meaningful process for determining when it might be appropriate to be deceptive. There is another important criterion to add: If a journalist uses deception in the news-gathering process, that deception must be disclosed to the public when the story is published. McLaughlin said the *Bay Guardian* demanded that Franklin include that full disclosure in his article. That level of accountability forces journalists to be judicious in their choice of exceptions to the truth-telling principle and requires them to be ultimately accountable to the public.

Journalists must accept that when they are less than honest about who they are in gathering information, whether it be through actively misrepresenting their identity, using hidden cameras or microphones, or passively deceiving someone, they are lying, pure and simple.

In the case of Jonathan Franklin's decision to pose as a mortician at the Dover Air Force Base, that lie must be balanced against the significant public policy interests inherent in this case and the responsibility of the media to hold the government accountable. Furthermore, Franklin's decision to misrepresent himself must truly be the last and only alternative available in gathering and reporting that information.

News organizations and individual reporters who consider using deception should also weigh both the short-term and the long-term consequences of their actions. It is possible that lying may provide access to significant information for a particular story; it also could keep government agencies honest. It is also possible that lying may erode the credibility of journalism and undermine its overall and long-term ability to function effectively as the primary information provider in society.

— from the Third Edition, Black, Steele and Barney

CASE STUDY 11:

Story or Stunt in Tampa?

Summary

The image had come to be seared into the collective consciousness of America as a portent of terror: a yellow Ryder rental truck parked in front of a bustling federal office building. Only this time, there was no bomb, no explosion, at least not in the literal sense. On this day, March 31, 1997, — by no mere coincidence the opening day of the trial of Oklahoma City bomber Timothy McVeigh—the Ryder truck in question was rented to a Tampa Bay-area television news team and parked in front of a building in downtown Tampa.

If the idea and the journalists' news judgment were questionable, at least the action taken by government officials and building security personnel was swift and decisive. As viewers of that evening's WTVT-TV newscast witnessed, a station reporter climbed out of the parked truck and started walking down the street. Security personnel quickly emerged from the federal building, detained the reporter and searched the truck. All of this activity was recorded by a WTVT photographer and aired in that evening's newscast.

> There were alternative reporting methods the television station could have taken to examine the status of security at the Federal building.

No legal steps were taken, but law-enforcement officials were quick to criticize the station for staging the event. WTVT-TV news director Daniel Webster — who was not involved in the planning, production or airing of the story — told the *St. Petersburg Times* the story was a test of the "status of public safety in Tampa." Saying that "if the scenario played out differently ... we might have done a piece that protected people's lives and led to a change in policies." Webster added that "if you had a belief that if you pulled a fire alarm and it didn't work, you might be exposing an issue of public concern."

U.S. Marshal Don Moreland, however, was quoted in the *Times* report on the stunt as saying, "In this case, I think a line was crossed." And officials at another local TV station were skeptical of the way WTVT approached the story, saying their own report on courthouse security was handled without having to stage an actual test of it.

Analysis

While the intent of the journalists in this story may have been noble — to examine the security status at the Tampa Federal Building — the reporting methods were poorly thought out and outright dangerous. The use of the Ryder truck was insensitive to family members of those who died in Oklahoma City and unfair to the Ryder truck company.

The greatest danger, however, was to public safety, exactly what the journalists were trying to protect. This staged event held all sorts of potentially significant dangers to citizens, the journalists involved, security personnel and public safety officers.

It's not inconceivable that workers in the federal building might panic at the sight of the Ryder truck outside. Passersby on the street might also react in fear, conceivably even attacking the journalists leaving the parked truck. Fortunately, the incident was well handled by security personnel, but it could have led to a shooting. In addition, firefighters or police officers could have been at risk in responding to someone's urgent call for assistance.

This case demonstrates the importance of strong front-end decision-making in a newsroom where managers and journalists seriously weigh the consequences of their actions. The risks in the actions of the WTVT journalists far outweighed the benefits. There were alternative reporting methods the television station could have taken to examine the status of security at the Federal building. While less visual, those approaches would have been safer and could have produced meaningful information.

This was a case where those involved ignored journalism ethics and completely forgot about common sense.

— from the Third Edition, Black, Steele and Barney

Deception

What the Codes Say

San Jose Mercury News

Under ordinary circumstances, reporters or photographers ought to identify themselves to news sources. There might be times, however, when circumstances will dictate not identifying ourselves. Only the executive editor or editor may approve such exceptions.

Philadelphia Inquirer

Impersonation is prohibited, as it undermines the trust that should be implicit in our relationship with the public. The Inquirer reports on the news; it tries not to create it, and it should never do so under false circumstances.

The Denver Post

We should be honest in carrying out all of our work. We should clearly identify ourselves in all situations.

If deception might be necessary to obtain critical information, it must be approved in advance by the Editor or Managing Editor/News. The information sought must be vital to the public interest and all other approaches to obtaining the same information without using deception must be exhausted.

Detroit Free Press

Ensuring the Truth Principle

"Seeking and reporting the truth in a truthful way" includes, specifically:

- We will not lie.
- We will not misstate our identities or intentions.
- We will not fabricate.
- We will not plagiarize.
- We will not alter photographs to mislead readers.
- We will not intentionally slant the news.

The Virginian-Pilot (Norfolk, Virginia)

It is our policy for reporters and photographers to fully identify themselves when covering a news event. Some situations will call for judgment. Openly announcing one's presence at the scene of certain news events could impede fair coverage. But reporters, editors or photographers should not lie or be deceptive when asked to identify themselves. Journalists are forbidden from posing as representatives of other professions, including but not limited to law enforcement, the medical fields and military.

The New York Times

Times reporters do not actively misrepresent their identity to get a story. We may sometimes remain silent on our identity and allow assumptions to be made — to observe an institution's dealings with the public, for example, or the behavior of people at a rally or police officers in a bar near the station house. But a sustained, systematic deception, even a passive one — taking a job, for example, to observe a business from the inside — may be employed only after consultation between a department head and masthead editors. (Obviously, specific exceptions exist for restaurant reviewing and similar assignments.)

7

Minimize Harm

Minimize Harm. It's one of the four major sections of the SPJ Code of Ethics. It's also a major factor in moral reasoning and ethical decision-making. Many ethical decisions, in journalism and elsewhere, are a struggle between doing one's duty and being responsible about the consequences of that action.

The important thing is to have that debate — either with yourself or preferably with colleagues — and to ask the right questions. A key pair of those questions is this: Who gets hurt if we tell this story? And does the benefit to the public of knowing that truth outweigh that harm?

The heavyweight in this balancing act is the truth. Telling the truth is a journalist's overriding duty. Considering the consequences is a tempering element — a smaller element, but nonetheless an important one.

In the simplest terms, minimizing harm requires being sensitive to the consequences of what you do as a journalist. "Recognize that gathering and reporting information may cause harm or discomfort," the code of ethics says, and remember that "[p]ursuit of the news is not a license for arrogance."

Before the code of ethics was revised in 1996, it didn't say much about minimizing harm. Years ago, we were more confident in our righteousness. But while the older SPJ codes of ethics don't actually use the words "minimize harm," they do include some evidence of sensitivity.

The 1984 version is an interesting document. This code of ethics has one section, out of six, labeled "ethics." It's all about conflicts of interest — the principles that are now part of the code's "Act Independently" section. Of course, there's much, much more to ethics than merely avoiding conflicts of interest.

There's another section in that 1984 code called "fair play." Parts of it correspond to the "Minimize Harm" and "Be Accountable" sections of today's code. It says "Journalists at all times will show respect for the dignity, privacy, rights and well-being of people encountered in the course of gathering and presenting the news." Journalists shouldn't "pander to morbid curiosity," it says, and should "make prompt and complete correction of their errors."

The "Fair Play" section represents about one-sixth of that 1984 code. By contrast, "Minimize Harm" is nearly a quarter of today's code. Add the "Be Accountable" provisions and you've got close to a third of the whole thing.

There is some sentiment in the profession that journalists shouldn't fret about consequences. It makes them timid. Throw it all out there and let come what may. Tell the story and run.

That attitude gives ammunition to journalism's critics, and it helps to explain dwindling trust. Civic journalism's response was to try to show the public that journalists do care, and to pay more attention to readers' and viewers' wants. The 1996 code revision, with its inclusion of "Minimize Harm," and "Be Accountable," was in part an effort to recognize that new sensitivity.

"Minimizing harm" means letting your humanity show through. Show a little compassion for the people who are affected by what you write. Remember that, for many people, being part of a story is a rare, even once-in-a-lifetime experience. They live with the consequences of what you've written long after you've moved on to other stories.

Minimize Harm (from the SPJ Code of Ethics)

Ethical journalists treat sources, subjects and colleagues as human beings deserving of respect.

Journalists should:

- Show compassion for those who may be affected by news coverage. Use special sensitivity when dealing with children and inexperienced sources or subjects.
- Be sensitive when seeking or using interviews or photographs of those affected by tragedy or grief.
- Recognize that gathering and reporting information may cause harm or discomfort. Pursuit of the news is not a license for arrogance.
- Recognize that private people have a greater right to control information about themselves than do public officials and others who seek power, influence or attention. Only an overriding public need can justify intrusion into anyone's privacy.
- Show good taste. Avoid pandering to lurid curiosity.
- Be cautious about identifying juvenile suspects or victims of sex crimes.
- Be judicious about naming criminal suspects before the formal filing of charges.
- Balance a criminal suspect's fair trial rights with the public's right to be informed.

Fairness Checklist

- Is the meaning distorted by over- or under-emphasis?
- Are facts and quotations in proper context?
- Have you given this story the length and display appropriate to its importance, and have you presented it with dignity and professionalism?
- Are the headlines and teases warranted by the text of the stories?
- Have you done your best to report all sides of the story, not just one side — or, just as problematic, two artificially polarized points of view?
- Have you been compassionate in your reporting?
- Have all relevant people, particularly those who may be affected or harmed by the story, been given an opportunity to reply? If they have not been reached or have not comment, have you explained why in the story?
- If sources are not fully identified, is there a justifiable reason?
- When substantive errors or distortions appear in your paper or on the air, do you admit and correct them voluntarily, promptly and with a prominence comparable to that given the inaccurate statement or statements?
- Are you fostering an open dialogue with your readers, viewers and listeners? Do others, both in the newsroom and outside it, feel the story is fair to those involved?

CASE STUDY 12:

TV Doctors in Haiti

WHAT: It didn't take long after the Haiti earthquake in January 2010 before news organizations, especially television, started sending in their medical experts. In almost every case these experts are in fact accredited medical doctors — fully capable of tending professionally to the injured and the sick. And not just capable of ministering to the needs of the victims, but professionally and ethically obligated to do it as well.

But these doctors are also journalists. And journalists have an obligation to a certain degree of detachment. They're expected to be impartial observers, not to be involved in the stories they cover.

Dr. Sanjay Gupta, CNN's medical expert, was the first to arrive, a couple of days after the January 12 disaster. He was soon followed by Dr. Richard Besser of ABC News, Dr. Nancy Snyderman of NBC News and Dr. Jennifer Ashton of CBS News. All four answered the basic ethical conflict by dividing their time between caring for patients and reporting on what they observed.

Dr. Snyderman said this in an e-mail to *Fortune* editor-at-large Patricia Sellers on January 19: "I have worked whenever possible triaging patients and sewing patients up, operating to clean dirty wounds. But there aren't enough hands on the ground. The bodies keep coming — in wheelbarrows, on mattresses and on shoulders."

Dr. Besser helped a pregnant woman in labor; Dr. Gupta performed surgery on a girl with a suspected skull fracture. Dr. Ashton helped surgeons operate on a girl in shock from a botched amputation. "When I see a situation where there's something I could do to help somebody, I'm going to do that," Dr. Besser told the *Los Angeles Times*. "It would be cruel and heartless to do anything but."

All of the physician-journalists soon faced criticism, though, that in reporting on their own efforts to fulfill their medical responsibilities, they were exploiting their good deeds and thus tainting their journalistic responsibilities. Journalism ethicist Bob Steele told the *Los Angeles Times*, "I think it's very hard for an individual who is professionally and emotionally engaged in saving lives to be able to simultaneously step back from the medical work and practice independent journalistic truth-telling." News organizations that focus on work being done by their own staff "at some point appear to be capitalizing for promotional reasons on the intervention by journalists," Steele added.

Question: What are the professional obligations of a medical doctor who is also a journalist — which takes priority, telling the story or tending to the victims?

WHO: The doctor-journalists themselves are the moral agents in these circumstances, the ones who have to decide which approach to take. Their employers also must decide what demands to put on them, including what stories to assign, what video to use and how much time to allow them to attend to ministering to victims of the quake. Those two — the doctors and their media employers — also are the key stakeholders in whatever decisions are made. Their professional reputations are under scrutiny. The people of Haiti, especially the quake victims, also have a major stake in the outcome of the decision; they can use help from even just a few extra skilled physicians, and the images that the media carry worldwide will increase awareness of their plight.

WHY: This is a clear example of the often-encountered dilemma between impartial truth-telling and minimizing harm. Both the SPJ Code of Ethics and the Statement of Principles of the Association of Health Care Journalists have similar language. The AHCJ principles recognize "that gathering and reporting information may cause harm or discomfort" and urges "special sensitivity ... when dealing with children, mentally handicapped people, and inexperienced sources or subjects." Neither deals specifically with the choice faced by doctor-reporters, but both are similar in intent to the Hippocratic Oath: "Whatever I see or hear in the lives of my patients ... I will keep secret, as considering all such things to be private."

Journalists are taught not to make themselves part of the story. And yet they often do. Travel writers, food critics and theater reviewers have been known to write in the first person. Columnists do it from time to time. And then there are those pieces where reporters tell what it's like to live on the street as a homeless person, or to try to get by on food stamps for a month. Reporters are human beings, too. Is it realistic to expect them not to act when they might save a life — or in this case, many, many lives?

There's another question here: Is it really helpful to inundate a disaster scene with journalists? Every news outlet, it seems, wants its own take on what happened, and how recovery efforts are going. But that coverage can get to be redundant, and reporters run the risk of getting in the way of people whose sole function is to try to provide assistance.

In an article published in *Electronic News*, Dr. Tom Linden, a medical doctor and journalism professor at the University of North Carolina, Chapel Hill, proposed three rules for physician-journalists covering disasters:

(1) When physician journalists face medical emergencies, their duty to treat might take precedence over their responsibility to report. When that's the case, the medical professional should perform health care duties as he or she sees fit. However, it's usually inappropriate for medical professionals to report about their own health care efforts. In most cases, this type of first-person journalism is self-centered and simply bad journalism. When physician journalists become the story, medical reporting loses its way.

(2) Standard practice for reporters in the United States is to seek a parent's or guardian's approval before interviewing and featuring a child in a radio or television news report. Those same standards should apply when physician reporters travel to trauma zones, whether they're in the United States or abroad.

(3) A physician reporter who treats a patient shouldn't feature that patient (or ask that patient for permission to be featured) on a radio or television report. Such a request puts the patient in an unacceptable bind. If the patient refuses consent, then the patient might fear that the physician will withdraw treatment. This fear might be especially acute in a disaster zone or in impoverished areas where limited or no other medical help is available. Moreover, physician journalists should bear in mind the Hippocratic Oath's admonition about keeping private what they 'see or hear in the lives' of their patients.

News executives might well chafe at these restrictions,

but physician journalists should stand their ground and not allow themselves or their patients to be used to boost ratings for commercial gain. The public has a right to know, but physician reporters have a duty to protect their patients from exploitation and to keep the boundaries between their dual professions intact.

HOW: The doctors covering this story decided they could be both physicians and journalists, although it wasn't an easy choice, and they continued to have their doubts. "I don't think our intention is ever to make the story about myself," Dr. Gupta told the Los Angeles *Times*. "I think people innately understand that there is a tremendous medical need down here, and if you can help, you should help." "Morally," Dr. Snyderman said, "I have a responsibility to help people. From a journalistic standpoint, I have a responsibility to tell stories. And in between is a very delicate balance that I wrestle with."

— SPJ Ethics Committee

CASE STUDY 13:

Publishing Drunken Drivers' Photos

WHAT: As the publisher/editor of a 5,700-circulation, chain-owned weekly newspaper in Anderson County, Kentucky, Don White often received phone calls from local residents begging him to keep their names off the court records page of the paper. After learning from an anti-drunken driving coalition that the battle against drunken driving had "hit a brick wall," White decided to heed the group's call for more innovative sanctions against drunken drivers.

When readers of *The Anderson News* picked up the December 31, 1997, issue of the newspaper, stripped across the top of the front page was a New Year's greeting and a warning. "HAVE A HAPPY NEW YEAR," the banner read. "But please don't drink and drive and risk having your picture published." Readers were referred to the editorial page where White explained that starting in January 1998 the newspaper would publish photographs of all persons convicted of drunken driving in Anderson County.

> Does fairness mean treating every individual convicted of drunken driving the same regardless of whether the person is an adult or a juvenile, or whether the person is a first or repeat offender?

"Most violators of the law dislike having their name in the local paper. We hope the certainty that their picture will also be published will keep more drunks off our highways," White wrote. He also published state and national drunken driving statistics and stories about seven people killed by drunken drivers.

In February 1998, White published 1-column by 3-inch-deep photos of two persons convicted of DUI during January. Both had been arrested before White announced his policy. In March, 12 mug shots appeared, followed by 20 in April and 11 in May. In May, White also revised his policy. Instead of publishing all DUI (driving under the influence) convictions in the county, he limited the photos to residents of Anderson County or surrounding counties where *The News* circulates. He also began publishing the photos weekly rather than monthly.

After a person charged with DUI was convicted or pleaded guilty, the county jailer (who is elected in Kentucky) supplied the information and the photo taken at the time of the arrest to the newspaper. Under each photo the newspaper printed the person's name, age, place of residence, date and time arrested, charge, blood alcohol level and date convicted. The paper published the photos regardless of the age of the offender and made no distinction between first offenders and those who had been arrested before for DUI. The only cases in which photos were not published were those where the DUI suspect was injured, taken to the hospital for treatment and, although charged, never processed at the jail and never photographed. Only once did White give any person special treatment. When the chairman of the county Democratic Party was convicted of drunken driving for the second time in five years, White published his mug shot and a story on Page 1 rather than on the district court page where the photos usually ran. Before someone's photo was published, the person's name usually had already appeared in the paper twice — after the arrest and after the arraignment.

Question: Is this an appropriate policy for a newspaper?

WHO: Circulation of *The Anderson News* apparently was unaffected by the policy. It's unclear whether publishing the photos directly affected DUI arrests or accident rates in the county. In 2003, Anderson was the only one of Kentucky's 120 counties to record no traffic deaths. For the years 1999 through 2003, however, the percentage of collisions involving alcohol in Anderson County was 4.7 percent, slightly higher than the state average of 4.4 percent for that time period. No one knows how many prominent local citizens did not drink and drive because of the policy. Some evidence is anecdotal. White knew of one group of teens who chose not to drive after drinking for fear their pictures would be in the paper.

Police told White one teenager tried to commit suicide after his DUI arrest because he feared his picture would be published. Some whose pictures appeared said the publication hurt their families, particularly their children. The management of the chain that owns *The Anderson News* did not interfere in White's decision to publish the photos. The policy applied only to drunken driving convictions and not to any other misdemeanor or felony offenses. Apparently, no other newspaper followed White's lead and adopted a similar policy.

WHY: Newspapers have an obligation to seek the truth and report it. But in what form should that truth be reported? Is a listing of DUI arrests and convictions sufficient to inform the community or does publishing photographs of those who are convicted or plead guilty further the goal of truth-telling?

. This case raises important questions about fairness and the role of a newspaper in a small community. Does fairness mean treating every individual convicted of drunken driving the same regardless of whether the person is an adult or a juvenile, or whether the person is a first or repeat offender? Is it fair to single out only those convicted of drunken driving while not routinely publishing photos of persons convicted of felony offenses such as rape or robbery?

Is the newspaper imposing an additional punishment on drunken drivers that other convicted criminals in the community do not face? Is it the newspaper's job to determine the community will benefit more from publication of the photo of someone arrested for a misdemeanor DUI offense than the photo of a convicted child abuser or sex offender?

Undoubtedly, reducing drunken driving is a noble goal for the newspaper, but should the newspaper purposely embarrass individuals in an attempt to achieve that goal? No one disagrees with the need to keep drunken drivers off the road. The disagreement is over whether publishing the photos will, in fact, achieve the newspaper's goal. Will the policy keep alcoholics off of the road? Will prominent people who would lose face in their community if their photos were published be more likely to refrain from drinking and driving? What about the impact on the families of those whose pictures appear in the paper?

> Without the cooperation of an elected county jailer, *The Anderson News* would not have been able to publish the photos.

HOW: One can argue that *The Anderson News'* DUI photo policy was designed to minimize harm to the community by reducing the number of drunken drivers on the county's highways. On the other hand, the policy did not minimize harm to those convicted. Particularly harmed by the policy were the families of those arrested and convicted of DUI who usually had nothing to do with the offense but were embarrassed and humiliated by their family member's public exposure. One father, who managed a local restaurant frequented by teens, said his children's friends didn't say anything after his name appeared in the paper reporting his arrest on a DUI charge. After he pleaded guilty and his picture was published, however, his teenaged sons "got rode over pretty hard" by their friends who recognized their father's picture. The man, who had a blood alcohol reading of .16 (twice the legal limit in Kentucky) when he was arrested, said, "I deserved everything I got (from the legal system). Thank goodness no one got hurt." But he didn't think the photos were fair or reduced the number of drunken drivers on county roads.

This case also raised questions about the relationship between a newspaper and public officials. Without the cooperation of an elected county jailer, *The Anderson News* would not have been able to publish the photos. The SPJ Code of Ethics admonishes journalists to act independently, but the policy and practice of *The Anderson News* would have been impossible without the cooperation of an elected official. *The News* was also dependent on the jailer for the accuracy of the photo identifications.

Author's note: In May 2006, White retired as publisher and editor of *The Anderson News*. His replacement is General Manager Ben Carlson. In a column in August 2006, Carlson announced he would no longer publish the photos. He wrote that publishing mug shots of those convicted "adds a level of punishment, or at least embarrassment, beyond what is imposed by a judge." In an interview, Carlson told the *Lexington Herald-Leader,* "I really don't think that the role of a community newspaper is to punish or embarrass anybody. It's to report the news and provide information." Carlson told the *Herald-Leader* he had no negative response from county residents when he announced the change. The state director for Mothers Against Drunk Driving said she was disappointed by the decision to change the policy. In 2008, only 15 alcohol-related accidents — none of them resulting in fatalities — occurred in Anderson County. That was the lowest number in the 11 years since White first published the photos, but it came two years after the policy was dropped. In eight of the 11 years, Anderson County had no fatal accidents involving alcohol and only three alcohol-related highway deaths occurred during that time. In 2007, as in 2003 and 2001, no one died on the county's highways.

— Elizabeth K. Hansen, SPJ Ethics Committee

CASE STUDY 14:

Naming Victims of Sex Crimes

WHAT: On June 5, 2002, 14-year-old Elizabeth Smart was abducted from her bedroom in Salt Lake City, Utah. Elizabeth's parents worked with local and national media to increase visibility of the case; public interest in the kidnapping of the attractive, accomplished blond teenager was immense. Nine months after the abduction, Elizabeth's younger sister, who had witnessed the kidnapping, remembered that the abductor's voice sounded like that of a vagrant who had done some work for the family some months before the kidnapping. That detail ultimately led to Elizabeth's rescue, which was a major media story nationwide.

Elizabeth's suspected kidnappers, a man and a woman, were charged with several crimes, including sexual assault. Their trial was indefinitely postponed, as both suspects were deemed mentally unfit to stand trial. Then in November 2009, the woman pleaded guilty, apologized to Elizabeth, agreed to testify against the man and was sentenced to 15 years in prison. A new competency hearing for the man was held in late 2009.

After Elizabeth was returned to them, her parents, Ed and Lois Smart, wrote a book about their family's ordeal. They and Elizabeth gave a number of interviews. Some reporters were sensitive in questioning Elizabeth about painful subjects. Others grilled her about the details of the time she spent with her captors, leaving her visibly upset. The Smarts authorized a made-for-television movie about Elizabeth's kidnapping and eventual rescue.

• • •

On May 16, 2005, a man, a woman and a teenage boy were found brutally murdered inside their rural Idaho home. Two children, eight-year-old Shasta Groene and her nine-year-old brother Dylan, were missing. For six weeks, police and volunteers searched for the children; their names and descriptions were widely distributed in hopes someone would recognize them and alert authorities. Eventually, that is just what happened. A waitress in a Coeur d'Alene, Idaho, Denny's restaurant recognized Shasta with a man who would later be identified as Joseph Duncan, a 42-year-old registered sex offender. Dylan's body was eventually found in a Montana campsite.

As the story unfolded, it became evident that the brother and sister had been sexually abused by their kidnapper. Although the identities of sexual abuse victims are usually shielded in the media, many media outlets continued to identify Shasta Groene in this case, since the children's identities had been widely circulated while the search efforts were ongoing.

• • •

On January 8, 2007, 13-year-old Ben Ownby disappeared while walking home from school in Beaufort, Missouri. A tip from a school friend led police on a frantic four-day search that ended unusually happily: the police discovered not only Ben, but another boy as well — 15-year-old Shawn Hornbeck, who, four years earlier, had disappeared while riding his bike at the age of 11.

After the boys' discovery, the families of both victims held press conferences at which the young victims were present and answered a few questions. Shawn and his parents appeared on *The Oprah Winfrey Show*, as did Ben's parents. Shawn's parents spoke to Winfrey about the mental changes their son had undergone and speculated that he had been sexually abused.

Media scrutiny on Shawn's years of captivity became intense. Shawn had apparently had a certain amount of "freedom" while he was being held. (He played games and spent time with friends.) So why, analysts asked, didn't he try to escape? Psychologists pondered the matter on air; one pundit even posited that Shawn preferred life with his kidnapper and had chosen to remain with him. Others cited the Stockholm syndrome in defending the young man for not attempting to escape years earlier.

Question: Should children who are thought to be the victims of sexual abuse ever be named in the media? What should be done about the continued use of names of kidnap victims who are later found to be sexual assault victims? Should use of their names be discontinued at that point?

WHO: Decision-makers in this case are reporters, editors/producers and management who have to weigh the potential to cause further harm to already-victimized minors against the desire to tell the whole story, pressure to improve ratings/circulation and pressure to beat other news organizations to the story. They are also under pressure from the public, which, accustomed to 24-hour, speed-of-light news availability, has come to expect immediate, detailed coverage of the big stories.

The stakeholders are obviously the children in question. These children have already been through more than most of us can even imagine. Is it a healing experience for them to share their stories with the world? Or will the scrutiny add further turmoil to their already-fractured lives, perhaps causing irreparable damage?

Other stakeholders include the children's families, who have been through the wrenching ordeal of losing a child and are sometimes eager to share their joy at being reunited with their children and to thank those officials and volunteers who helped bring their children home. In the Smart and Hornbeck cases, the parents gave their consent for their minor children to be interviewed and were present during the interviews.

WHY: Does the charge to "seek the truth and report it" in the face of enormous public interest outweigh the potential for causing further harm to children who have already been victimized? It is a journalist's job — and obligation — to tell compelling stories in detail. But is there ever a point when it is better for a journalist to step back, give the story's subject her privacy, and, if necessary, tell the clamoring public to mind its own business? Even if the child declares that he wishes to speak in an interview or press conference, given the child's age and what he has been through, is he really in a position to make that choice?

On the other hand, in the Smart and Hornbeck cases, the journalists had permission from the children's parents to interview them. The children were apparently willing to be interviewed. The children or parents could have ended the interviews at any time.

In the Groene case, the child's identity was already very well known, particularly in Idaho. It would have been impossible to remove her name from the news stories that had already been

> Which is more important, the obligation of the journalist to tell the story well, or the obligation of the journalist to minimize harm to the abused child?

published, so referring to her by oblique descriptors would have seemed pointless at best, and disingenuous at worst. After all, you can't un-name a name any more easily than you can un-ring a bell. Further, some journalists reasoned that it would be irresponsible to refrain from informing the public that the search for these children was, in fact, at an end.

The first guideline in the code of ethics of the Society of Professional Journalists is "seek the truth and report it." But the second guideline is "minimize harm." Items under that dictum include "avoid pandering to lurid curiosity" and "be cautious about identifying juvenile suspects or victims of sex crimes." With words like "seek," "minimize," "avoid" and "be cautious," however, there is always room for interpretation. One can take caution, and then go ahead, if he or she truly believes it is the right thing to do, without having breached the code of ethics.

So the question remains: Which is more important, the obligation of the journalist to tell the story well, or the obligation of the journalist to minimize harm to the abused child?

HOW: Do you release the name of a child who is thought to have been abused? Do you interview the child? Increasingly, we are seeing instances of this scenario playing out in the media. A precedent has been set, so we may continue to see cases like this unless news organizations change their policies.

This issue is not black and white; it is a wide range of grays. Every case is different, and a journalist could certainly choose either course while remaining true to the SPJ Code of Ethics. In some cases, the best course of action might be to name the child, but refrain from publishing graphic details about the abuse the child endured. Perhaps in other cases, there is no pressing public interest for the child's identity to be released, and his or her privacy is the utmost consideration.

Most importantly, journalists must closely examine their own motives. Whatever path they choose, they should be guided by professional ethics and never simply by a desire to be first with a detail that will increase ratings or circulation.

— Amber Orand and Sara Stone, Baylor University

CASE STUDY 15:

Admiral Boorda Suicide

Summary

When he committed suicide on May 16, 1996, Admiral Jeremy Boorda was the Navy's top officer, a highly decorated veteran of the Vietnam era who had risen from the enlisted ranks to command NATO as it engaged in its first offensive action.

Boorda killed himself roughly an hour before he was to be interviewed by *Newsweek* correspondents about whether he had worn a medal for valor that he hadn't earned. In the aftermath of the tragedy, *Newsweek* and other news organizations were accused of hounding Boorda to his death, which provoked the magazine and other media members to do a little soul-searching over the question: Is any story worth a life?

Although the Pentagon did not blame *Newsweek*, it was clear that Boorda changed his lunch plans and went home to kill himself upon learning that reporters were on their way to ask him unsettling questions. Boorda's suicide note, *The Washington Post* reported, "indicated he was not

> Acknowledging the sometimes grave consequences that journalism can produce, Alter also raised the issue of "whether the story was worthy or not. Was it too trivial to pursue?"

taking his life in the belief he had been caught in a lie, but out of fears that the media would accuse him of one and blow it out of proportion." Navy spokesman Admiral Kendall Pease said, however, "*Newsweek* did nothing wrong."

Some media critics, however, did blame *Newsweek* and other news organizations that had begun to investigate Boorda for what syndicated columnist Nat Hentoff called a story that "had no legs." *Newsweek* acknowledged that letter writers complained vociferously about the magazine's role, and some canceled subscriptions.

In a "full accounting" by its media critic, Jonathan Alter, the magazine looked inward to examine whether it had violated some unwritten but understood ethical tenet. Alter chronicled how the story idea had been generated: a Washington-based outfit called National Security News Service provided documents and photos showing Boorda began wearing the valor pin in the 1980s, then stopped. He described the reporting: part-time contributing editor David Hackworth had been working on the story with Washington bureau chief Evan Thomas and national security correspondent John Barry. His conclusion was that *Newsweek*'s position was "defensible."

Acknowledging the sometimes grave consequences that journalism can produce, Alter also raised the issue of "whether the story was worthy or not. Was it too trivial to pursue?" Although Hentoff and others believed so, some current and former military officers disagreed. Among them was Hackworth, a retired Army colonel often referred to as the nation's most highly decorated officer. Accompanying Alter's article was an essay by Hackworth titled "Why Medals Matter." Referring to an officer's wearing of decorations he is not entitled to, Hackworth wrote: "There is no greater disgrace."

Hackworth's involvement in the story included this ironic footnote: Almost a year to the date after Boorda's suicide, CNN and CBS reported that Hackworth also had military decorations he hadn't earned. Hackworth told CNN he had learned he was not entitled to a Ranger tag and a second Distinguished Flying Cross. Hackworth said he had listed the medals on the résumé posted on his personal page on the Internet but removed them. CNN reported that Hackworth might have made an honest mistake — just as Boorda claimed he had.

Analysis

This is a troubling case study about journalistic fairness. Whenever the public jumps to the conclusion that the media have caused egregious harm, it is time to take stock — regardless of the merits of the public's opinion.

It may be a mark of lingering Vietnam-born media paranoia among the military over what most civilians would consider a trivial story: A man at the top of the military ladder takes his own life rather than face a reporter's questions.

Reporters often must weigh the effect of reporting a story when determining whether audiences need any particular information. Each time a reporter inquires into an individual's personal behavior there is risk that the source will react in an extreme way. It's unlikely *Newsweek* reporters, however, could have anticipated Admiral Boorda's suicide.

Still, reporters must have been aware that their story would be more than an embarrassment to Boorda. It was bound to damage an otherwise honorable officer's professional reputation.

A former officer, who himself was later found to have worn undeserved medals, took a strict stance in calling such behavior "no greater disgrace" — a difficult statement for most civilians to comprehend.

Truth is important, and comprehensive media reports relating to public figures are doubly important.

But, the suicide aside, harm to Boorda's reputation may have been difficult to justify when considering the usefulness of the information to *Newsweek* readers. On the other hand, scrutiny of public figures and such mundane behavior as wearing unearned medals is critically important if citizens are to make informed judgments about their leaders.

If Boorda had told the reporter he would commit suicide if the story ran, would the reporter have been justified in killing the story? Such threats do occur. In this case, the *Newsweek* reporters would probably have been puzzled at the extremity of the response. Their puzzlement, however, might have led to more thorough understanding of and better reporting on the military, a complex institution whose value system is not well understood by all journalists.

In the aftermath of Boorda's suicide, public discussion of the matter was effective in holding *Newsweek* accountable, whatever the magazine's justification. The soul-searching conducted by *Newsweek*'s Alter was commendable — not just as a PR effort on behalf of the magazine but as an ethical postmortem. It's likely reporters familiar with the Boorda case will make greater efforts to determine the impact of their stories on their sources as they decide whether the story is worth the potential harm.

— from the Third Edition, Black, Steele and Barney

CASE STUDY 16:

Abortion Coverage on Deadline

Summary

Journalists covering the abortion issue often find themselves facing ethical dilemmas. That was the case July 3, 1989, the day the U.S. Supreme Court upheld a Missouri law restricting abortion. It was clearly **the** news story of the day, and news producers at WCCO-TV in Minneapolis wanted to give the abortion issue a strong play on their 10 p.m. newscast. They decided to focus on a woman having an abortion that day.

The station contacted Minneapolis abortion clinics. Some agreed to ask their patients if they would be willing to be interviewed. At about 6 p.m., one woman agreed. Her appointment was for 6:30, so the news crew rushed to the clinic.

According to WCCO-TV news producer Julie Kramer, the "woman had no restrictions as far as questions. She asked only that her last name not be used and her face not be shown." The station agreed.

Kramer described how the events of the evening unfolded:

"The crew came back with the tape between 8 and 8:30 p.m. A debate began then over whether the story should air. Some thought it was too inflammatory. Others thought it tasteless. Others thought it was blatantly pro-choice. The crew was baffled. When they'd left, the newsroom seemed enthusiastic about the story.

"The 10 p.m. producer didn't want to air it that night, suggesting that it could run the next evening, or maybe never. An anchor insisted that the other side be given comparable time in the same section. The news director was called at home. He was concerned about the controversial nature of the piece.

"The field producer and the photographer couldn't spend as much time arguing in favor of the story as they'd like because they needed to spend their time producing and editing the story. The producer felt that since the news of the day, the Supreme Court decision, was written with both views in section one, it was not necessary to balance every abortion view in the newscast with the opposing side.

"The news director decided that to be fair, we should broadcast a string of sound bites from an interview earlier in the day with the local archbishop. After the piece was edited, the producer had the photographer change some suction scenes she felt were too graphic."

The story aired on WCCO's 10 p.m. newscast that night, followed by the interview comments from the archbishop.

Analysis

This case is an example of ethical decision-making under deadline pressure, and it's important to note that the story did make it on the newscast that night. The journalists at WCCO-TV were faced with making some tough calls, weighing consequences and considering alternatives on an important story. They did not succumb to paralysis of analysis.

There were several issues at play. Fairness was a factor, as some in the newsroom felt the story was biased toward the pro-choice position on abortion. Interestingly, one could argue the opposite, suggesting that the graphic scenes of the abortion and the revelation by the woman that this was her second abortion reinforced the pro-life position.

It is an issue not easily resolved. Perhaps the best a journalist can do in such a situation is to recognize one's personal biases, do collaborative decision-making to gain diverse input, and present factual information from competing sources. Sometimes an imperfect alternative is chosen to resolve a fairness struggle, as in this case with the use of the archbishop's interview to provide a competing perspective on abortion in the same newscast.

Balance is a noble goal, elusive though it is. Yet, to believe that

> Perhaps the best a journalist can do in such a situation is to recognize one's personal biases, do collaborative decision-making to gain diverse input, and present factual information from competing sources.

every story can be perfectly balanced can restrict good journalism. Instead, it is productive to recognize that each story can be fair, although **balance** might better be achieved over time and through continuing coverage of an issue.

Another issue in this case deals with "taste," which is truly an ethical issue because it deals with the potential for harm to individuals as well as the obligation to tell the truth. To show video of an abortion procedure certainly raises the possibility of offending some viewers by harming their sensibilities or even emotionally traumatizing them. At the same time, it's important to present as clear and compelling pictures of the procedure as possible in order to bring the viewers an accurate account of what took place.

Abortion is a highly controversial and important public policy issue in our society. Journalism best serves the public when it provides meaningful information on such important issues, even when some might be offended. It is possible to minimize that harm to viewers, however, by choosing alternatives that allow for a clear understanding of what happened, yet protect to some degree the sensibilities of the public.

In the end, the principle of truth-telling must take precedence over the principle of minimizing harm, except in those exceptional situations where the harm is truly extreme and clearly outweighs the value of the information that is to be left out of a story.

In most cases, journalists can resolve these competing obligations, honoring both. In the case of the WCCO coverage of the abortion, the photographer shot the video with alternative editing possibilities in mind. He recognized that he must be sensitive in how he took pictures, both out of respect for the woman undergoing the abortion and eventually for the viewers who would see the videotape. Yet he knew that he must provide enough video to give the story context as well as accuracy.

Another alternative for minimizing harm while providing potentially offending information is to provide a warning. Introductory comments by the anchor might alert viewers to the nature of the upcoming material, preparing them for its impact and giving them the choice not to watch.

Another issue in this case was how the reporter and photographer dealt with the woman having the abortion. What are the pros and cons of agreeing to the woman's request that her last name not be used and her face not be shown?

The authenticity of all news reports is enhanced by fully revealing the identities of those involved in stories, be they sources of information or subjects of coverage. Yet it's clear that to avoid using individuals as mere means to a journalistic end, reporters must sometimes grant confidentiality and anonymity to protect those who are quite vulnerable.

Making such ethical decisions on fairness and balance, taste and confidentiality places great demands on individual journalists and news organizations. These decisions can be made best by individuals who think about ethics on a regular basis, not just when a crisis occurs. Ethical decision-making is a craft and a skill, much like writing or editing or taking pictures. If journalists develop and practice this skill, then they can make good decisions on tough issues, even when those calls must be made on deadline.

— from the Third Edition, Black, Steele and Barney

CASE STUDY 17:

When the Crime is Incest

THE SITUATION: Sexual abuse is one of the most sensitive topics to report. The victims often want to avoid publicity, but reporting sex crimes may help prevent future sex crimes and direct victims to sources of help. Reporters must strive to show respect for the subjects of their stories.

A story published in July 1995 in *The Wabasha* (Minnesota) *County Herald*, a weekly newspaper in a town of about 2,500 people, offers a case study of the steps that should be followed from start to finish. The newspaper reported the sentencing of a father who was convicted of incest. The victim was his only daughter.

The daughter complained that the newspaper's report was insensitive, and the Minnesota News Council ruled in her favor. The complaint would likely have never reached the Minnesota News Council had the principles underscored at the hearing been practiced by the newspaper in pursuing the story.

> In hindsight, as revealed at the News Council hearing, the decision to rely only on the county prosecutor resulted in a significant omission in the story.

The News Council's near unanimous decision to uphold the complaint should not be interpreted as a blanket condemnation of the newspaper or that the staff was callous in its decision to identify the victim as the daughter. The publisher and editor said it was a gut-wrenching decision.

ISSUES AND ANALYSIS: A case like this presents numerous questions for evaluating whether any story is fit for publication.

Is It News?

Values frequently collide when editors seek to balance victims' rights with a responsibility to inform. There was no doubt that reporting the father's sentencing stirred painful childhood memories for the victim. But from the editor's standpoint, the story held the individual accountable for his crime. The seriousness of the crime warranted front-page coverage, he said.

Part of the article was about the judge's apparent leniency in the punishment. Further examination, however — principally, talking to the victim — would have revealed the daughter's role in advocating a shorter sentence. The father was sentenced to one year in jail even though state guidelines recommended 13 years in prison. The father also was placed on 30 years' probation.

The story could have prompted a review of sentencing patterns in sex-abuse cases. It also could have raised the overall awareness of sexual abuse, especially if it included follow-up stories on the signs of sexual abuse and where to turn for help.

Even If It's True, Should We Publish It?

Must all facts be reported? The sex-abuse case offered instruction. The editor pointed out that he printed exactly what was in court documents. His intent was to prevent sensationalism and to circumvent gossip about what had happened in the family. It's fair to ask, however, whether all details were necessary for public examination.

The family brought the complaint to the News Council on the basis of two issues: identifying the child and giving excessive detail.

The descriptive narrative of charges often is the more sensitive and bigger problem when reporting from court summaries. In this case, simply reporting the charges — repeated instances of abuse during several years — would have allowed readers to deduce the victim was a family member. (But that is not always true in such circumstances. Extensive cases of abuse also have been reported between an adult and a babysitter or neighborhood youth.) In any case, the community still would have had a clear picture of the abhorrent circumstances had the newspaper not identified the victim as the daughter.

A CHECKLIST for Evaluating Sensitive Issues

How many editors have faced reporting bad news — or, put another way — making an uncomfortable news decision? Pressed by a reader for the rationale, you've replied, "That's our policy," or "It doesn't meet our guidelines." Yet, in the calm and privacy of your office, you reflect, "We could have done a better job."

The examples of tough issues are numerous, especially in community newspapers. Stories can range from following teacher negotiations or publishing salaries of public officials to reporting business layoffs or interviewing families of homicide victims.

All of these incidents are being talked about in the community. They have an impact on people. They are sensitive issues. And they are news. They should be reported if newspapers are to represent themselves as a living history of their hometowns. Reporting these stories in a responsible fashion is a requisite for community newspapers to remain relevant, especially during these rapidly changing times.

It's natural, and healthy, for newsrooms to pause and consider whether readers are served by the reporting of certain news. Here is one checklist, and accompanying rationale, that advocates the publication of challenging stories.

Is it true? Newspapers routinely report why athletes are "missing in action" — whether due to an injury, a family emergency or a college recruiting trip. Sitting on a bench for violating school or high school league rules is equally newsworthy.

What is the impact of an event? It's standard procedure at most schools to call in counselors in the wake of an untimely death of a classmate, whether the death is due to natural causes or a suicide. The death automatically becomes conversation in homes. Can newspapers ignore the story?

Is the report fair? Teacher salary negotiations often are emotional and acrimonious. At the same time, the salaries can represent 75 percent of a school district's budget. Newspapers are performing a vital service by keeping a community abreast of contract talks, giving equal attention to all sides of all issues.

Is it a public or strictly private issue? A closure of a major employer has a tremendous economic impact on a community. The news begs for explanation and interpretation.

Will the story make a difference? A newspaper's attention to a fatal accident, including a photo, can become a springboard for action to install traffic signals at a dangerous intersection.

Will the truth quell rumors? A newspaper receives word from an elementary school student that a high school teacher lost all his fingers in a lab experiment — the "news" clearly spreading quickly. An investigation reveals that the teacher lost a fingertip, and a story sets the record straight.

How would you justify your decision to readers? Certain stories are expected to generate reader reaction, and editors should be prepared to answer questions. The circumstances might provide excellent fodder for a column to readers.

How would you treat the story if you were the subject? This question is not intended to prompt rejection of a story. Rather, it's a reminder to treat the story with sensitivity.

In the end, fairness and consistency should be guiding principles for any story, and they are especially important when dealing with sensitive subjects.

Another element — discussion — is common to all of these questions in deciding whether and what to publish. All decisions are stronger if the options are talked about with as many individuals as possible — people within and outside of the newsroom. Discussion doesn't mean consensus will be developed, but it assures that editors will get many perspectives before making a final call.

— *Jim Pumarlo, SPJ Ethics Committee former editor, The Red Wing (Minnesota) Republican Eagle, 1982–2003*

What If You Were the Subject?

Had the publisher and editor pictured themselves as the subjects of the story, they may have changed the final version. There's no better test than editors putting their own names in the headline. If editors have opportunity, they also should discuss approaches to stories with their families or other people they hold in high regard.

Did You Talk with the Subject of the Story?

Editors should try to interview the involved parties, or at least alert them to the story. Most individuals expect to be contacted as part of the news-gathering, but that does not always occur, as illustrated in this case. The newspaper's failure to talk to the victim directly almost certainly altered the story's presentation.

The editor and publisher said they spoke to each other and to the prosecutor, who had urged full disclosure. They did not talk to the family or a mental health therapist, and they did not seek a woman's perspective. The editor said he had all the information and only a weekend to write the story.

In hindsight, as revealed at the News Council hearing, the decision to rely only on the county prosecutor resulted in a significant omission in the story. The victim herself had asked that her father be given a lenient sentence so, in her words, her family could be reunited and try to get back to living a normal life.

The newspaper may have had only a few days to sort through the court appearance and sentencing, but the staff had months to sort through questions and prepare the coverage. The father had been charged with the crime a year earlier.

Editors may even consider sharing a story in advance with key participants. Many journalists reject the idea of letting someone preview a story, and for good reason. The practice can result in problems, not the least of which is setting a precedent. But sometimes pre-publication review — with explicit ground rules established in advance — can head off serious problems.

Reviewing a story with the individuals involved does not assure that everyone will leave the room on the same page. It's likely, however, that all parties in the sex-abuse case — the victim, the community and the newspaper — would have been served better had a discussion occurred.

Is the Report Fair?

Reporting the facts does not necessarily guarantee balance. Omission of certain information, or failure to get a response from a party, can put a completely different slant on a story, especially in crime and court news.

It's easy to produce a story from a police report or criminal complaint. Getting a comment from the accused is not as easy. If a response is tracked down, comments often are tacked on the end of a story and appear almost as an afterthought. The sex-abuse report may have fulfilled expectations of the prosecutor, but few others. In fact, the victim — who was represented by the prosecutor — was most upset by the coverage. In a story as important as this one, including the comments of others would have produced a stronger and more accurate story.

Lastly, don't be afraid to admit an error in judgment or a mistake. It's the right thing to do, and it goes a long way toward restoring credibility.

Is it a Public or Strictly Private Issue?

The Wabasha County Herald and the victim agreed that the story was important. The editor said he believed that by fully reporting the incest, the newspaper would discourage others from committing the crime for fear of publicity. He also said the newspaper had been sensitive to the well-being of the girl by choosing not to run a story when her father was first charged with the crime a year before sentencing. The girl, who said she first wanted to keep the case secret, said she decided she wanted to help others. The differences, of course, surfaced in how the story was reported.

The impact of such stories on victims cannot be overstated, as pointed out by Dr. Frank Ochberg, a psychiatrist and adjunct professor who helped launch and sustain the Victims and the Media Program at Michigan State University's School of Journalism. "Victims in our society already feel that they have been labeled as losers, weak and pathetic, so when you add the stigma of sexual assault, it is easy to see how vulnerable this makes them," said Ochberg, an expert on posttraumatic stress disorder who has treated many victims.

Most newspapers have policies that protect the identity of victims, but that can become difficult in small towns where word spreads quickly. Community newspapers still should make the effort.

Will the Story Make a Difference?

Both *The Wabasha County Herald* and the victim had agreed — or at least had hoped to agree — the story could have positive effects. The editor said the publicity given the perpetrator would deter others from carrying out a similar crime. And the victim said she hoped the publicity would help others who might be in similar situations.

Newspapers must give equal attention to how a story will affect those directly involved as well as the good provided to the broader community. An equally large part of the sex-abuse story was the reason the judge handed down a punishment far less than that recommended by sentencing guidelines. It can be argued that residents needed to know it was an incest case to put the county attorney's comments in context and to hold everyone in the criminal justice system accountable. Even to that point, the story identified the case as first-degree criminal sexual conduct, which in itself underscores the severity.

Will the Truth Quash Rumors?

The opportunity to quash rumors is one of the strongest arguments editors can present to an otherwise unwilling or uncooperative news source. If a rumor has reached the newspaper, rest assured it has circulated throughout the community. One word of caution, though: Rumors are never-ending, especially in small towns. Editors must establish that a particular rumor is significant enough to warrant a story.

Sex-abuse reports are especially problematic. *The Wabasha County Herald* believed the story would put rumors to rest. Even the victim's therapist in this case encouraged newspapers to bring the problem to public attention.

Does a Story Meet Journalistic and Community Standards?

All newspapers strive to protect victims, but it is not always possible. Consider these three cases, which all occurred during the span of a few months at *The Red Wing (Minnesota) Republican Eagle*:

- A defendant, in what the judge characterized as a highly unusual request, asked for a three-hour furlough from jail once a week to visit with his daughter, the victim. It was difficult to report the court proceedings without identifying — but not actually naming — the daughter.

- A father was on trial for alleged sex abuse, but his attorney claimed what really was at issue was a custody battle between parents. The mother and daughter, the alleged victims, lived an hour away from Red Wing.

- A father was sentenced for sexual abuse that occurred during the course of 15 years. The newspaper identified the victim as a son, since he no longer lived in Minnesota. At an attorney's suggestion, the story also made it clear the abuse did not involve children who still lived in the area.

The Minnesota News Council took two actions on the complaint against *The Wabasha County Herald*. One was to uphold the victim's complaint. The council also urged the newspaper to consult others, including sex-abuse therapists, to develop a policy for covering such sensitive stories. That's sound advice for any newsroom. The policy may not be black and white, but it will give the newspaper a basis for making sensitive decisions that still serve the need of informing readers.

— Jim Pumarlo, SPJ Ethics Committee
former editor, The Red Wing (*Minnesota*) Republican Eagle, *1982–2003*

Minimizing Harm

What the Codes Say

The Virginian-Pilot (Norfolk, Virginia)

FAIR PLAY

In our commitment to fair play, we:

- Treat all sources the same, whether friendly or hostile. We evaluate all sources based on the newsworthiness of their information. We report stories involving *The Pilot*, Landmark Communications and its executives as rigorously as any other.

- Report all sides of a story. We are upfront with readers about what we don't know and about evidence that contradicts the main finding of a news story.

- Give people accused of wrongdoing a full and immediate opportunity to respond to all charges. We also report the final outcome of such allegations — for example, the verdict after an arrest — and give the outcome comparable play to the original story.

- Do not make promises to sources about where, whether or when we will run a story or photo.

GUIDING QUESTIONS:

What if the person accused of wrongdoing in a story were your mother? Would you feel the story was fair?

What if *Columbia Journalism Review* wanted to interview you about the methods you used to get a story or photo? Would you be comfortable defending your conduct?

American Society of News Editors

Fair Play. Journalists should respect the rights of people involved in the news, observe the common standards of decency and stand accountable to the public for the fairness and accuracy of their news reports. Persons publicly accused should be given the earliest opportunity to respond. Pledges of confidentiality to news sources must be honored at all costs, and therefore should not be given lightly. Unless there is clear and pressing need to maintain confidences, sources of information should be identified.

National Public Radio

NPR journalists must treat the people they cover fairly and with respect. They always keep in mind that gathering and reporting information may cause harm or discomfort, and they weigh that against the importance of the story.

NPR journalists show sensitivity when seeking or using interviews of those affected by tragedy or grief. They show special sensitivity when dealing with children and inexperienced or unsophisticated sources or subjects, or individuals who have difficulty understanding the language in which they are being interviewed.

The Denver Post
Fairness

A strong sense of fair play must imbue our writing, accurately reflecting motives of sources. The tone and language of stories must be even-handed and avoid loaded phrasing.

Even under deadline pressure, it is imperative that we allow news subjects ample time to respond and react to issues, events and, most important, allegations against them. We should make every possible attempt to reach them, both at home and work.

We should accurately characterize their response or lack of response. "Would not comment" may be preferable to "refused to comment." However, it may be appropriate to characterize a public official, who typically is obligated to respond, as refusing to comment when given ample time and opportunity.

We also should never characterize anyone as refusing to return phone calls if he or she had little time to respond.

We owe it to our readers to disclose in detail how and when we tried to reach the subjects of news stories.

Treatment of Inexperienced Sources

A common challenge is communicating with people inexperienced in dealing with reporters.

But the rights of people ensnared in news events must be respected.

Ordinary people have greater rights to privacy than public figures. And our use of their words, or descriptions of their behavior, can have unintended consequences.

We should clearly identify ourselves to inexperienced sources, such as crime victims, children and others, and be willing to explain to them the context of their portrayal in stories. Such disclosure respects the victim's dignity. It also builds trust.

San Jose Mercury News
FAIRNESS

The *Mercury News* strives to operate with fairness, accuracy and independence.

It strives to be diligent in its pursuit of the truth without regard to special interest and with fairness toward all. Although the law does not require it, the *Mercury News* whenever possible seeks opposing views and solicits responses from those whose conduct is questioned in news stories.

Editors and reporters should make news decisions without regard to the connections or outside activities of editorial employees, the publisher or employees of any other department.

Detroit Free Press
Exercising fair play

- We will treat people with dignity, respect and compassion.
- We will correct errors promptly.
- We will strive to include all sides relevant to a story and not take sides in news coverage.
- We will explain to readers our journalistic processes.
- We will give particular attention to fairness in relations with people unaccustomed to dealing with the press.
- We will use unnamed sources as the sole basis for published information only as a last resort and under specific procedures that best serve the public's right to now.
- We will be accessible to readers.

8

Diversity

O nly recently have news media codes of ethics and books on journalism ethics begun to mention issues related to diversity. It is clear, however, that diversity issues have an important place in any discussion of journalistic ethics.

Diversity is clearly a part of accuracy and fairness, whether it relates to avoiding stereotypes or redefining news to better reflect a multicultural society.

Diversity is about the makeup of news organizations and who is making decisions. Diversity is about the way story ideas are developed and who does the reporting. Diversity is about inclusiveness in choosing sources and about giving voice to the voiceless.

Diversity means talking to people who are different from you, using people of different races, ages, religions and political beliefs in your reporting. Their viewpoints will enrich your story-telling.

There is no shortage of horror stories about news media thoughtlessly running roughshod over the sensitivities of various groups in society — ethnic, racial, religious, sexual, physical ability, etc. While lessons can be learned from mistakes, the authors of this book believe we learn best from success.

Therefore you will find a relatively positive tone in much of this chapter, including a number of suggestions for news organizations and for individual journalists relating to both staffing and story content. Case studies show how print and electronic journalists can and should practice diversity.

Diversity Checklist
The following questions, protocols and recommendations for handling issues of diversity come from the Poynter Institute for Media Studies in St. Petersburg, Florida.

Putting Diversity to Work in Your News Organization

By Kenneth Irby
Diversity Director, The Poynter Institute

1. Inclusion
Who is on your staff? Who's on the freelance list? Who is reading your paper, watching your broadcast, listening to your station or navigating your site? What examples are you holding up as evidence of good work? What sources are being used by the journalists in your organization (books, articles, agencies, websites)?
    ... and

2. Combating Prejudice
How are you helping your readers/viewers/listeners learn about the world around them and to recognize and work against prejudice, ignorance and stereotypes that get in the way of good journalism and good management? How can you help them to communicate better across difference? How do we help our readers, viewers, listeners and staffers challenge existing news values and newsroom practices that exclude, stereotype and marginalize and mislead?
    ... and

3. Improving Craft
How do we help journalists increase truth-telling by bringing in seldom seen faces, seldom heard voices and seldom shown places in your daily reports? Capturing diversity in the presentation of content is key. How do we help journalists and readers/viewers/listeners recognize when people and perspectives are missing in our daily reports? How do we help them strengthen their craft and understanding so that images and language are sharper, more precise, and fairer to the people we serve?
    ... and

4. Leading Change
How are you helping your staffers and readers/viewers/listeners increase the diversity of people who they report on, hear and see? How are you doing as employers at hiring, recruiting and promoting people with diverse backgrounds? How are you managing diversity in your shop? How can you help people see the connection between a diverse team and high performance (excellence) in the newsroom?

Guidelines for Racial Identification

By Keith Woods
Former Poynter Dean

The use of racial identifiers in the media was for decades a means of singling out those who were not white. The practice helped form and fuel stereotypes and continues today to push a wedge between people. We can handle this delicate material better if we flag every racial reference and ask these questions:

1. Is it relevant?

Race is relevant when the story is about race. Just because people in conflict are of different races does not mean that race is the source of their dispute. A story about interracial dating, however, is a story about race.

2. Have I explained the relevance?

Journalists too frequently assume that readers will know the significance of race in stories. The result is often radically different interpretations. That is imprecise journalism, and its harm may be magnified by the lens of race.

3. Is it free of codes?

Be careful not to use *welfare, inner-city, underprivileged, blue collar, conservative, suburban, exotic, middle-class, Uptown, South Side,* or *wealthy* as euphemisms for racial groups. By definition, the White House is in the inner-city. Say what you mean.

4. Are racial identifiers used evenly?

If the race of a person charging discrimination is important, then so is the race of the person being charged.

5. Should I consult someone of another race/ethnicity?

Consider another question: Do I have expertise on other races/cultures? If not, broaden your perspective by asking someone who knows something more about your subject. Why should we treat reporting on racial issues any differently from reporting on an area of science or religion that we do not know well?

CASE STUDY 18:

When Sources Won't Talk

WHAT: It began as a letter to the editor from a former editor. It ended with a record number of online postings and apologies from a fraternity and sorority.

Jamilia Gates, former news editor for *The Parthenon*, the student newspaper at Marshall University, learned that a campus sorority and fraternity had sponsored a thug- and gangsta-themed party. Gates, who is black, wrote in her letter that the party was an insult to black students and not an appropriate campus activity.

"Pictures from this party were posted all over Facebook. Pictures of representatives from these organizations showed members grabbing their lower limbs, with gum wrappers in their mouth representing gold teeth, baggy clothing, backwards hats and permanent-marker tattoos saying 'Thug Life,'" she wrote. "The people in those photos were basically displaying light-hearted racism."

> Such a story could stir racial divisions on campus and risk the charters of both Greek organizations.

Question: The SPJ Code of Ethics offers guidance on at least three aspects of this dilemma. "Test the accuracy of information from all sources and exercise care to avoid inadvertent error." One source was not sufficient in revealing this information.

"Diligently seek out subjects of news stories to give them the opportunity to respond to allegations of wrongdoing." The newspaper editors knew the Greek community had often complained about *The Parthenon*'s so-called negative coverage of Greek life.

"Tell the story of the diversity and magnitude of the human experience boldly, even when it is unpopular to do so."

How could the editors maintain credibility and remain fair to both sides yet find solid sources for a news tip with inflammatory allegations? Such a story could stir racial divisions on campus and risk the charters of both Greek organizations.

WHO: The newspaper's editors sat on the letter for a couple of days hoping the Greek affairs reporter could get details. Meanwhile, the editors found proof of the party in photos published on Facebook.

Managing editor Brian Dalek said: "As the person usually overseeing the opinion page and letters, the staff and I did want to verify that the party did, in fact, take place before publication. There was a little bit of concern that having

THE PARTHENON

WWW.MARSHALLPARTHENON.COM

MARSHALL UNIVERSITY'S STUDENT NEWSPAPER — THURSDAY, OCTOBER 9, 2008 — VOL. 110 NO.25 © 2008 THE PARTHENON

■ GREEK AFFAIRS

Greeks issue apology, student body president says move on

BY MEGAN ARCHER
THE PARTHENON

Members of Marshall's greek community are offering apologies in written letters to The Parthenon after an African-American student strongly criticized a recent ethnic-themed party in a letter to the editor, which was published in the The Parthenon on Monday.

Jamilia Gates, senior print journalism major from Erie, Pa., and author of the letter, said she stands behind what she said even if students are misinterpreting her view of the party that occurred Sept. 26.

"People don't like to hear the truth," Gates said. "I just voiced my opinion and said what people are too scared to say."

The party, which was hosted by members of Alpha Chi Omega and Sigma Alpha Epsilon, boasted a "Gangster and Thug" theme. Pictures could be viewed by any member of Marshall's Facebook community for a period of time following the event.

The chapters of Alpha Chi Omega and Sigma Alpha Epsilon apologize in written letters published in The Parthenon Thursday. Both letters say the organizations meant no offense to any culture or ethnicity on campus.

The letters also emphasize each organization's standards for the way the group wishes to be represented on Marshall's campus.

Stephen Hensley, dean of student affairs, said Gates had the right and obligation to state what she feels.

"Racial issues are important to all of us because we all live amongst one another," Hensley said. "When issues like this arise, people have the right to defend their opinions."

Hensley said it was a mistake for the involved parties to hold an event of that nature, and they should have considered the impact of their decisions.

Yolanda Whitfield, a sophomore business and marketing major from Charleston, is the president of The Black United Students at Marshall and was another Marshall student who took offense to the activities of the party. Whitfield said when planning events as president of one of Marshall's organizations, she always asks herself three questions.

"I ask myself 'Will this benefit my organization, will this represent my organization in a positive way and will this represent Marshall in a positive way?'" Whitfield said. "The activities of the party did not benefit or represent their organization or Marshall in a positive way."

SEE **GREEK** | PAGE 5

Letters to the Editor
Page 2 | The Letters to the Editor submitted by Alpha Chi Omega and Sigma Alpha Epsilon can be found on the Opinion page.

Teacher group won't endorse candidate for W.Va. governor

BY LAWRENCE MESSINA
THE ASSOCIATED PRESS

CHARLESTON—A major teachers' group believes Gov. Joe Manchin will be re-elected, but it has decided not to endorse his bid for a second term. It isn't endorsing any of his opponents, either.

The West Virginia Education Association differs with the governor over teacher pay, hiring practices and overall public education funding.

The group considered questionnaire answers from Manchin as well as from GOP nominee Russ Weeks and Jesse Johnson, the Mountain Party candidate, before declining to endorse any of them, President Dale Lee said.

With chapters in all 55 counties, Lee says that his group applauds Manchin's efforts to help thousands of educators switch retirement plans earlier this year. These

---

a former editor submit the letter would lead to some in the Greek community on campus to see the paper as singling them out, as they had perceived in the past."

Members of the fraternity and sorority did not respond to the Greek affairs reporter's repeated requests for interviews.

"The photos were only taken down when we tried to get the Greek chapters' perspective on the party before we ran the letter," Dalek said. "After the initial inquiries, the reporter was basically shunned."

WHY: Knowing that further delays would detract from the event's news value, the editors made the unusual decision to break a news story in the letters column and published Gates' letter October 6, 2008.

Dalek said: "We did wait until we actually found several pictures on Facebook that appeared to have the theme of the gangsta/thug party. Sure, it could have been any party at Marshall, but we saw several pictures that actually had the name of the Greek chapters in the background. My only regret is that we did not print these photos or save them for proof that we did see photos before they were taken down."

HOW: Their strategy worked. Publication of the letter forced members of the fraternity and sorority to respond to *The Parthenon* reporter — but only off the record. They still didn't want to acknowledge the party. Over the next two days, the phone messages, online posts and letters from the Greek community flew. Online posts supported both sides — this type of behavior is unacceptable on a college campus versus no harm was intended as it was just a party.

Finally, the student government president urged both organizations to issue written apologies. Still, they refused to go on the record with the reporter who was finally able to pull together a story with reaction to the incident.

"After the publication of (Gates') letter, Sigma Alpha Epsilon members submitted a letter that gave an apology on the taste of the party. Just hours before the page was sent to print, however, the chapter's president informed us that he had never seen the written apology and his signature was actually forged. They pulled the letter, thankfully, but it also gave us some clarification that there were individuals in the fraternity who were likely to be insensitive to different cultures based on the fact that they forged signatures as well. We no longer had second thoughts about the original letter by Jamilia Gates' take on the story," Dalek said.

Alpha Chi Omega's letter stated: "The sisters of Alpha Chi Omega would not and did not set out to hurt anyone's feelings or be insensitive to anyone's culture. We greatly regret choosing a theme with even the potential to be offensive ... Please know that we have learned from this experience. We will share this valuable lesson with others in our organization. And we'll make every effort to ensure that it never happens again."

Sigma Alpha Epsilon submitted its letter: "Our fraternity prides itself on our creed, 'The True Gentlemen,' and our decisions regarding the social event did not live up to the beliefs to which we strive ... We are committed to reaffirming our actions to reflect those of a gentleman in order to better ourselves and our community."

The editorial board opted to follow up with an editorial October 10: "Hopefully this is the end of this controversy, but something can be taken from the situation. As individuals and as student groups at Marshall, we all need to take into account the impact of our decisions ... With the Internet, mobile videos and photos posted on MySpace and Facebook, anything you do can be a thorn in your side, and not just on a college campus."

The editors took a gamble in using the opinion page to break a story. Their savvy use of social networking sites, however, allowed them to independently confirm the party occurred. By the time Gates' letter was published, the photos had been removed.

The unusual strategy allowed the newspaper to cover an event with important ramifications to the campus. Had editors waited on a news story to cover it, the story would have been lost.

— *Nerissa Young, SPJ Ethics Committee and*
Parthenon *adviser, Marshall University*

CASE STUDY 19:

The 'N' Word

In April 1996, Don Follmer, spokesman for the speaker of the House in North Carolina, called a group of protesting University of North Carolina housekeepers and students "niggers and wormy kids" in what he thought was a private conversation with Associated Press reporter Dennis Patterson.

Follmer uttered the racial slur in the doorway of Patterson's office in the North Carolina General Assembly building's press room. Another reporter overheard the remark and told others. No journalists, including Patterson, reported the remark until two weeks later when *Raleigh News & Observer* reporter Joseph Neff heard about it. Neff pursued the story. He discussed it with the newspaper's state editor and managing editor, both of whom agreed that Follmer's racist comments were newsworthy.

> Follmer's admission, however, was not enough to eliminate the controversy that his comments had stirred on the university campus and in state government.

Neff confronted Follmer about the remark, and Follmer admitted he had used the racial slur. Neff wrote a front-page story about the comment, and three days later, North Carolina House Speaker Harold Brubaker fired Follmer.

Neff said he never had any doubts that he should report Follmer's conversation with Patterson.

"The speaker of the House is the second most powerful person in state politics," Neff said. "And you have his spokesman standing in a public place, very loudly making racist jokes about state employees. To me, this was a no-brainer."

Neff said Follmer had used "nigger" during an interview with another *News & Observer* reporter a year earlier but the reporter chose not to use the racial slur in a story.

"Anyone in the '90s should know better," Neff said. "It isn't a word you toss around like that."

Follmer said the "niggers and wormy kids" comment was made in jest while "letting off steam." He said he was "under a lot of stress" that day and protesters who had entered the General Assembly building were disruptive. "It just got away from me," Follmer said. "I used an unfortunate word in a private setting. I just popped off in a private conversation."

Follmer's admission, however, was not enough to eliminate the controversy that his comments had stirred on the university campus and in state government.

Neff questioned Follmer's boss, Brubaker, who said his staff was "color-blind" and never used racist language. Follmer said he advised Brubaker to fire him, and the House speaker did.

Patterson declined to comment on why he didn't report Follmer's remark. In an interview with Neff, he said he sometimes engaged in "politically incorrect" banter with Follmer but that he had never used racial slurs. In a story distributed by the AP, Patterson said he had told Follmer to "be careful" with his remarks but didn't consider writing about them.

"It was a casual conversation, not an interview, and I was working on something else," Patterson said in the AP story.

Follmer, a 20-year journalist before switching to state politics, said he had overheard numerous conversations that included racist and foul language but chose not to report them. "If I had been in that boy's shoes, I never would have reported the story," said Follmer, who has retired and lives in the North Carolina mountains. He blamed the story on the popularity of "gotcha" journalism and "political correctness."

"These days people will take an inflammatory statement like that and try to smear somebody," he said. "They need to lighten up. Just report the news. And have a sense of humor."

Consider this situation from two perspectives: That of the reporter who overheard the remark and that of the Associated Press reporter and editor who decided to do make a story of the remark. Who has the stronger ethical position? What would you have done?

— from the Third Edition, Black, Steele and Barney

CASE STUDY 20:

A Columnist's Edge Cuts Skin-Deep

Summary

In contemporary sports journalism, *The Miami Herald*'s Dan LeBatard is widely known as a talented, hip, young columnist with an acerbic writing edge that, he proudly proclaims, "sells papers."

So when LeBatard was directed to write a piece during the 1997 NBA playoffs bashing the Knicks and New Yorkers in favor of his hometown Heat — standard sports-page fare for intercity rivalries — what he sent was a postcard from the edge.

Or, from over the edge, his editors would say in apologizing for a column they called "inappropriate ... offensive" and "a failure of the editing process."

Reaction to LeBatard's column, in which he joked that even New York moms are named Vinny and in which he described Knicks center Patrick Ewing as having "a face used by cavemen to scare woolly mammoths," resulted in a protracted public debate in the *Herald* and in the New York press about racial and ethnic stereotyping, with colleagues and competitors alike turning critic on LeBatard.

> From the narrower perspective of one editor, or even a few, it is difficult to foresee how a broader range of readers might react to anything that smacks of the controversial.

The column, *Herald* executive editor Doug Clifton wrote in the paper the following week, had raised eyebrows in the sports department before publication, but "the debate didn't go on long enough or proceed high enough up the chain." Sports editor Dave Wilson described the editing process — the column was read by a deputy sports editor and at least two copy editors, including an African-American — as not "thorough enough." There was, Wilson said, "a major meltdown in the editing process."

The most provocative passage proved to be that which poked fun at Ewing's appearance. To some readers, and to the editors at *The Daily News* in New York, where LeBatard's column was run reciprocally as part of the hyped coverage — and to Clifton — the passage about Ewing, who is African-American, was "racially insensitive." *The Daily News* printed LeBatard's column but deleted the Ewing reference, but the next day a *Daily News* writer printed the passage in his own column, in which he denounced LeBatard as a racist and called for his firing.

Fellow *Herald* columnist Richard Steinbach, who is African-American, also castigated LeBatard in print, but another African-American columnist at the *Herald*, Leonard Pitts, while maintaining LeBatard had been too zealous and defending Ewing's looks, denied the remark had any relevance to race and suggested the furor boiled down to: "Can you call a black man ugly?"

For LeBatard, and his colleague Pitts, racism in this instance was in the eye of the beholder. LeBatard, a Cuban-American who acknowledges having been the target of ethnic prejudice but claims not to feel its sting as others might, maintained that there was nothing racial in the caveman reference, citing white athletes who have the same facial characteristics. "Why can't it just be about an athlete?" LeBatard wonders aloud. "Why does anyone have to read 'black' into it?"

Executive editor Clifton saw things differently, writing that LeBatard had "gratuitously" offended "vast classes of people," and pre-empting the counter-claim that the newspaper's concern was mere misguided political correctness by labeling that argument "a false debate."

In retrospect, sports editor Wilson said, the editing process in place wasn't thorough enough. His department has "tightened up the checks and balances — either I or another senior editor gets a look at all columns as early as possible."

"The real tragedy here," Wilson added, "would be if there were no lessons learned. In fact, there were hard lessons learned."

Months after the storm, LeBatard said he remained "confused" by the episode and gun-shy about using all the ammunition in his arsenal of wit. "I can understand being cautious about what I say," the columnist said, "but I don't want to be afraid of what I say. You do that to a columnist, you take away his edge."

Analysis

As the diverging views of Steinbach and Pitts, two African-American columnists at the *Herald*, show, whether some comments might be racially insensitive is often in the eyes of the beholder. But the overwhelming public and media response to LeBatard's column about New Yorkers and the Knicks, particularly his unflattering remarks about Patrick Ewing, are evidence enough that the remarks could be found offensive.

Despite a reasoned argument that LeBatard's reference to Ewing's resemblance to an ugly "caveman" was never meant to be, nor could have been, construed as racial stereotyping, the fact that so many people drew a racial inference raises the concern that the *Herald* did not give enough thought to how such pejorative comments might be perceived and did not have in place a process for flagging such problems.

From the narrower perspective of one editor, or even a few, it is difficult to foresee how a broader range of readers might react to anything that smacks of the controversial. In such cases, it helps to engage in collaborative decision-making. And it helps to collaborate early in the process during the assigning and planning stages of a story, column or project — as well as later, on deadline, when second thoughts about the appropriateness of language, for instance, might occur to either writer or editor.

The collaborative process ought to allow for diversity, and not merely diversity of ethnicity or race; in the LeBatard case, the columnist and one senior editor who approved the piece are members of a minority group, and so is one of the copy editors who read the column. True diversity means a variety of minds and voices. Combined with the truth-telling aspect of voicing what one really thinks, diversity is essential to collaborations.

In the case of the *Herald*'s tabloid-style treatment of the playoffs package, the implications of mimicking a tabloid should have set off alarms among those who conceived of the idea and those who knew it was in gestation. Because the image of the tabloid today often evokes questions of taste and propriety in the minds of most people, editors who choose even to parody one should have been exceptionally careful to scrutinize the content of the package's every component, as well as the impression it gave overall.

Although principals involved in the editing of the LeBatard column — including the writer himself — disagree in their recollection of just what was edited out or kept the same, and why and how, all agree that the level of editing and discussion was minimal. In this case, "negligible" might be a more accurate description. Even though three gatekeepers read and, by allowing LeBatard's column to pass through, at least tacitly approved of it, it is clear that in retrospect, *Herald* management regrets that none of the editors pressed whatever concerns they may have had.

Ironically, in the post-mortem discussions, according to sports editor Dave Wilson, the copy editors have been excluded from accountability and exculpated of blame. Such a top-down, non-collaborative approach can be self-defeating. Every journalist in the process from content generation to publication has some moral and legal, as well as professional, stake in the outcome; each should be viewed positively as a collaborator.

In many newsrooms, columnists traditionally have been granted greater leeway in pushing the outside of the envelope. In part, that may be because individual journalists maintain a fierce independence and pride of authorship in their work and do not lightly accept the questioning of it. In part, the freedom given columnists may stem from a lack of understanding of the protectedness of opinion in libel law. LeBatard and his editors agree that the substantive editing of his Knicks column amounted to a simple request to delete and LeBatard's rejection of that request.

In any case, often at the end of the process, rank-and-file copy editors and copy desk chiefs feel they have neither the authority nor the support to question what assigning editors and department heads appear to have approved. Such organizational thinking reduces the work of gatekeepers to mere fact-checking, when instead the work calls for moral wherewithal as well.

Newsroom managers would be better served, as would writers and editors equally, by having an ongoing editing process that allows for frank and constructive discussion, the goal of which is not to censor, but to publish — and to publish in as responsible a way as possible.

— from the Third Edition, Black, Steele and Barney

CASE STUDY 21:

Portrayal of the Disabled

Summary

It was the type of story that television reporters are often assigned without any advance preparation. Reporter Doug Miller of KHOU-TV in Houston, Texas, was covering a story involving disabled individuals taking part in a water sports event.

Miller and his photographer could easily have shot some video and gathered a few facts and made the story into a 30-second voice-over for the evening newscast. Or they could have done a short report focusing on the difficulties of disabled people in participating in such an event.

But Miller went beyond that. He and his photographer produced a story that concentrated on the feeling of freedom these individuals experienced while in the water. Most were unable to walk and used wheelchairs for mobility. In the story, they expressed the feelings of elation they experienced during their first time free-floating in the water.

What could have been a routine story merely showing the event or a potentially negative story detailing the individuals' difficulty in getting around on land became an informative and visual story about inspiration and success.

> News organizations can improve their coverage of the disabled by considering various reporting alternatives such as first-person narratives, photo essays and series reporting.

Analysis

Telling the truth in a story is much more than just providing facts. This case is an example of a journalist who took the time to recognize the value of a meaningful and fair portrayal of a group of individuals who don't always receive such media coverage.

By focusing on the positive aspects of the human condition, journalists can provide a more enlightened outlook about people who are often regarded as afflicted or handicapped. Reporters and photographers must be willing to try to see situations from the perspective of the subjects of the story. To those who are disabled, an ordinary trip to the beach can be an adventure filled with excitement and wonder.

News organizations can improve their coverage of the disabled by considering various reporting alternatives such as first-person narratives, photo essays and series reporting. Additionally, it is important to report continuously on how well society treats those with disabilities, in the job market and in building access. In that reporting, journalists should examine their use of language and images in stories to prevent unfair stereotypical portrayals of the disabled.

Beyond that, news organizations should ensure their daily reporting includes people with disabilities in routine coverage of all events, whether interviews with stockbrokers, reporting on school programs or athletic competitions. Newspapers and broadcast stations should also hold themselves accountable in this respect, taking the initiative in hiring and promotion practices to ensure that individuals with disabilities are represented within the news organization and that their voices are regularly heard in the decision-making process.

—from the Third Edition, Black, Steele and Barney

CASE STUDY 22:

The 'Art' of Darkness

WHAT: On June 27, 1994, both *Time* and *Newsweek* ran cover photos of O.J. Simpson, the former football and movie star who had been arrested 10 days earlier as a suspect in the stabbing deaths of his wife and a male acquaintance of hers. Both magazines used essentially the same photo — a police mug shot taken at the time of Simpson's arrest, after a bizarre, long-distance, slow-motion car chase followed worldwide on television.

Newsweek used the mug shot without altering it. *Time* used a darker, coarser image, symbolizing Simpson's fall from grace. Given three choices for a cover, *Time*'s managing editor, James R. Gaines, said he chose one by Matt Mahurin, whom Gaines described as "a master of photo illustration."

Gaines wrote in a "To Our Readers" note the following week that he had found Mahurin's work "quite impressive. The harshness of the mug shot — the merciless bright light, the stubble on Simpson's face, the cold specificity of the picture — had been subtly smoothed and shaped into an icon of tragedy. The expression on his face was not merely blank now; it was bottomless. This cover, with the simple, nonjudgmental headline 'An American Tragedy,' seemed the obvious, right choice."

But the reaction was swift, and angry.

"I have looked at thousands of covers over the years and chosen hundreds," Gaines wrote.

> "I have never been so wrong about how one would be received. In the storm of controversy over this cover, several of the country's major news organizations and leading black journalists charged that we had darkened Simpson's face in a racist and legally prejudicial attempt to make him look more sinister and guilty, to portray him as 'some kind of animal,' as the NAACP's Benjamin Chavis put it. A white press critic said the cover had the effect of sending him 'back to the ghetto.' Others objected to the fact that the mug shot had been altered at all, arguing that photographs, particularly news photos, should never be altered."

There certainly was no racist intent, Gaines wrote, nor did the magazine or artist intend any suggestion of guilt. A week after the uproar, he still defended the cover:

> Our critics felt that Matt Mahurin's work changed the picture fundamentally; I felt it lifted a common police mug

shot to the level of art, with no sacrifice to truth. Reasonable people may disagree about that. If there was anything wrong with the cover, in my view, it was that it was not immediately apparent that this was a photo-illustration rather than an un-altered photograph; to know that, a reader had to turn to our contents page or see the original mug shot on the opening page of the story. But making that distinction clearer will not end the debate over the manipulation of photographs. Nor should it. No single set of rules will ever cover all possible cases. It will remain, as it has always been, a matter of subjective judgment.

Question: Was the decision to use this cover a defensible one? Did *Time* respond appropriately?

WHO: Gaines, the managing editor, made the decision to use the photograph, after Mahurin, the artist, made the decisions on how to make the image more compelling. They are the moral agents, the decision-makers in this case. They are also stakeholders, be-

> Most photojournalists, in particular, argue that news photographs must be totally authentic. Manipulation alters the truth of what happened.

cause their reputations — and their magazine's — are affected by their decisions. Others affected clearly include Simpson and the families of the victim, as well as the African-American community, potential jurists and even the entire judicial system. You may be able to think of others.

WHY: The principles involved here include a journalist's overriding responsibility to the truth — to be accurate and, as the SPJ Code of Ethics puts it, "honest, fair and courageous in gathering, reporting and interpreting information."

Certainly, there was a controversial amount of "interpretation" in developing this image. But should any news photo, in particular a police mug shot, be manipulated? Should journalists' decisions be guided by racial or other sensitivities of their audiences? Does the fact that the image was manipulated diminish the argument some journalists make that one should "tell the story and run" and not be cowed by the possible consequences?

HOW: *Time* clearly did not go casually into the decision to alter this cover. The managing editor's explanation in the July 4, 1994, issue explains the reasoning. But not many people agreed with what was done. Most photojournalists, in particular, argue that news photographs must be totally authentic. Manipulation alters the truth of what happened.

And yet, news images continue to be changed. In March 2005, the National Press Photographers Association took *Time*'s competitor *Newsweek* to task for publishing a cover picture of a smiling Martha Stewart, her head perched on a model's body. "NPPA finds it a total breach of ethics and completely misleading to the public," said Bob Gould, then-president of the organization. Rich Beckman, head of the School of Journalism and Mass Communication's visual communication program at the University of North Carolina in Chapel Hill, went on to list several other bad examples of photo manipulation, all of them in the decade since the flare-up over the Simpson cover:

"We've had the head of former Texas Governor Ann Richards placed on the body of a model sitting astride a motorcycle on the cover of *Texas Monthly* in July 1992, Oprah Winfrey's head placed on Ann-Margret's body on the cover of the August 26, 1989, issue of *TV Guide*, and in July 2003, *Redbook* published a cover photo of actress Julia Roberts that *USA Today* revealed to be a composite created by sticking the head of a year-old photograph of Roberts atop the body from a four-year-old photograph of her."

"I wonder how many heads have to be attached [to other people's bodies] before the industry learns its lesson," Beckman said.

— SPJ Ethics Committee

Case Study 23:

Prejudiced and Persistent

WHAT: A reader of *The Durango* (Colorado) *Herald* complained to the Society of Professional Journalists in the spring of 2010 that the family-owned newspaper was regularly printing "hateful" letters to the editor attacking homosexuality. The particular sequence of events that appeared to spur the complaint was set off by a letter praising a parochial school in another Colorado community, the liberal university town of Boulder, for refusing admission to a child with lesbian parents. The letter, published March 24, 2010, included statements like this: "Satan is alive and well. This is why it is so important for Christ-based churches to offer special counseling to help the gay and lesbian community, including children trapped in their immoral existence."

Numerous letters were printed in response. Most of them challenged the initial letter, but one supporter wrote: "I am sick and tired of having sexual perversion crammed down my throat. Enough is enough. Sodomites are the ones filled with hate and evil — not God-fearing Christians."

> Lesbian, gay, bisexual and transsexual individuals are offended and hurt. Their critics want to continue to be able to express their beliefs publicly.

This is the sort of language that drove the complainant to the SPJ Ethics Hotline. She said the *Herald* had even "created an editorial policy to justify" the practice. "The letters are so hateful that the community began to bombard them [the *Herald*] with requests not to print them, and that," she surmised, "is what inspired the policy." She asked if ethical journalists should ever publish such letters and complained that the newspaper's editorial defending its publication of such letters was "so weak." She did give the *Herald* some credit, though, for at least listening to the complaints. "I have written a response to the policy that was published in the paper, a group of us went and met with the editorial page editor, and I wrote a letter to him after our meeting because I did not think that we had made an impact," she said in her e-mail to the Hotline.

Question: What guidelines should a newspaper have for printing letters to the editor that attack a particular group?

WHO: The decision-makers here, the moral agents, are the *Herald*'s publisher, Richard Ballantine, and its editorial page editor, Bill Roberts. They are responsible for setting the newspaper's policy on letters to the editor. The people most

There are three things that no one can do to the entire satisfaction of anyone else: make love, poke the fire, and run a newspaper. **William Allen White, 1917**

Opinion

4A

THE DURANGO HERALD

durangoherald.com   Bill Roberts, Opinion Page Editor ✆ 375-4560 ✉ letters@durangoherald.com   Wednesday, March 31, 2010

On publishing 'hateful' letters

A number of readers – see Page 5A – have responded to a letter published March 24 in the *Herald*. Most describe it as "hateful," and several have urged the *Herald* not to print further letters from that author or from authors they deem homophobic.

They are reasonable complaints from people honestly concerned about hurtful speech and intolerance. But they miss the point.

The *Herald* tries to keep the discussions on its Opinion page civil, if not always cordial, but there are some topics that are in themselves inherently ugly. The perceived need on the part of some Americans to limit the rights of their gay and lesbian neighbors is one example.

For starters, the *Herald* limits letter writers to 350 words and one letter per month. That some choose to address the same topic repeatedly may make it seem as if they are accorded more space. They are not.

But they are edited. The assertion that homosexuality is both forbidden by the Bible and a threat to society is theologically shaky and offensive to many. It is not an epithet.

As for whether anti-gay sentiments are a suitable topic, there are two reasons for printing such letters. The first is simply to educate readers about the diversity of thought in the community – good and bad. But admittedly, that goes only so far. The *Herald* would not print a letter proclaiming the inferiority of a given racial group.

But the equality of people of different races is settled law and a firmly established cultural ideal. The status of gay and lesbian Americans is another matter entirely. Issues such as "don't ask, don't tell," lesbian parentage and gay marriage are hotly contested public issues of a kind racial minorities have not faced in decades.

The discussion surrounding those questions cannot be limited to those who support full equality and opponents who express their homophobia only in euphemisms. It must also include those who would deny other's rights because they believe homosexuality is morally wrong and offensive to God.

They may be on the wrong side of history, but it is their country, too.

affected by their policy include members of Durango's homosexual community as well as the people writing the letters. Lesbian, gay, bisexual and transsexual individuals are offended and hurt. Their critics want to continue to be able to express their beliefs publicly. The community itself, and its image, have a stake here, too. Durango is not large, so it might be surprising that it has an LGBT community. About 16,000 people live within the city limits; the *Herald*'s countywide circulation area is about 50,000. But Durango is one of a number of scenic and sophisticated small towns that dot the American Southwest, attracting tourists, artists, galleries, students and good restaurants. It's the cultural hub of southwest Colorado. Its daily newspaper, owned by the same family since 1952, has a reputation to be concerned about — in particular, a reputation for an expansive world-view that contributes to Durango's level of sophistication.

WHY: This is a classic ethical struggle between freedom of expression and the ideal of minimizing harm. In a March 31, 2010, editorial defending the *Herald*'s letters policy, editorial page editor Roberts, after what he called "considerable discussion" with the publisher and editorial board, wrote: "The *Herald* tries to keep the discussions on its Opinion page civil, if not always cordial, but there are some topics that are in themselves inherently ugly. The perceived need on the part of some Americans to limit the rights of their gay and lesbian neighbors is one example." The reasons for printing such letters, he said, are "to educate readers about the diversity of thought in the community — good and bad," and to permit debate about a controversial subject that covers hot-button issues like military service, gay marriage and adoption. The *Herald*, he conceded, would not be as permissive on issues of race, but racial equality "is settled law and a firmly established cultural ideal"; the issues still facing the homosexual community are still "hotly contested ... of a kind racial minorities have not faced in decades."

This did not satisfy the woman who complained about the policy. "I cannot imagine *The New York Times* ever printing the types of letters that the Herald prints on a regular basis," she wrote to SPJ. "... My point is that I do not understand why gays and lesbians should be treated different." Another letter, published in the *Herald* on April 27, asserted that "religious belief is no justification for slander and hate-mongering. Homophobic hate speech, which these letters represent, is not 'discussion'; it is intimidation, pure and simple, and should not be tolerated."

SPJ's Ethics Hotline, staffed by volunteers, doesn't formally investigate complaints, but it does offer opinions and advice. In this case, the woman who complained was told that the editorial defending the *Herald*'s policy appeared to be "a very thoughtful explanation of why journalists feel compelled to give voice to ideas and sometimes actions they don't agree with." She was invited to give more potentially damaging details about the letters' contents, but she did not reply. The facts in this case study were researched afterward.

Personally, Roberts said, he believes that sexuality is innate, not a lifestyle choice, "and as such should be treated much like race." But the half-dozen or so conservative Christians writing the anti-gay letters "really are offended," he said, by the growing acceptance of something they see as "profoundly immoral."

HOW: The *Herald*'s policy on letters to the editor is similar to that of many publications that try to keep polemicists from dominating their op-ed pages. It limits letters to 350 words and writers to one letter a month. "That some choose to address the same topic repeatedly may make it seem as if they are accorded more space," the *Herald*'s editorial said. "They are not." The discussion surrounding issues affecting gays and lesbians "cannot be limited to those who support full equality and opponents who express their homophobia only in euphemisms," the editorial continued. "It must also include those who would deny others' rights because they believe homosexuality is morally wrong and offensive to God. They may be on the wrong side of history, but it is their country, too."

Discussion: Is there such a thing as fair criticism in this delicate subject area? Should there be more restrictions on letter writers who get to be predictable and repetitious? Is it fair to treat attacks based on sexual orientation different from criticisms based on racial or ethnic identity? Would you have a different, more specific, policy for letters to the editor?

— Fred Brown, SPJ Ethics Committee

Diversity

What the Codes Say

The Virginian-Pilot (Norfolk, Virginia)
DIVERSITY

We will accurately and fairly reflect the diversity of gender, color, ethnicity, class, generation, geography and other attributes that distinguish our communities.

This standard requires our staff to go beyond the usual suspects when seeking sources. The ideal is to have the community's diverse groups represented in whom we cite, regardless of the theme or topic being covered. For example, there are minority health care professionals in Hampton Roads; health and medical stories should, therefore, include such minorities among the sources consulted. The principle holds true for business, religion, education, consumer and political stories.

Reporters, editors and photographers will accomplish this by ensuring that their source lists include women, minorities and representatives of other communities. There is no easy way to do this. Staff writers must be as purposeful about it as they are now in ensuring that names are spelled correctly.

In the drive for diversity, avoid using minority sources as tokens.

RACIAL AND ETHNIC IDENTIFICATION

- We identify someone's race or ethnicity only when it is important to understanding the story.
- Identify race evenly. Stories that deal with racial conflict or identify people by race because that's the topic should identify all the characters in the story by race.

  GUIDING QUESTIONS
  - Is race or ethnic identity relevant? Can I explain the relevance in the story?
  - How will this information help readers understand this story?
  - Am I stereotyping a race or ethnic group, or just catering to some readers' idle curiosity?

CRIME STORIES

Two basic tenets of good journalism — accuracy and precision — require us to identify a suspect's race only as part of a detailed physical description.

A suspect's identifying information should exclude that suspect from all but a narrow group of people. We should ask authorities to provide more meaningful details.

Poor examples: "A 6-foot tall Hispanic man in his 20s"; "A 5-foot-8 black male of medium build." These vague descriptions don't provide valuable information to help readers assist police.

Good example: "An olive-skinned male, 25 to 30 years old, 5 feet 7 inches, weighing 130 pounds, with thinning hair, wearing blue jeans and a Dallas Cowboys hat and driving a black Caravan."

"Hispanic," "Latino" and "Filipino" should never be used as a physical description. Those words describe ethnicity — not color. Imagine describing someone as "Italian-looking" or "Jewish-looking."

GUIDING QUESTION

– Is the physical description specific enough to help a reader identify a suspect?

KGNU (Boulder, Colorado)

Seek out more than one, two or three perspectives on an issue. The more interviews, research and diverse resources you use in your program, the closer you will come to "the truth."

Hearst Newspapers

In our news columns as well as in our reporting, we will treat people with dignity and respect. Recognizing that there are multiple points of view in most stories, we will make every effort to include all sides relevant to a story. We must make a particular effort to seek comment from those portrayed in a critical manner...

Hearst Newspapers seeks to maintain a safe and supportive workplace where employees are treated with respect, where diversity is valued and where decisions on employment and career advancement are based on equal opportunity. Employees are expected to support and uphold these principles.

9

Conflicts of Interest

The success of a free press is reflected in the ability of journalists to honor a primary loyalty to the public. Journalistic principles of truth-telling and independence work together to honor that loyalty. To seek truth and report it as fully as possible, journalists must be independent.

Journalists must remain free of associations and activities that may compromise their integrity or damage their own or their organization's credibility. (Don't forget: Credibility is what others think of us; ethics is what kind of people we actually are. One is image, the other substance.) Journalists must seek out competing perspectives without being unduly influenced by those who would use their power or position counter to the public interest.

Conflicts of interest occur when individuals face competing loyalties to a source or to their own self-interest, or to their organization's economic needs as opposed to the information needs of the public.

Journalism carries a terrific responsibility in our society. No other profession does what journalism does. No other individuals have the primary and constitutionally protected role of regularly informing and educating the public in a meaningful way on significant issues. To abdicate that responsibility, to put awards or friends or self-interest or economic gain ahead of public benefit, is unacceptable and unethical.

Editors and reporters in small towns face particularly difficult challenges because of the unique nature of their personal and professional loyalties. They are far more likely than their metropolitan colleagues to be tugged by ties of friendship with sources, commitments to local institutions, and the simple fact that they come face to face with their readers on a daily basis. In rural communities, there tends to be a vacuum in leadership, which often impels communities to draft all competent and willing citizens — including journalists. And the readers have a proprietary interest in the newspaper (not legal, but social). In this setting, the journalist may have a responsibility to be a part of the community and may behave in ways that would be a conflict of interest in a larger community.

The cases in this section, while not reflecting the full range of potential conflict-of-interest issues, raise essential questions about obligations and competing loyalties. The accompanying excerpts from codes of ethics provide specific guidelines various news organizations use to guard against conflicts and to ensure journalistic independence. More than half of all the sections in the news media codes reviewed for this project were devoted to conflicts of interest, and we offer a generous sampling of that soul-searching.

Conflicts of Interest: Checklist

Because of the enormous responsibility journalists have to the public, they must be aware of any situations that create a real or perceived conflict of interest. Individual journalists must weigh their obligations against the impact of:

- involvement in particular activities.
- affiliation with causes or organizations.
- acceptance of favors or preferential treatment.
- financial investments.
- outside employment.
- family and friendships.

Newspapers and broadcast organizations play a dual role in a community, as journalists and as corporate citizens. While these roles are not mutually exclusive, media leaders must

INDIFFERENCE VS. IMPARTIALITY

As journalists, we know better than to get involved in a story we are covering. But what does that mean, exactly? Some reporters will say not getting involved means you should always be totally detached — an observer, never a participant. Yes, reporters should be impartial. They shouldn't take sides. They should avoid the appearance of conflict of interest. Yet there's a difference between impartiality and refusing to get involved. Journalists faced that question in their coverage of Hurricane Katrina. In the end, many reporters found themselves siding with the victims. There's nothing wrong with that. In fact, it's preferable to stony detachment. I'm in favor of showing some humanity, and opposed to getting in the way of those whose real job is to give help.

Let me qualify that. A certain amount of badgering is justifiable and necessary. Aid officials are going to have press conferences to tell us their side of things — and they should. We'd insist on it if they didn't, and part of their obligation is to be accountable to their critics.

The media are a conduit for those criticisms. In serving as the public's representative, asking the tough questions, reporters should be impartial. But asking those questions also makes them a part of the story. Involvement is unavoidable. And it's not taking sides to ask the questions that need to be answered.

Getting involved, like most ethical questions, is a matter of degree.

The easiest ethical decision is to avoid covering an organization or an activity in which you — or a spouse, significant other or close friend — have a personal stake or are a regular participant.

But what if it's your hometown that's being destroyed? Certainly, you have a personal stake in that story. And what if you are covering a developing story and find yourself in a position to prevent injury or death? Doesn't your mere presence as a chronicler of the event change the event itself? Would the story be different if you weren't there — and isn't that a kind of involvement?

Hurricane Katrina was a story in which many reporters decided to get involved. Maybe they couldn't help themselves. They broke down and cried on the air. They asked angry questions, showing more than the expected journalistic aggressiveness, going beyond assertiveness to emotional anger. And sometimes they did more.

NBC's Kerry Sanders gave food to a very ill 91-year-old man on the floor of the triage center at New Orleans International Airport. Sanders slept at the airport and the next morning reported that people near him had died during the night.

Chris Merrifield, a promotions producer for WWL-TV in New Orleans, waded into chest-deep water to pull a driver through the window of his sinking car. The station's assistant news director, Chris Slaughter, told *USA Today*: "The kid just reacted. We're proud of what he did. I would hope all of our people would do something like that rather than let someone drown."

So where, exactly, is it written that reporters should not get involved? It may be one of those things we believe to be so obvious that it doesn't need to be spelled out. It's not specific in the SPJ Code of Ethics, although some code language comes close:

"Professional integrity is the cornerstone of a journalist's credibility."

"Distinguish between advocacy and news reporting."

"Journalists should be free of obligation to any interest other than the public's right to know."

"Avoid conflicts of interest, real or perceived."

"Remain free of associations and activities that may compromise integrity or damage credibility."

But the code of ethics also reminds us to "minimize harm.... Ethical journalists treat sources, subjects and colleagues as human beings deserving of respect." Sometimes showing that respect comes in the gathering of news, and sometimes it may involve minimizing the harm in the actual unfolding of the news — right there, on the spot.

The code also says, "Show compassion for those who may be affected adversely by news coverage."

That could be expanded to say "affected adversely by events." The question of appropriate involvement, if involvement is ever appropriate, is another of those fine-line ethical issues. It's more modest and thus more noble to help quietly and behind the scenes than to do it with cameras rolling.

But all of what happened in the Katrina disaster, in New Orleans and elsewhere, was an important part of this huge and historic story, including the media's anger and compassion.

— *Fred Brown, SPJ Ethics Committee*

guard with vigilance their organizations' stewardship roles in society. They also must ensure that their primary obligation to the public is not eroded by other legitimate goals, such as:

- a quest for economic gain.
- the interest of being a good corporate citizen.
- the concern for their own employees.
- the need to be competitive in the marketplace.

In the end, individual journalists would do well to ask themselves:

- Am I being independent?
- Could my action harm my integrity or my organization's integrity?
- Is the mere appearance of a conflict enough to diminish my credibility?
- Am I willing to publicly disclose any potential conflicts?

CASE STUDY 24:

The Embedded Reporter

WHAT: When the United States ousted the Iraqi army from Kuwait in 1991, it kept reporters far from the front lines of the conflict. By the time the U.S. invaded Iraq in 2003, it was persuaded to allow reporters to be "embedded" with military units. But there were rules: reporters could not drive their own vehicles, military commanders could impose temporary restrictions on electronic transmissions back home, a military public affairs escort might be assigned, datelines would have to follow ground rules of local commanders, bright lights generally would be barred during night missions, embargoes might be imposed, specific troop numbers could not be disclosed, the names of individual soldiers could be released only with their consent. And pictures of wounded or dead soldiers were to be withheld for 72 hours or until the dead soldier's family had been formally notified. In all, the policy and list of rules regarding embedded reporters runs to 13 pages.

> "Rules are what people who decide them say they are."

Was it possible, within those rules, to offer a journalistically accurate description of a military unit's activities? Given the sometimes-extreme situation of the battlefield environment, can one retain a detached nature?

Question: Do you surrender your journalistic independence by agreeing to be embedded into a military unit? And therefore should you refuse the opportunity?

WHO: Bill Nemitz, a columnist at the *Portland Press Herald/Maine Sunday Telegram*, returned to his roots as a reporter, going on three tours of duty as an embedded reporter working alongside Maine National Guard Units. Nemitz said it was his idea, approved by his managing editor, Eric Conrad, and Editor Jeannine Guttman who agreed he should go.

Being an embedded reporter also meant a heightened contact with a stakeholder group other than readers and editors, namely the troops themselves. Nemitz said he began to notice he would find very few soldiers to talk to at the time each day when his stories were posted to the *Press Herald* website because, he discovered, they were off at computers reading what he'd written. And some troops became upset that his stories "blew their cover" — not their operational cover, but the reassuring e-mails some troops were sending their families describing conditions in Iraq. Nemitz's reporting sometimes painted a more dangerous picture. Nemitz said he had no choice but to be accurate for his readers' sake. But he also sent a message to the troops by getting their

commander to go on the record with a quote saying he always told it like it was to his family.

Only once, in describing a formation used by the troops, did he get after-the-fact criticism from an officer who believed the formation Nemitz reported about was a matter of "operational security" off-limits to reporting. Nemitz said after that he was more conscious of what might constitute "operational security," though he believed sometimes the military's rules about such things "imply the enemy is oblivious."

WHY: For Nemitz, embedding was going to be the best way to capture the local angle of the war story: Maine was facing the largest call-up of its National Guard troops since World War II in support of the Iraq invasion. As Nemitz put it, "If we didn't cover it, they would disappear not to be seen or heard until the deployment was over, or unless something really bad happened."

HOW: Though embedding under the Department of Defense system challenges journalists with the kind of rules normally an anathema to independent reporting, Nemitz said he was always driven by the fact that, even in the confines of the embedded environment, the story was worth doing, worth telling. He said on his three trips, he felt he had unfettered access to anyone in the unit he was covering. He found the unit commander willing to help steer him to the right people to talk to and never felt the commander acted as a gatekeeper.

In one instance he was refused permission to interview a wounded soldier, but that refusal came from an officer of another unit the soldier was with. It affirmed a truth Nemitz said he found on his three visits to Iraq: "Rules are what people who decide them say they are."

"Source cultivation and maintenance," he said, was the key, and, in that way, made reporting as an embedded reporter with military units no different than other reporting assignments. Nemitz added, "If I felt I was being prevented from what I thought was an accurate portrayal I would have gone home."

— *Irwin Gratz, SPJ Ethics Committee*

CASE STUDY 25:

'Reigning' on the Parade

WHAT: Frank Whelan, a features writer who also wrote a history column for the Allentown, Pennsylvania, *Morning Call*, took part in a gay rights parade in June 2006 and stirred up a classic ethical dilemma. The situation raises any number of questions about what is and isn't a conflict of interest. Whelan, 56, and his partner of 25 years, Bob Wittman, were the co-grand marshals of a gay pride parade. His newspaper prohibits employees from taking part in "public demonstrations in favor of or opposed to a cause." His editors say Whelan didn't seek their permission to participate in the event. A subsidiary publication co-sponsored the parade, but *Call* editors say they didn't know of Whelan's involvement until they saw a press release. Two days before the parade, they warned him that his role would be a conflict, a breach of the paper's code of ethics, and that there would be "consequences" if he participated. Whelan said their roles as grand marshals were a celebration of his and Wittman's long-term relationship.

> What do you think are appropriate limits — if any — on a journalist's political involvement?

Question: What should those "consequences" be for Frank Whelan?

WHO: Consider the decision-maker and the parties affected by that person's decision. Put yourself in the position of the editor who must decide how — or whether — to punish Whelan. As for those affected, the major stakeholder obviously is Whelan. Others include his partner, the parade organizers, proponents and opponents of gay rights. The newspaper's reputation is hugely at stake. And, of course, its readers have a stake in this situation, too, but not nearly as great as the newspaper's.

WHY: The first four principles of the "Act Independently" section of the SPJ Code of Ethics seem particularly applicable here. It's unprofessional, and unethical, to engage in activities that "may compromise integrity or damage credibility." But there are other questions that should be asked. Is "gay pride" a political cause? Was the parade a demonstration or merely a celebration, intended to advocate or merely to entertain? The newspaper notes that a website promoting the parade said naming Whelan and his partner grand marshals "supports the need for Marriage Equality."

A reporter shouldn't be an active advocate for a particular point of view about a subject he or she is covering. But how far does that go? If a political reporter can cheer for the hometown team, should a sports reporter be able to back a political candidate? How many rights must journalists give up when they accept the idea that they should be detached observers? Would we feel differently about this if it had been an anti-abortion parade? What about an Italian-American reporter marching in a Columbus Day parade?

Isn't it better to acknowledge — and disclose — one's interests than to deny them? Avoiding membership or participation doesn't guarantee objectivity. Some reporters who make a great show in the newsroom of avoiding any ties to anything can be among the most biased in their reporting.

HOW: In this case, you'd want to be fair to a longtime employee — minimizing harm, in other words. Is a suspension in order? Paid or unpaid? A change in assignment, perhaps? Or would that be too harsh? The important thing is to ask the right questions (and by no means is this an exhaustive list), to satisfy yourself that your solution is the best outcome — and to be able to explain it. Put it in writing to be sure it makes sense.

Whelan, upset by his employer's reaction, took two days off after which the paper told him it would consider that an unpaid suspension. "I basically walked out the door," he said in January 2009, even though he was asked to return after the two days.

Whelan filed three lawsuits: sexual discrimination in violation of a city ordinance, age discrimination and defamation. All three claims were settled out of court, he said. The *Morning Call*'s owners, the Tribune Co., agreed to pay two years of severance to Whelan and two years of medical benefits for him and his partner, he said.

Morning Call editor Ardith Hilliard, who was editor during the controversy, wrote in an e-mail that she could not comment on the matter because it was a legal one.

— Fred Brown and Nerissa Young, SPJ Ethics Committee

CASE STUDY 26:

Controversy over a Concert

WHAT: Three former members of the Eagles rock band came to Denver during the 2004 election campaign to raise money for a U.S. Senate candidate, Democrat Ken Salazar. John Temple, editor and publisher of the *Rocky Mountain News*, advised his reporters not to go to the fundraising concerts. In a memo to the staff, Temple said:

"Since our longstanding policy precludes all newsroom employees from making political donations, none of us will be able to attend these concerts, or any others that occur this political season. The obvious exceptions are reporters, columnists and photographers covering the concerts, both as entertainment events and political stories."

> This is a case in which a news organization must weigh its actions according to the principles of truth-telling and independence.

Some reporters and editors interpreted the directive as implying that their bosses didn't trust them. Some said the only issue should be whether their work is fair and accurate, not about what they do in their off time. At staff meetings requested by the Denver Newspaper Guild, reporters asked all manner of questions, Temple said: What if my spouse goes, or gives a donation? What if I never cover politics or have a byline in the paper? Why can't we buy tickets to this concert when we can go to concerts by other artists who may then use the money for political donations?

Temple, writing about the situation in two different columns, said a newspaper's first obligation is to its readers. It should avoid anything that might compromise — or appear to compromise — its impartiality and integrity.

Question: Is it fair to ask newspaper staffers — or employees at other news media, for that matter — not to attend events that may have a political purpose? Are the rules different for different jobs at the news outlet?

WHO: In this case, the decision was made by the top executive at the *Rocky Mountain News*. His decision clearly affected his employees, and it was intended to look out for the interests of the newspaper's readers. In Temple's eyes, the public had a major stake in this decision. Also affected, but perhaps not so much, were the entertainers, the Democratic (and Republican) parties and candidate Ken Salazar.

WHY: One of a journalist's biggest challenges is how to put aside personal preferences and prejudices in order to deliver impartial, fair information. Elections raise ethical questions for reporters, and the answers to those ethical questions are usually inflexible: Avoid any display of partisanship, including donating money to candidates, even indirectly. Some media companies discourage employees from participating in partisan politics in any way; some individuals have gone so far as to declare publicly that they do not vote, to avoid even the slightest appearance of bias. That may be going too far, but journalists do give up some of their constitutional rights if they want to practice their profession ethically. Ironically, this is a profession protected by the same First Amendment that grants the right to any citizen to support, by word, deed or cash, the people they'd like to see elected.

HOW: Temple's decision wasn't well-received by many in his staff. Reporters are well aware that some newspaper owners and publishers contribute to political campaigns. Editorial pages endorse candidates. Some members of the public, too, argued that Temple was too concerned with appearances. "I suspect that if and when you and your management put as much thought and effort into changing the reality of political bias on your staff as you do worrying about the image which your staff projects, you won't have to be concerned about either the reality or the image," one reader wrote.

What do you think are appropriate limits — if any — on a journalist's political involvement? Does it differ from job to job? What sort of a policy would you set for your staff if you were managing a media outlet — or yourself, if you were a weblog with a staff of one?

— Fred Brown, SPJ Ethics Committee

CASE STUDY 27:

A National Guard Trip

Summary

When, if ever, should a reporter accept a free trip in order to cover a story? Is that "junket journalism," or can it be a legitimate way to cover important events?

The *Bangor Daily News* bureau chief in Presque Isle, Maine, received an invitation to join employers and public officials who were flying to a National Guard training site in Gagetown, New Brunswick, nearly 200 miles away. Military issues are important in that region. There are 1,000 Guard members in Aroostook County in northernmost Maine, an area that has also been home to a bomber base targeted for closing.

The helicopter trip was sponsored annually by an organization whose sole purpose is to educate employers, public officials and the public about the National Guard. A Guard spokesman said the trip would help foster understanding between employers and Guard members.

> News organizations benefit from having clear guidelines on such issues as conflicts of interests, junkets and freebies.

The bureau chief was interested in joining the group to talk to employers about the problems and benefits of having employees who are members of the Guard. She also was interested in seeing the training site in Gagetown, one of the largest training facilities in Canada.

There are no commercial flights between Presque Isle and Gagetown and no bus service. A chartered flight would have cost about $1,000. Driving to and from the training site would take the better part of a day.

The newspaper contacted a representative of the group sponsoring the trip and asked if the paper could pay the reporter's way for the helicopter trip. The newspaper was told it couldn't pay.

The bureau chief consulted with her editors, and the decision was made to send her on the helicopter trip anyway, after determining what stories she would develop as a result of the trip.

Analysis

This is a case in which a news organization must weigh its actions according to the principles of truth-telling and independence. The journalists involved also must consider the consequences of their decisions, both short-term and long-term.

Some questions to raise when mulling over this type of dilemma:

- Can the newspaper fulfill its news-gathering and reporting responsibilities to the public if the paper is accepting a free trip from the people being covered? On the other hand, can the newspaper properly inform its readers about potentially important stories if its coverage is limited by economic or logistical reasons?

- How valuable is it for the community to understand, through the newspaper, the program that involves many of its citizens every summer? Is the story valuable enough that the paper should risk compromising its integrity or damaging its credibility by accepting the free trip?

- Where does the "free" stop? If the sponsoring group also was offering free meals to those making the helicopter trip to the training site, should the newspaper accept those free meals?

- How would reasonable people respond to this dilemma? Would they agree that the benefit of covering the National Guardsmen outweighs the risk that a free trip might cause the reporter to unduly favor the Guard in that or subsequent stories? Or that she might be overly critical in her reporting in an effort to prove her independence?

- What other alternatives might the newspaper have considered to cover the story while also recognizing economic concerns? Could the newspaper have used a freelance reporter? Could the story have been reported from Presque Isle without going on the free helicopter trip? Could the reporter have driven to the training camp, possibly reporting several stories on the way to help justify the travel time involved?

Finally, when a decision has been reached, the news organization would do well to hold itself accountable by sharing its decision-making with its readers:

- What level of disclosure should the newspaper make when reporting the story? Should the story include specific mention that the reporter traveled at the expense of the sponsoring organization? Should an editor write a column explaining the decision-making process the paper followed?

News organizations benefit from having clear guidelines on such issues as conflicts of interests, junkets and freebies. Such guidelines provide guideposts for making good decisions. Guidelines also provide standards for consistency, combating the tendency to "slide down the slippery slope" by taking every case as something new.

When it comes to junkets and freebies, is it harder for a small news organization to take the high road on ethics than it is for a larger organization?

—from the Third Edition, Black, Steele and Barney

CASE STUDY 28:

KQED and the Vintner

Summary

When executives at San Francisco public television station KQED announced to their board of directors that the station was planning a documentary on Napa Valley vintner Robert Mondavi, they never anticipated the uproar that would be ignited by the proposed program.

In a report, the board was told that the station hoped the documentary would air on PBS' "American Master Series" and that a $50,000 research grant had been secured from the nonprofit American Center for Wine, Food and the Arts, a potential underwriter for the program as well.

> Perhaps the major transgression here is that KQED was unwilling to recognize and therefore unwilling to disclose the extent of the program's funding connection to the industry being covered.

The funding sounded fishy to KQED board member Sasha Futran, a part-time journalist who researched the American Center for Wine, Food and the Arts and discovered the center was financed primarily with a $5 million donation from Robert Mondavi and had close personal ties to his winery. Mondavi was chairman of the center's board. The American Center's marketing director called Mondavi its "visionary." The center's executive director previously had been vice president of Robert Mondavi Winery.

Futran called the documentary "paid programming," adding, "Someone is paying for a documentary about themselves. This raises some very serious journalistic questions of ethical integrity."

Station executives defended the project. They said the documentary would focus on the growth of the wine industry, using "Mr. Mondavi as a frame of reference." They also said:

- the $50,000 was research money, not production money;
- the show itself would be cultural programming ("lifestyle and growth of the Napa Valley") and therefore didn't have to adhere to the stricter PBS standards for funding public affairs shows;
- the American Center had more than 100 benefactors in addition to Mondavi and was not a stand-in for the Mondavis; and
- "neutral" contributors would be solicited for the remainder of the documentary's $600,000 cost.

Both the station and the American Center told news reporters that KQED would retain total editorial control.

Faced with a barrage of unwelcome publicity, station executives eventually canceled the program and returned $50,000 to the American Center. The station president, however, defended the funding of the proposed documentary, saying "Questions about the American Center's funding, raised publicly by a member of KQED's board of directors, created an inaccurate perception of conflict and have resulted in negative news coverage, damaging the project's viability."

A week later, the *San Francisco Chronicle*, citing numerous KQED internal documents, disclosed that the station's agreement with the American Center was the result of negotiation with marketing officials at Mondavi and that all preliminary correspondence to the station was on the letterhead of the Robert Mondavi Winery, not the American Center. The *Chronicle* also reported that KQED had pitched the documentary to the winery as a highly flattering portrayal of the vintner, titled "Robert Mondavi — A Profile."

PBS funding guidelines caution against problematic "connections between the funder's interest and the subject of the program." KQED sought the opinion of lawyers, who echoed the station's assertion that "the Center was not given any of the indicia of editorial control or supervision which concerns PBS under its guidelines."

KQED's board later voted to adopt a short ethics policy described as a distillation of PBS guidelines. Critics said the new guidelines were vague and left the door open for the same kind of misjudgments that they said characterized the proposed Mondavi documentary.

Analysis

Conflict of interest, which involves seducing journalists from the object of their primary loyalties — their audience — has two flash points: the actual subverting of the message by the source and the appearance of luring the producers from that loyalty by the source.

In this case, it would appear a strong case could be made for the appearance of conflict, station protestations notwithstanding, because the money came from an entity that was an offspring of the industry from which the show's subject comes.

As more information became available, it appeared the conflict of interest was actual. It is difficult to foresee how the station, given terms of funding, could remain independent in the production. The cards, as so often happens, were stacked in favor of the funder, to the harm of a vulnerable audience relying on the producer's integrity.

On the other hand, economic realities being what they are for public television stations, the lure of being able to shine the light on a seldom-seen industry, biased though it may be or may be perceived to be, has some validity.

Yet, it appears clear the wine industry would have borrowed the integrity of the television station through funding if the ties had not been disclosed. As so often occurs when media are manipulated, this leads to a deliberate deception, by omission of information, of a vulnerable audience expecting to take at face value the station's declaration about the documentary's pedigree.

New economic realities can be expected to seduce producers into convincing themselves, and trying to convince others, that hard-won funding is pure and divorced from the content of the program.

Indeed, more funders are insisting on guiding the programming they pay for, increasing the probability of conflict of interest.

One solution when a station finds itself trapped into such a coalition is to disclose the conflict, clearly telling audiences the favorable programming was paid for by the subject of the story or his friends.

Perhaps the major transgression here is that KQED was unwilling to recognize and therefore unwilling to disclose the extent of the program's funding connection to the industry being covered. Whistle-blowing notwithstanding, KQED did not demonstrate the level of accountability called for by the SPJ Code of Ethics.

In an ideal world, a disinterested automakers' association would provide funding for a vintner's documentary, clearly demonstrating a low possibility of either the appearance or fact of conflict. In the world of new realities, however, perhaps the disclosure of ties may be the best that can be hoped for in an increasing number of circumstances.

— from the Third Edition, Black, Steele and Barney

CASE STUDY 29:

Independence and Car Dealers

Summary

A front-page story in the *Hartford* (Connecticut) *Courant* cautioned readers about high-powered sales tactics that could be used by local auto dealers during an upcoming "car-sales blitz." The article appeared the same day as ads began running promoting car sales during Presidents' Week. One dealer called the article "grossly untrue and slanderous." Some irate dealers began pulling their ads from the paper.

In response, then-publisher and editor Michael Davies sent a letter of apology to the auto dealers and their advertising agencies. Davies told the dealers he was angry the story appeared without his knowledge or the review of a top editor — and on Page 1 at that.

He labeled as "unfair" a line in the story that began, "Experts agree that not all dealers are out to rip off consumers." This statement angered dealers who said this line implied that only a few dealers are honest. The "experts agree" reference had been inserted by an editor on the originating desk.

Davies pointed out that the topic itself is newsworthy and that other stories in the *Courant* had been favorable to auto dealers. A reporter was assigned to do a story on the auto dealer protest. The *Courant* also invited several of the dealers to the paper to discuss how news is produced under deadline. This invitation was not unique, as the paper had often invited business people and other members of the public to the paper to voice concerns or complaints. Four or five dealers accepted that invitation and gained a better understanding of how the paper operated. Some dealers, however, kept their advertising out of the paper, and some took their ads to competing media — although most of them eventually were wooed back.

Davies' actions reportedly strained existing tensions between the business and editorial sides of the paper and had a chilling effect on some coverage. Reporters said they found themselves being more cautious on certain stories. Line editors said they began checking with top editors on stories involving big advertisers.

> All elements have to live in some harmony in a community, making it necessary for journalists to understand and respect the economic role that auto dealers play.

Analysis

The virtues of editorial independence and the financial health of the newspaper come into conflict in this case. Media organizations are profit-making endeavors and must support themselves financially in a free enterprise economy. Journalists and the public, however, worry about business "buying" the news functions of the media with advertising, thereby damaging the credibility of the news side.

Most advertisers do not realize they are buying the media's credibility when they buy space or time. They feel they are merely buying the audience, and that they have paid for the right not to have their advertising dollars neutralized by criticism.

Reporters and editors, on the other hand, have a moral obligation to empower audiences with everyday decision-making skills, whether political or economic, such as buying an automobile.

Perhaps the story would have caused less conflict if it had been made more palatable to the auto dealers. More interviews with the dealers and more research might have provided the necessary cautionary information while softening what was viewed as a condemnation of all car dealers in Hartford.

As it is, the community may have reason to believe the newspaper is not credible when it comes to the auto industry. All elements have to live in some harmony in a community, making it necessary for journalists to understand and respect the economic role that auto dealers play.

Publishers and ad salespeople, on the other hand, have an obligation to regularly explain to advertisers the information and persuasion functions of the newspaper.

Several questions might be raised when considering the conflicts in this type of journalism:

- What is the ethical value of separation between editorial and business-advertising departments of a newspaper?
- Would routine discussions among editors and reporters about the story have raised cautionary questions before the story ran and created the furor?
- How could an editor ethically arrive at a decision to delay running the story until after the special automobile promotion?
- Would such a discussion have resolved the problem so an important story could be run and the publisher-editor would not have felt the need to write an apologetic letter to auto dealers and ad agencies?
- What are the alternatives to appeasing the advertisers?
- Should the publisher appease the advertisers, back his staff, seek another solution or back off altogether?

- Both ethically and practically, would it be wise for editorial and advertising departments to confer more often to head off such problems?
- What role should senior editors play in reviewing stories of this sensitive nature, and how should they discuss this issue with the publisher and with the business side of the paper?
- What compromises are ethically acceptable when the financial and editorial functions of the newspaper conflict, as they did in this case? What should be the major considerations for each side?

— from the Third Edition, Black, Steele and Barney

CASE STUDY 30:

CNN Conflicted

Summary

Many media observers and television news consumers agree that CNN earned its stripes while reporting developments from the Persian Gulf War in 1990. The news organization's stature grew as, around the clock, correspondents dutifully filed stories no other media outlet could or would. CNN's journalistic reputation also blossomed during coverage of natural disasters and major trials in the mid-1990s.

By 1997, celebrity appeared to have gone to CNN's head.

Hollywood and Madison Avenue came courting, and CNN was seduced. Reporters and anchors began appearing as themselves in otherwise fictionalized films such as "The Lost World: Jurassic Park" and in an advertisement for Visa credit cards.

In a Visa print ad targeted at Generation X, 29-year-old CNN correspondent Jonathan Karl's wallet was featured. Scribbled notations detailed his recent Visa purchases, at least one of which revealed his profession (expenses incurred while covering the presidential inauguration), and his press credentials are prominently displayed. Overall, the ad was plainly an endorsement of Visa and of some of the merchants listed in his purchases.

A spokesman for the agency that created the ad told *The Wall Street Journal* that Karl was not paid for the ad but that CNN executives who approved of his action thought it might bring him valuable exposure. They argued that Karl had done no wrong, since he sought the approval of his bosses.

In summer 1997, CNN correspondents and anchors appeared in the "Jurassic Park" sequel and in "Contact," a movie about scientists preparing to make contact with life from another planet. CNN explained that the idea was similar to "product placement" of name-brand soft drinks and cars, for example. Some CNN journalists, such as White House correspondent Wolf Blitzer, refused to appear in the movies.

The blurring of the line between reporting the news and selling a product raised the specter of an incident in 1992 in which Lou Dobbs, then the managing editor of business news for CNN, was strongly reprimanded by

> Journalists face enough skepticism from the public without adding to it by muddying the waters between news and entertainment, between fact and fiction.

Tom Johnson, the news organization's president, for appearing in promotional videos for Wall Street firms — a gig that earned him $5,000 to $10,000 per assignment. At the time, Johnson called for a "full review of all outside projects" by CNN journalists to examine whether employees had compromised journalistic integrity.

When the issue resurfaced in 1997, provoking criticism from media observers and colleagues, Johnson decided to enact a policy that restricts its journalists from appearing in movies. (A July 15, 1997, *Washington Post* article said that ABC, CBS and NBC already had such policies.)

Johnson's swift actions earned praise in a news release from the Society of Professional Journalists, quoting a letter from its president, Steve Geimann. "It's about time that CNN pulled the plug on turning its responsible, professional journalists into Hollywood stars," Geimann wrote to Johnson. "Your action sends an important signal to other professional journalists that the separation between fact and fiction is what makes journalism an important and honored profession, and what makes movies fun and amusing."

Karl had been given approval by senior executives. But Johnson claimed no prior knowledge of the advertisement and later disapproved, according to a *Journal* article. Johnson also determined that the ad violated CNN policy, and he made it clear to senior executives that it should not happen again, *The Journal* reported.

Analysis

CNN deserves credit for responding with clarity and conviction in these instances, albeit after it hit some land mines along the way. Each of these cases involves the journalist principle of independence. As presented in this handbook, **journalists should act independently, remaining free of associations and activities that may compromise their integrity or damage their credibility.**

Journalists face enough skepticism from the public without adding to it by muddying the waters between news and entertainment, between fact and fiction. It might seem good fun (and perhaps good marketing) for a news organization or its journalists to be featured in a movie or an advertisement. To do so, however, raises significant possibilities of conflict of interest or erosion of credibility.

How can a journalist or his news organization be perceived as fair in covering any stories about a major credit card company if that journalist was a pitchman for the company? What happens to a journalist's reputation and her news organization's credibility in covering Wall Street issues when she moonlights for one of the financial firms on her beat? How can a news organization legitimately cover the film industry if that news organization is a player rather than an observer?

Yes, journalists and their organizations can keep saying, "We maintain objectivity. We have not been compromised by our involvement." But it is impossible to prove that point. Journalists cannot prove they haven't bent too far one way or the other. Journalists cannot defend their decisions for what they did cover and what they didn't cover.

And, if journalists are fending off challenge and criticism, they are distracted from what they are supposed to be doing — reporting the news.

CNN's experience in these cases points out the importance of news organizations having clear policies and protocols for matters of journalistic independence and conflicts of interest. Guidelines and decision-making processes protect both the organization and the individual.

The best time to handle an ethical issue is before it becomes an issue.

— from the Third Edition, Black, Steele and Barney

CASE STUDY 31:

Writing Checks, Getting Exclusives

WHAT: It's called "checkbook journalism," and it's something serious journalists say is wrong. You shouldn't have to pay your sources for giving you information. And yet sometimes the lines are blurred. Is it legitimate, for example, to buy a murder victim's diary from her family, a diary that might provide clues about whether her former boyfriend stalked and killed her? What about the fairly routine business of flying talk show guests to New York City so they can appear on your broadcast? When does a journalist cross the line between legitimate newsgathering expenses and, as the SPJ Code of Ethics puts it, "bidding for news"?

On more than one occasion in late 2009 and early 2010, the SPJ Ethics Committee criticized television networks for what the committee felt were clear instances of "checkbook journalism." The circumstances are different, and there's a big difference in the amounts of money involved, but two cases in particular afforded opportunities for a spirited discussion — from both a journalistic and humanitarian perspective. We'll look at both cases in this and in the following case study.

> Under what circumstances, if any, should a news organization provide financial assistance to a news source?

The first is the case of David Goldman. Goldman is a New Jersey man whose Brazilian wife, Bruna Bianchi Goldman, took their 4-year-old son, Sean, to Brazil in June 2004 for what was supposed to be a vacation with her family. They never returned. Mrs. Goldman divorced her American husband — though they were still legally married under U.S. law — and married a Brazilian lawyer but later died, giving birth, in August 2008. After her death, her family and Brazilian husband took steps to adopt Sean, and David Goldman stepped up his efforts to win custody of his son. The international custody battle was fought up to the highest levels of both U.S. and Brazilian courts. Finally, in late December 2009, the chief justice of the Brazilian supreme court ruled that Sean should be returned to his biological father, David, by the morning of December 24. That evening, Christmas Eve 2009, NBC News brought the boy and his father to the United States on a chartered Gulfstream jet. Reporter Jeff Rossen and a cameraman were with them on the plane. They did interviews during the flight, and after the plane landed in Orlando, where father and son spent Christmas at Disney World. They then flew to New York, where "Today" show host Meredith Vieira had an exclusive interview with David on December 28, the Monday after the holiday.

From the beginning, NBC had followed this story closely. David Goldman first appeared on NBC's "Dateline" program in January 2009. And, while there was widespread interest in what happened to Goldman and his son — there is still a Bring Sean Home Foundation that seeks to resolve "international abductions" — NBC seemed to have a closer relationship to the father than any other news outlet. In fact, NBC said David Goldman had appeared on "Today" 17 times in the year since the story first aired on "Dateline." Not that there's anything wrong with that; any medium in a competitive environment justifiably seeks an edge. And on balance, what NBC did in flying Sean and his father back to the U.S. on Christmas Eve seemed to have much more popular support than criticism. Several online comments on various sites called it "a Christmas miracle." SPJ's Ethics Committee, though, was "appalled"; Chairman Andy Schotz, in a statement, said, "The public could rightly assume that NBC News bought exclusive interviews and images, as well as the family's loyalty, with an extravagant gift."

Question: Under what circumstances, if any, should a news organization provide financial assistance to a news source?

WHO: The decision-makers in this case are the people in NBC management who decided to invest tens of thousands of dollars in this story — especially when it came down to chartering the private jet that brought Sean and his father from Rio de Janeiro to the United States. Among the stakeholders in that decision, no one is more affected than the father and son. If the network hadn't flown them out, they might have been stranded in Brazil — or at the very least hounded by international media at their departure from and arrival at commercial airport terminals, and possibly even during the long flight itself.

The family Sean left behind in Brazil also was deeply affected by NBC's decision. The child they had raised for five years had been taken from them by the law and spirited away by a television network. "My heart is empty and broken because our love is missing," said Sean's maternal grandmother, Silvana Bianchi. She called the Brazilian court's custody ruling "a heinous crime." In April 2010 she flew from Brazil to New Jersey to try to see Sean, but a judge denied her immediate access. Maybe later, said David Goldman, but not yet.

Clearly, NBC's reputation is also at stake in this decision. Some saw the trip as a noble humanitarian gesture, an unusual show of empathy from what often are perceived as the cold-hearted media. From that perspective, the decision greatly helped the network's image. Yet others, no doubt a smaller and less vocal number, saw it as a bad example of callous exploitation. NBC's competitors also were affected; they were kept at arm's length from the drama by NBC's exclusivity agreement. Others with perhaps a lesser stake in the network's action include the Bring Sean Home Foundation and lawmakers such as U.S. Rep.

Chris Smith, R-N.J., who sponsored the International Child Abduction Prevention Act of 2009. You may be able to think of others who could be considered stakeholders in this decision.

WHY: In this case, the network's expressed desire to minimize harm, or perhaps to be proactively compassionate toward the Goldmans, conflicts with the journalistic ideals of independence and impartiality. Here are pertinent excerpts from the news release SPJ issued about the situation — a statement that got more coverage, online and in print, than many SPJ releases get, suggesting a broad public interest in the case:

"By making itself part of a breaking news story on which it was reporting — apparently to cash in on the exclusivity assured by its expensive gesture — NBC jeopardized its journalistic independence and credibility in its initial and subsequent reports. In effect, the network branded the story as its own, creating a corporate and promotional interest in the way the story unfolds. NBC's ability to report the story fairly has been compromised by its financial involvement....

"The news media's duty is to report news, not help to create it. The race to be first should not involve buying — directly or indirectly — interviews, an unseemly practice that raises questions of neutrality, integrity and credibility. 'Mixing financial and promotional motives with an impartial search for truth stains honest, ethical reporting,' (ethics committee chairman Andy) Schotz said. 'Checkbook journalism has no place in the news business.'"

Schotz and SPJ President Kevin Smith called on NBC to explain its decision, "as well as the terms of any deal it made with the Goldman family." And, they added, the network is "ethically bound" to disclose its "active role in the story in each of its future reports on the Goldmans." An NBC spokeswoman did respond by e-mail after the news release, primarily to ask if SPJ would be using remarks made by Goldman's attorney or making similar criticisms of other networks. SPJ also linked to a story about a more formal network response on a website called Multichannel News. One of the points NBC made is that the chartered jet already was scheduled to return network staffers from Brazil; the Goldmans merely were invited along. "NBC News has not and will not pay for an interview," the network's statement said.

Some ethics committee members felt SPJ's public criticism should have been held until NBC had had a chance to tell its side of the story. At least one ethics committee member wrote on the ethics blog that he felt it was unfair, and he called the statement "an unwarranted and humiliating pillory of NBC." But other committee members — in a clear example of how different, well-intentioned people can reach different conclusions when presented with the same situation — felt it was important not to wait too long, and NBC already had been given two or three days to respond to a request for a statement.

The main principle at issue here is impartiality. The exchange of money, favors or anything of value inevitably affects the tenor of the news-source relationship. Most journalists understand that they shouldn't accept anything of value from a source; most employers' codes of ethics make that quite clear. Is it, then, equally as wrong for a source to accept anything of value from a journalist? One argument against paying people is that they then might feel compelled to say what they think you want to hear. Of course, that can happen in the absence of payment, too — merely the opportunity to appear on national television might make some people eager to please. The big three morning shows — and the afternoon shows, too — routinely fly people to New York, feed them, and put them in nice hotels so that they can appear in a broadcast. It's a form of checkbook journalism, even though it's less expensive than a private chartered jet flight from Rio to Orlando. None of the main players in this scenario were in any way destitute. Goldman had pursued a successful career as a model. If he could not have paid to charter a jet, his case had attracted enough notoriety that some other organization might have donated a corporate aircraft for the flight.

There's also a question of favoritism to consider here. Was NBC being unfair to the family Sean had lived with for five years? Do they matter less because they're Brazilian and not American? You might also want to consider whether the critics of this action, including SPJ, were too quick in their judgment. It probably wasn't good public relations for SPJ, but journalists will argue that they shouldn't base their actions on what the public thinks. The long- and short-term consequences of that attitude certainly merit discussion.

HOW: Obviously, NBC decided that paying to transport a father and his son back to the United States on Christmas Eve was a legitimate, even compassionate thing to do. And it did mention, several times on air, that the flight was an NBC charter. SPJ, although it wasn't a stakeholder in the original decision, became part of the continuing story when it issued its widely circulated statement. Did both organizations achieve the outcomes they hoped for? What do you think?

— SPJ Ethics Committee

CASE STUDY 32:

Expensive Home Movies

WHAT: In August 2008, ABC paid $200,000 to the family of a dead Florida toddler for exclusive use of family photos and home videos. The apparent murder of Caylee Marie Anthony had attracted international media attention. Caylee disappeared in June 2008, two months shy of her third birthday. Her body was found six months later, buried near the family home. Caylee's mother, Casey Anthony, was indicted in October 2008 for first-degree murder, but continues to maintain her innocence. One reason for all of the interest in the case is that Casey from the beginning was reluctant to give critical information to authorities. Caylee wasn't reported missing until a month after she was last seen. On July 15, 2008, her grandmother, Cindy Anthony, reportedly called 911 when Casey would not tell her where Caylee had been.

In March 2010, during a pretrial hearing in Orlando, Casey Anthony's attorney revealed that ABC News had made the payment to Anthony's family seven months earlier. ABC, in a statement after the hearing, said the payment was for exclusive rights to "an extensive library of photos and home video for use by our broadcasts, platforms, affiliates and international partners. No use of the material was tied to any interview."

Question: Should ABC have paid for this exclusive access?

WHO: ABC network officials had to approve this expenditure; they're the decision-makers, the moral agents. They are also among the people affected, the stakeholders, because their action drew criticism from journalism ethics watchdogs. The chief stakeholders, though, are the Anthony family. Competing media outlets also have an interest in this decision because of the exclusivity of the agreement; they won't have the same access that ABC has to these scenes from a childhood cut short.

WHY: The SPJ Ethics Committee, as it did in the NBC/Goldman case, condemned the payment as another example of the bad practice of "checkbook journalism." In this case, though, it was a direct cash payment, not providing an expensive service, as in the Goldman case. "Paying someone while covering them breaches basic journalistic ethics," said Andy Schotz, chairman of the committee. ABC spokeswoman Cathie Levine said the network wasn't paying for an interview, but for exclusive rights to certain materials, which is a common practice for broadcast news organizations. But she also acknowledged that "we should have disclosed it to our audience." In the future, she said, the network would make it a policy to disclose such payments as part of its reporting. Indeed, it could be argued that paying for photographs or other images is no different than paying for a freelance article, or a cell phone picture that an onlooker snapped of a spectacular explosion. But critics of the arrangement with the Anthony family would argue that the difference here is that there's an ongoing relationship with the source of the material — a news relationship that should be free of the influences that money brings. "The public," said the SPJ statement, "can legitimately question a news organization's credibility and doubt whether its reports are fair and accurate."

HOW: ABC defended its contract with the Anthonys and promised to make any similar arrangements in the future part of its future coverage. But apparently that was open to interpretation. ABC did not disclose the $200,000 payment during an interview with Casey Anthony's parents on "Good Morning America," because, said spokeswoman Levine, "we haven't licensed anything from either of them so there was nothing to disclose." She pointed out that there was a disclosure during a "20/20" interview with a former girlfriend of Joran van der Sloot, accused of murdering one woman and suspected in the disappearance of another several years ago. The difference, said Levine, is that "we licensed material from her [the former girlfriend]."

There continue to be multiple examples of this questionable practice. In May 2009, ABC paid for plane tickets for Anthony Rakoczy of Pennsylvania to fly to Florida to pick up his daughter and then return home with her after a fake kidnapping attempt. Levine, the ABC spokeswoman, said reporters covered both legs of the trip and disclosed the donated air travel in both stories. Shortly after the Goldman flight from Brazil, CNN, ABC and the *New York Post* bought rights to an image taken by Jasper Schuringa aboard a flight from Amsterdam to Detroit during which a terrorist attempted to set off a bomb hidden in his underpants. Schuringa, a Dutch citizen who was hailed as a hero for overpowering the terrorist, also was criticized for attempting to profit through the sale of his cellphone photos. In June 2010, the *New York Post* published its best estimates of a couple of recent payments for interviews, including "at least $100,000" to Joran van der Sloot's mother for appearances on "Good Morning America" and "Nightline" and "about $340,000" paid by NBC's "Dateline" for an interview with the mother of the late Michael Jackson. Regardless of what one might think of the *Post*'s own standards, the tone of the report was critical, noting that network policies usually forbid paying for interviews. "One commentator called the no-pay policy TV's equivalent of the 55-mph speed limit," the *Post* said " — a rule no one really pays much attention to."

— *SPJ Ethics Committee*

Conflicts of Interest

What the Codes Say

KHON-TV (Honolulu)

All members of the KHON news staff shall govern their personal lives and such non-professional associations as may impinge on their professional activities in a manner that will protect them from conflict of interest, real or apparent.

In order to preclude a real or apparent conflict of interest, news personnel should, under no circumstances, allow their names, voices or likenesses to be used in connection with any form of commercial advertising.

As professional journalists, all members of the news staff, reporters, talent and cameramen are prohibited from accepting gifts, favors, merchandise, travel or accommodations which may be offered regardless of whether any type of consideration may be asked in return. In the case of items or services of minor or insignificant value, the News Director should be consulted if there is any question of propriety.

Violations of this Code of Ethics may result in either dismissal or some other disciplinary action.

Association of Food Journalists

(1) Gifts, favors, free travel or lodging, special treatment or privileges can compromise the integrity and diminish the credibility of food journalists, as well as that of their employers. This includes commercially sponsored contests. Such offers should be avoided. An example is a contest promoting specific food products that is open to food journalists only.

(2) Similarly, food journalists should not use their positions to win favors for themselves or for others.

(3) Secondary employment, political involvement, holding public office or serving in organizations should be avoided if it compromises the integrity of a food journalist.

(4) Because the editorial space allotted to food journalism is not an extension of advertising, brand names or names of specific companies or interest groups should be used only in a newsworthy context or for purposes of clarification.

(5) Food journalists should use their bylines only in conjunction with material that they have written. Material from other sources incorporated in a story should be credited.

(6) To assure accuracy, so-called news communications or press releases should be substantiated.

(7) Expression of opinions, editorials or special articles devoted to the writer's own views should be clearly labeled as such and thus easily distinguished from the news reports.

(8) Because of the controversial nature of many food-related topics, food journalists accept the obligation to acknowledge opposing views on such issues.

PLEDGE: The Association of Food Journalists encourages observation of these standards by all newspeople. The Association further urges news media managements to support the decision by food journalists to uphold this code.

The Virginian-Pilot (Norfolk, Virginia)

PERSONAL LIFE
Business conflicts

- Staff members may not have financial investments in companies they cover. This is particularly important with regard to local companies. In general, mutual funds are excluded from this prohibition because they hold stock packages rather than individual investments. Reporters and editors who regularly handle mutual-fund stories should consult their team leader.
- Investments, loans or other outside business activities that could conflict with the newspaper's ability to report news must be avoided.
- Use of inside knowledge for personal gain is prohibited. Staff members should not enter into a business relationship with news sources.

Gifts, favors, events

Employees must never become obligated to news sources, advertisers, suppliers or any person or organization by receiving gifts or favors. Situations will arise that call for judgment. We need not be reduced to arguing with sources over who will pay for a cup of coffee or a hot dog. If you have any doubt, check with your team leader.

- We do not accept free or discounted trips, dinners, entertainment, gifts or admission to events. When there is a clear journalistic purpose in attending an event, a staff member should buy a ticket and obtain company reimbursement.
- Press passes are limited to those assigned to cover an event and other staff members with a clear journalistic purpose for attending. Team leaders will determine appropriate staffing. Extra passes should not be given to friends or family.
- Staff members can attend media-day events only if they are involved in news coverage.
- Items delivered to staff members should be returned, donated to charity or sold through company events that benefit charity. Review copies of books,

movies, computer software and music may be kept by the reviewer. Material not scheduled for review falls under the return-or-donate rule. When possible, let gift-givers know their gifts were donated.

- Items of no significant value — desk trinkets, pens, etc. — may be kept.

San Jose Mercury News

Employees shall not use their positions with the *Mercury News* to get any benefit or advantage in commercial transactions or personal business for themselves, their families, friends or acquaintances.

For example, they shall not use company connections to:

- Get information or a photograph for purposes other than those of the newspaper.
- Expedite personal business with, or seek special consideration from, public officials or agencies, such as police.
- Seek for personal use information not available to the general public.
- Get free, or at a reduced rate not available to the general public, considerations such as tickets, memberships, hotel rooms or transportation.

Employees shall not use the company name, reputation, phone number or stationary to imply a threat of retaliation or pressure, to curry favor or to seek personal gain.

For example, it is improper for an employee to write a personal letter of complaint to a merchant on company stationery, or to arrange a personal purchase at wholesale or discount rates through the public relations office of a corporation.

The Denver Post

Employment with *The Denver Post* should never be used to win favorable treatment.

This includes a special price for something, preferential treatment or other benefits.

Such situations must be avoided regardless of whether the person or establishment offering the benefit is involved in the employee's area of coverage.

Examples might include:

- Seating at a restaurant, entertainment or sporting event
- Discounts for merchandise, travel or other items or services for purchase
- Injecting your employment at *The Denver Post* into legal or other disputes in which the employee is involved

If employment at *The Post* surfaces in the normal course of conversation, or if an employee is recognized by name or other association and is offered special treatment — as opposed to access to a newsmaker or news event — decline as graciously and professionally as possible.

Denver Post editorial employees may take advantage of DNA-negotiated price breaks on merchandise or services. However, if a potential conflict arises regarding a discount involving an industry covered by a reporter, a supervising editor should be immediately consulted.

...

Press parking plates and free parking spaces should be used by *Post* staffers only during the coverage of breaking news, to facilitate deadline reporting and writing, or to gain access to news sites or crime scenes. They are not to be used for all-day free parking.

In general, *Post* staffers should avoid other forms of free press parking. Reporters working at Denver International Airport, for instance, should expense parking and not accept free validated parking for time they work at the airport. The same principle applies to other news venues. Exceptions are allowed for the coverage of sports events, where parking often is included with press credentials and where close proximity to a stadium or arena is an assist for photographers hauling heavy equipment and offers safety and security advantages for staffers leaving arenas late at night.

The Washington Post

We have adopted stringent policies on these issues, conscious that they may be more restrictive than is customary in the world of private business. In particular:

We pay our own way.

We accept no gifts from news sources. We accept no free trips. We neither seek nor accept preferential treatment that might be rendered because of the positions we hold. Exceptions to the no-gift rule are few and obvious — invitations to meals, for example, may be accepted when they are occasional and innocent, but not when they are repeated and their purpose is deliberately calculating. Free admissions to any event that is not free to the public are prohibited. The only exception is for seats not sold to the public, as in a press box. Whenever possible, arrangements will be made to pay for such seats.

Society of American Travel Writers

(excerpts from 2006 revised code of ethics)

SATW members shall maintain the highest standards of professionalism on press trips and sponsored activities.

Rules:

1. No member shall deliberately misrepresent the status of an assignment in order to secure participation in a press trip.
2. All assistants accompanying a member on a press trip shall be fully qualified assistants; all others accompanying a member must be identified as

guests. The participation of guests on press trips is subject to the restrictions of the host and at no time shall a guest attend in place of a member.

3. A member shall personally pay for all services required by that member that are personal, or over and above the services voluntarily provided by the host.

4. Members shall not engage in conduct that embarrasses the host.

SATW members shall avoid all real or perceived conflicts of interest.
Rules:

1. Content providers shall be open with editors/publishers about their own activity that could compromise or might appear to compromise their integrity on a given assignment, including non-editorial writing, researching or consulting, political involvement, holding office or serving in organizations dealing with the same or a similar subject matter, and/or association with a travel destination, service firm or supplier.

2. Members shall avoid accepting or giving gifts and promotional items of more than a nominal value.

The Philadelphia Inquirer

(Preamble and one of numerous sections: The Inquirer's *entire code section on conflicts of interest comprises 3,400 words)*

A staff member's foremost professional obligations are to *The Inquirer*. As employees of *The Inquirer*, staff members are obliged to make certain that no outside personal, philosophical or financial interests conflict with their professional performance of duties at *The Inquirer*. Additionally, staff members should avoid activity that could create the appearance of a conflict with those professional duties. All interpretations as to what conduct may be appropriate in a particular situation will stem from this fundamental premise.

This policy is not intended to unnecessarily limit staff members' participation in the life of the community. They should feel free to take part in such activities as neighborhood organizations, youth organizations, school organizations, or churches, synagogues or mosques. However, staff members should recognize a need to use discretion when these activities might lead to taking sides in a public controversy, and they should not cover or make news decisions about organizations of which they are members.

...

Political activity. Staff members are encouraged, even urged, to exercise their franchise as citizens to discuss matters of public interest and to register and vote in referendums, primaries and general elections. But because their profession requires stringent efforts against partiality and perceived bias, staff members should not be involved in any political activity beyond that.

Specifically, staff members are not to post yard signs, attach bumper stickers, or wear buttons supporting a candidate or cause. Staff members may not make contributions of money or time to candidates, parties or groups taking a partisan stance. This includes attendance at events, such as concerts, performances, and screening of movies or other programs, whose purpose is to raise money for a candidate, party or cause. It also includes going door to door, making telephone calls or sending e-mails, or any other activity that could be defined as canvassing on behalf of a candidate or party.

Also, in no circumstances may a staff member work or act as an adviser, for pay or as a volunteer, in a political campaign or organization. Any request for a leave of absence to join in partisan activity will not be granted. If a person to whom a staff member is related by blood or marriage, or a close friend, is involved in a political campaign or organization, the staff member should refrain from covering or making news judgments about that campaign or that issue.

Detroit Free Press

Maintaining independence

- We will remain free of outside interests, investments or business relationships that may compromise the credibility of our news report.
- We will maintain an impartial, arm's length relationship with anyone seeking to influence the news.
- We will avoid potential conflicts of interest and eliminate inappropriate influence on content.
- We will be free of improper obligations to news sources, newsmakers and advertisers.
- We will differentiate advertising from news.

  ...

Being independent

"Maintaining independence" helps establish the impartiality of news coverage. To clarify two points:

- News staff members are encouraged to be involved in worthwhile community activities, so long as this does not compromise the credibility of news coverage.
- When unavoidable personal or business interests could compromise the newspaper's credibility, such potential conflicts must be disclosed to one's superior and, if relevant, to readers.

Outside Activities

The Virginian-Pilot (Norfolk, Virginia)

"The independence of our editors, reporters and photographers is not for sale...."

PUBLIC LIFE

Staff members are encouraged to participate in professional, civic and cultural activities. To ensure that our credibility is not damaged, staff members have a special responsibility to avoid conflict of interest or any activity that would compromise their journalistic integrity.

Politics and social causes

- Newsroom employees should not work for a political candidate or office-holder on a paid or voluntary basis. Participation in public demonstrations for political causes is forbidden.

- Taking a public stand on controversial social, religious or political issues is prohibited. This includes signing of petitions, either on paper or online. Staff members may not write letters to the editor.

- Holding public office or accepting political appointment is prohibited, unless specifically approved by the editor or publisher.

- If a staff member has a close relative or friend working in a political campaign or organization, the staffer should refrain from covering or making news judgments about that campaign or organization. A loved one's activities can create a real or potential conflict for a staff member. In those cases, inform a team leader and take steps to avoid conflicts.

- Donating money to political campaigns and parties is prohibited. Donations to or memberships in organizations with political agendas should be carefully considered.

- Staff members should use common sense when displaying bumper stickers, pins, badges and other signs. We should avoid items that promote causes.

Civic activities

- Membership in a social or civic organization normally does not result in a conflict; however, staff members should not cover or make news decisions about groups they belong to. Such activities should be disclosed to a team leader.

- Paid or volunteer public relations work for any organization whose operations are covered by the newspaper is prohibited.

- Membership on boards of charitable or cultural organizations that are covered by our newspaper — the SPCA, United Way, theater groups, etc. — should be approved by a deputy managing editor.

- It is inappropriate for staff members to appear publicly on behalf of a civic group or themselves. An exception can be made when an organization's policy or action directly affects the employee. In this case, talk with your team leader.

The Washington Post

We avoid active involvement in any partisan causes — politics, community affairs, social action, demonstrations — that could compromise or seem to comprise our ability to report and edit fairly. Relatives cannot fairly be made subject to *Post* rules, but it should be recognized that their employment or their involvement in causes can at least appear to compromise our integrity. The business and professional ties of traditional family members or other members of your household must be disclosed to department heads.

San Jose Mercury News

Because the newspaper should be perceived as impartial, staff members should avoid outside activities that could conflict with their jobs. Under no circumstances should a general assignment reporter, for example, work for a political campaign, either for pay or as a volunteer because it could be interpreted by the public as *Mercury News* involvement in the campaign. Likewise, a drama critic should not serve as a fundraiser for the San Jose Repertory Company because it might indicate a built-in bias on the part of the writer. In many cases, it would be a clear conflict to accept appointive office or run for elective office. In other cases, it may not be a conflict. For example, there would be no problem for most staff members in holding office as president of a school PTA. But if the education reporter were to hold the same office, a conflict would be present. There is no desire to unduly restrict staff members' exercise of the rights and duties of citizenship. But we must recognize that the reputation of the *Mercury News* is important to us all, and that a full discussion of possible conflict is essential to avoiding public embarrassment.

Staff members should avoid advertising or blatantly espousing viewpoints on public issues while at work, such as wearing an anti-nuclear button while covering a rally. Reporters and editors should be aware that such blatant espousal casts doubt upon their impartiality. Staff members should also avoid signing petitions or otherwise identifying themselves with causes they are expected to cover.

The Denver Post

Because politics is the primary fault line along which our critics attack us, the greatest attention must be paid by all newsroom employees to remain impartial in political discourse when representing the newspaper. Newsroom employees are encouraged to vote and engage in private debate as long as their views are expressed as their own and not representing the views of the newspaper.

To avoid conflicts of interest, employees should take great care in joining any group, but especially organizations that engage in political advocacy. While a membership may seem benign, it could place the employee or *The Denver Post* in a conflict if the organization or its mission becomes involved in controversy.

Newsroom employees should avoid joining organizations or institutions they cover or about which they make editorial decisions.

Employees should take care in considering whether to attend any rally, march or demonstration, especially those events that are overtly political.

Employees may not run for public office or be appointed to any public boards or commissions if such service will create a conflict of interest or is exploitation of the employee's connection to *The Denver Post*.

If an editorial employee has a close relative or friend working in a political campaign or on a ballot initiative, the employee should refrain from covering or making news judgments about that campaign or ballot proposal and disclose the relative's or friend's involvement to a senior editor.

It is not the newspaper's intention to attempt to control private lives, but an employee's involvement in an organization or activity could compromise the individual's professional credibility and the newspaper's. Therefore, newsroom employees should notify a supervisor of any such potential conflicts so that appropriate assignments or disclosure can be made, if necessary.

10

Photojournalism

Some might say that the photojournalist has the toughest job of all when it comes to journalism ethics. Photos and video images tend to generate the most heated of debates within newsrooms. And it's clear that the ire of the public can easily be provoked by a single photo or a short piece of video.

Making ethical decisions about what pictures to take and what to publish or broadcast is no simple matter. The very nature of gathering and reporting the news means that photographers are regularly expected to go into situations involving tragedy, to cover clashes between groups of people, to record the public actions of people who wish to protect their privacy. And photo editors, television producers and others who decide what images the public ultimately will see face equally difficult challenges. The Internet's capacity for seemingly unlimited photo displays has magnified the problem.

The case studies in this section run the gamut, from recording the horrors of violent accidents to revealing the identities of minors; from documenting deplorable behavior to changing images to protect the sensitive.

What the photojournalists did with their cameras and in their editing is quite interesting. How and why they decided to do what they did is highly instructive.

Additional photojournalism ethics dilemmas can be found in other chapters of this book, nested within the framework of issues on accuracy and fairness, deception, diversity and privacy.

Photojournalism Checklist

Questions to ask before taking a still or moving image:

- Am I invading someone's privacy? If so, is it for an appropriate reason?
- Is this a private moment of pain and suffering that needs to be seen by our readers or viewers?
- Does this image tell the story I want? Would another be more appropriate?
- Am I shooting at a distance that is not intrusive or potentially revictimizing individuals?
- Am I acting with compassion and sensitivity?

Questions to ask prior to publication or broadcast:

- Do I need more information about facts or context?
- Is there information missing from the content of the image?
- What is the news value of the image?
- What is the motivation for publishing the photo or broadcasting the video image?
- What are the ethical and legal concerns?
- Who will be offended? Does such offense outweigh the value of presenting the image?
- What are the possible consequences of using the photo or image?
- How would I react if I were in the picture?
- Can alternative ways to present the information minimize harm while still telling the story in a clear way?
- Will we be able to justify our actions?

CASE STUDY 33:

Illegitimate Image

The development of computer technology gives photographers the ability to sharpen, enhance and even fabricate reality. A little knowledge, a computer and the right software allows you to insert your face into the huddle of the Indianapolis Colts, find you a place at the table with the president as he meets with his cabinet, and put you on a movie set with George Clooney. Political campaigns have used the techniques to distort the associations of their opponents.

But what if photojournalists use the same practice? What is the ethical implication when a photojournalist is presented with the opportunity to turn something less than amazing into a Pulitzer Prize-worthy photo with a few clicks of the computer?

Is it ethical to alter a photo if it means producing a more compelling image?

WHAT: Brian Walski, a former staff photographer for the *Los Angeles Times*, digitally combined two photographs taken in Iraq to form one fantastic photo featuring a British soldier gesturing with his gun at an Iraqi civilian man carrying a child. In both original photos, the soldier and civilians are visible; however, in one, the civilians are more in the background than the foreground while the soldier is facing them and looking quite intimidating. In the other original photo, the civilians are more desirably visible while the soldier appears at a distance and is paying less attention to them. The manipulated photo was the only one submitted by Walski and it ran on the front page of the *Los Angeles Times*. An employee at another publication noticed some duplication in the doctored photo and notified top editors at the L.A. *Times* who investigated and then immediately terminated Walski.

Question: Is it ethical to alter a photo if it means producing a more compelling image?

WHO: Walski is the moral agent, the original decision-maker, in this scenario. Walski had more than 20 years of photographic experience under his belt, four at the L.A. *Times*, before being let go as a result of what he called a "complete breakdown in judgment." The photograph was widely published by other newspapers throughout the United States, making those unsuspecting publications fall victim to this journalistic crime, tarnishing their reputations and credibility.

WHY: In an apology to his former colleagues, Walski blamed fatigue and stress for what he did. It's a plausible explanation although it overlooks the skill and deliberateness, and amount of time no doubt, it took to manipulate the photo. Those in the news business can certainly identify with the pressure that Walski must have been faced with. It is no secret that the American public has become increasingly more difficult to shock and awe, placing greater expectations and demands on those responsible for drawing in readers. The average reader could argue that since the photo was created using two unaltered photos featuring the same content with just slightly different placement, the alteration was not really a bad offense. What do you think?

HOW: How could publication of a manipulated news photo happen? Editors certainly don't expect their staff photographers to manipulate photos so that they are more pleasing to the eye; but there are plenty of bad examples.

The University of Wisconsin altered the cover photo of its 2001-2002 admissions application by including the photo of an African-American male in order to appear to be a more ethnically diverse community. Its goal was to attract, or, perhaps to not deter, any minority students from applying. While the intent may have been noble, the end did not justify the means. Other examples include instances when photographers or editors:

- swapped heads and bodies to produce more pleasing images
- removed distracting objects such as poles, signs, wires, etc.
- engaged in digital cosmetic surgery
- merged two completely unrelated photographs to produce a scene or situation that never actually occurred.

The latter issue is the big problem. The manipulation of a photograph, even by removing a telephone pole that only interferes in the scene, produces an untrue picture of reality.

Some view these occurrences as outrageous violations of journalistic ethics that others in the profession work so hard to uphold. But does it make a huge difference if someone uses Photoshop if it produces a clearer picture or an image that tells the story better? The National Press Photographers Code of Ethics includes the following guidelines:

- While photographing subjects do not intentionally contribute to, alter or seek to alter or influence events.
- Editing should maintain the integrity of the photographic images' content and context. Do not manipulate images or add or alter sound in any way that can mislead viewers or misrepresent subjects.
- Respect the integrity of the photographic moment.

Is there ever an instance when it is all right to alter the content of a photo? You be the judge.

— Brittainy Daniels and Sara Stone, Baylor University

CASE STUDY 34:

Too Graphic?

WHAT: A father drives 100 miles from his rural home to Shepherdstown, West Virginia, home of Shepherd University, and shoots his two sons, who are students, in their dormitory parking lot before killing himself. All three are dead at the scene.

*The (*Martinsburg, West Virginia) *Journal,* the nearest daily newspaper, is 15 minutes from the community, and its photographer is first on the scene. Chief photographer Ron Agnir arrives before the bodies have been covered. He and his assistant, a part-time graphic artist, shoot hundreds of images, and some of those images are transmitted across The Associated Press wire. *Journal* editor Maria Lorensen considers which images to use. Shepherdstown and Martinsburg are close-knit. They are places where wrecks on the nearby interstate make Page 1.

> The code encourages journalists to show good taste and avoid pandering to lurid curiosity.

Meanwhile, at the other end of the state in Beckley, *Register-Herald* editor Carl Antolini is reading the story and looking at the AP photos, which include shots of the bodies before they were covered where bullet holes are plainly seen, and shots of the bodies after they are covered. Like his colleague, he works for a newspaper that covers a rural, close-knit area where such a murder would be Page 1. His town also includes a college.

Question: Which photo is least likely to upset readers while capturing the horrific nature of the incident?

WHO: Both editors must consider the effects of the photos on readers. Lorensen must consider the students, family members and friends of the victims who will see the photos and the long-term damage they may do to the community and *The Journal's* credibility. Antolini must consider the shock value on a community not directly connected to the incident but culturally related to it by geography and mores. A college campus shooting is newsworthy wherever it occurs and could happen in his own community.

WHY: Several principles in the Society of Professional Journalists Code of Ethics are in play. The admonition to seek truth and report it is paramount, along with its subordinate guidance to make certain that headlines, news teases, promotional materials, photos, video, audio, graphics, sound bites and quotations

The top photo was taken by Tetyana Portyanko and ran on Page 1 in the *Journal.*

The lower photo was taken by Ron Agnir, chief photographer of the same paper (*The Journal,* Martinsburg, West Virginia). It ran on Page 1 in *The Register-Herald.* Used with permission.

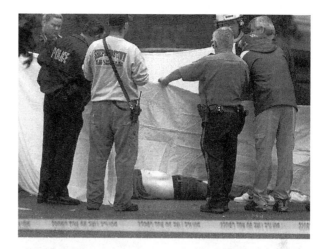

do not misrepresent. They should not oversimplify or highlight incidents out of context.

Yet, seeking truth and reporting it must be balanced by minimizing harm. The code encourages journalists to show good taste and avoid pandering to lurid curiosity. Further, it recognizes that gathering and reporting information may cause harm or discomfort. Finally, the code encourages journalists to show compassion for those who may be affected adversely by news coverage.

HOW: Lorensen chose to run a photo of the partially covered body of one of the victims where two bullet holes plainly could be seen. It was Page 1 above the fold. A photo below the fold showed grieving students. A Page 2 photo, in black and white, showed police officers around the covered body of a victim. Lorensen said she believed the Page 1 photo showed the truth of what happened without being too graphic.

Antolini passed on the photo showing the bullet holes because he said he it was too graphic for his community. Instead, he ran in color and below the fold on Page 1 the photo that his colleague used on Page 2 in black and white. In the color photo, the victim's blood could clearly be seen on the sheet covering his body.

Interestingly, Lorensen said she passed on that photo because the obvious blood on the sheet was too graphic.

This case study illustrates the difficulty in choosing images. What one editor chose not to use in full color on Page 1 because it was too graphic was another editor's choice for Page 1. Their reasons for the choices were identical — to avoid further traumatizing readers while showing the compelling tragedy in a small college town.

As this case study so well articulates, there is no "right" or "wrong" photograph of a tragedy. Well-intentioned editors in two communities made opposite choices in the interest of protecting readers, and both had sound reasons for their decisions.

It's important to examine images carefully and go through a decision-making process to answer why you are choosing one over another. Going through the process to identify the reasons achieves another principle of the code: Clarify and explain news coverage and invite dialogue with the public over journalistic conduct. Editorials and letters from the editor are good options to explain news coverage contemporaneously.

— Nerissa Young, SPJ Ethics Committee

CASE STUDY 35:

Tragedy at Ohio U.

Summary

In the early hours of April 12, 1996, a vehicle carrying five Ohio University students overturned on a highway on-ramp near the main campus in Athens, Ohio. None of the students were wearing a seat belt. The driver, it was later determined, had a blood-alcohol level more than twice the legal limit. At least two passengers also were intoxicated. The vehicle, a Jeep Wrangler with a canvas top, rolled several times during the crash. Students were thrown from the vehicle some 100 feet. Three died at the scene, and a fourth died 36 hours later at a Columbus, Ohio, hospital. The fifth student was critically injured.

Two reporters and a photographer from the university's independent newspaper, *The Post*, were on the scene shortly after the accident. The facts and images they gathered were vivid, powerful and disturbing. The photographer recorded the accident site from numerous angles and shot several photos of the dead students. Although

> *The Post* received more than 100 phone calls and 30 letters to the editor condemning the photograph's publication.

authorities had not released names of the accident victims, the reporters learned that they were Ohio University students. After inspecting the vehicle, which sustained little damage in the crash, investigators emphasized to the student reporters that the crash victims had not used seat belts and that the use of seat belts might have prevented the tragedy.

At 4 a.m., *Post* editor Joe Shaulis and his staff met with reporters and the photographer to determine the substance of the coverage. The most compelling decision concerned which photographs to publish with the story. The photographer presented two choices he felt were the most representative of the scene. The first contained a large pool of blood next to the Jeep's canvas top, a spiral notebook and a sandal belonging to one of the crash victims. The second photograph showed the body of one victim surrounded by a coroner and police officers. Much of the body was covered by a sheet, but the victim's pants and sweatshirt were visible. The sheet was blood-stained around the victim's head.

Facing a 6 a.m. press start, Shaulis and his staff had to decide which photographs to use quickly because the front page and at least one inside page had to be redesigned and composed. The editors selected the second image, the one containing the body, because they felt it was the less graphic of the two. They reasoned that the photo conveyed the story's impact without resorting to sensationalism.

The published picture sparked controversy. *The Post* received more than 100 phone calls and 30 letters to the editor condemning the photograph's publication. Readers aimed much of their criticism at photo editor John Martin, who shot the crash photos. It was the most intense public response to a story the paper had received in at least four years. Most of the letters and phone calls accused the paper of pandering to sensational and voyeuristic tastes. Some readers questioned the propriety of publishing a graphic image in a small, close-knit community such as Athens. The public outcry was so intense that the accident itself was nearly lost in the controversy over the community's response to the photograph.

In its next edition, *The Post* devoted its entire editorial page to the accident and explained the mechanics of its decision to publish the picture. Shaulis and Martin laid out for readers the reasons they believed the photo warranted publication. Shaulis wrote:

> Only an image could convey the seriousness and the impact of an accident... This picture has lasting value. It will make people think about the accident and why it happened. It will make them think about how any O.U. students could have died in the middle of the night, in the middle of a highway.

Martin explained how difficult it had been to view the accident scene and how he and other editors had considered the feelings of those who would be harmed by publication.

After the paper disclosed its reasons for publishing the picture, the tone of the overwhelming majority of the letters to the editor shifted from negative to positive. One reader wrote, "If a picture of an accident scene will make one person think twice about doing anything unsafe in an automobile, you should print it." Another reader wondered, "How many lives were saved because people had the image of that picture in their minds as they drove home for the weekend?"

Analysis

This case puts all four principles of the Society of Professional Journalists' Code of Ethics to the test: truth-telling, minimizing harm, being independent, and being accountable. The lessons in ethics were learned well by *The Post* staff and by the Ohio University community.

The inevitable backlash in this case demonstrates how the use of images can increase the intensity of debates about privacy, compassion and reporting of tragedies. Greg Lewis, a former news photographer who moved on to teaching at Fresno State, has written that images of tragedy have more impact than words because the photo leaves so little to the imagination. A photograph, he said, "forces an image on the reader, one he or she cannot control. Its presence on the page is almost impossible to ignore, and its reality can be overwhelming." Use of high-impact images often provokes allegations of sensationalism and lack of consideration for the families of victims, and while these are serious allegations, they must be weighed against the role of the journalist in society.

The moral dilemma places the duty of journalists to disseminate information that may be of significant instructional value to a mass audience in direct conflict with a duty to refrain from inflicting unnecessary harm to those who already have suffered significant emotional distress. The conflict is sharpened when it is framed by the effect of publication on members of small communities, where media play a significant role in defining and reflecting the perspectives of community members.

As information is necessary if individuals are to exercise control over their own lives, the benefits of information distribution are of sufficient value to justify potential harms that distribution may inflict. The need to distribute as much truthful, compelling and accurate information as possible about a local tragedy must be balanced against the need to reduce, or refrain from inflicting, unnecessary harm on family members and friends. In smaller communities, journalists must also consider harm to the news media's ability to fulfill a role that research shows is significant for community newspapers: to be a mirror of the community's perspectives and values.

Lewis observed that the question of whether some images ought to be published will likely never be answered. Journalists, he said, must set their own standards, "standards that are realistic, carefully thought out, and that you can live with." With that in mind — and motivated by the need to avoid *ad hoc* rationalizing and rely instead upon moral philosophy — the following set of guidelines is proposed to serve as a justification model for journalists faced with a dilemma similar to that which confronted *The Post*:

1. Does this image reflect significant instructional value? How might its publication prevent harm to readers? Is an image necessary to illustrate the instructional value of the story?
2. Is it possible to present the image in such a way that it reflects its instructional value without inflicting undue emotional distress on readers or on the families of victims?
3. Does the image truly qualify as news of instructional value? Or is it the result of a "news event," staged for its shock value?
4. Should disclosure play a role in this case? Would explanation of the reasoning process that preceded publication help to diffuse the controversy?

In working through this case, and others like it, the initial questions in Steps 1 and 3 must be answered in the affirmative to justify publication. Any decision to publish a disturbing image hinges on its instructional value, which is the primary consideration of Step 1. Does the image, by its compelling nature, warn others of imminent harm or danger, or is it exploiting tragedy for the sake of meeting traditional, non-moral news values? If the impact is of great instructional value, the journalist has a moral duty to publish, notwithstanding the harm or criticism that may follow. (It is very important to note that harm to others and criticism of the newspaper are very different considerations. Making a decision merely to avoid criticism is far less moral than making a decision that minimizes harm to others.) In the absence of clear instructional value, there is no debate, and the images that are disturbing or that could inflict unnecessary harm should not be published.

If there is instructional value, and Step 1 has been passed affirmatively, Step 2 suggests that journalists seek ways to present the image so that its instructional value is clear, while at the same time seeking to minimize emotional distress of readers or families of victims. This step, when coupled with the first, meshes nicely with the initial guiding principles of the SPJ Code of Ethics: seek truth and report it, and minimize harm. Research shows that positioning of images below the fold or inside the paper seems to reduce the impact of the disturbing images. Color is also problematic; where images of bodies or blood are concerned, it may be advisable to consider printing in black and white rather than in color. (The rival Athens *Messenger*, the town's commercial newspaper, had more time than *The Post* to weigh alternatives and selected a black and white photo of a state police officer examining blood stains on the highway.)

Next is the issue of journalistic independence. As journalists move to Step 3, they may wish to consider the motives of people who attempt to manipulate coverage by creating "news events" as a way of making public statements. Instructional value rarely exists in such pseudo-events. The same is true of "news events" staged for their shock value.

In the media's self-examination after the public suicide of Robert Budd Dwyer, the Pennsylvania state treasurer indicted in connection with a bribery scheme, the question of manipulation was raised frequently. Did the besieged official exploit the media to make a statement with his suicide? Obviously, that was his intent. While his death and the accompanying circumstances were "news" according to traditional, non-moral criteria of news judgment, the instruction value of the graphic images that depicted the moment of death and its aftermath was nil. On the other hand, it is unlikely that even the most accurate description of the one-vehicle accident in *The Post* case could have served the same instructional purpose without the accompanying photograph. Thus, in the absence of clear and decisive instructional value that goes beyond the realm of manipulation for shock value, we recommend that media seriously consider the motives behind such events and reject those that fail to meet the instructional-value test.

Finally, consider the issue of media accountability. After the first three steps of the model have been considered and adequate justifications for publication have been identified, it is likely that disclosure of the journalists' intent and reasoning process will help readers understand why they saw disturbing images in their newspaper. Certainly this is true of *The Post* case. The decisive shift in the tone of the public's response demonstrates the value of disclosure in educating readers about the reasoning for publishing in such cases. *The Post* case also suggests that disclosure will be especially valuable in smaller towns, where the newspaper plays such a vital role in communicating community values and perspectives to readers.

The initial wave of criticism focused on reaction to the photo and its effect on friends and families of the victims. Before disclosure, readers focused on criticizing *The Post* to the point that they seemed to have overlooked the accident and the deaths of four students. Disclosure prompted support for the decision to publish the photo; the intensity of that support was such that it nearly ended the controversy. Letters to the editor supporting the paper's decision indicated that their authors understood the instructional value of the picture. Disclosure fulfilled, at least in part, its aim of educating readers who may have believed that such images have no place in a small-town newspaper.

— by Paul Husselbee; a longer version of this case study was drafted for the Newspaper Research Journal

CASE STUDY 36:

'An Indelible Photo'

Summary

Seconds after a Northern California jury convicted Richard Allen Davis of murdering 12-year-old Polly Klaas, a press-pool photographer took a picture of Davis, who held up both of his middle fingers. The *San Jose Mercury News* decided to publish the picture of the obscene gesture on its front page accompanied by a "Dear Reader" box soliciting reader response and explaining its reasoning for running the controversial photograph.

Mercury News executive editor Jerry Ceppos told readers that the picture showed Davis' "contempt for the system that convicted him."

"Ever since Davis' arrest, I've wanted to know about the character of a man who could kill Polly Klaas," Ceppos wrote in a front-page column. "Ever since it became clear the jury would convict him, I've wanted to know how he would react, what he's thinking.

> Sometimes reasonable individuals pursuing the same goal radically disagree on a course of action.

"Even though it's unclear who the target of the gesture is, I believe the photograph tells us something about Allen's contempt for the system that convicted him. While the picture is vulgar, it does give us some insight. In fact, I suspect that it will become one of those indelible photographic images that will come to represent a terrible episode in American life."

Ceppos concluded the column, writing, "I'd be interested in your views, too."

More than 1,200 readers responded by fax, phone and mail (this was before most people had e-mail) — 815 were in favor of running the picture and 431 against.

In a subsequent column, Ceppos wrote that he was grateful for the relationship he had fostered with his readers, saying it was clearly "their newspaper." He added that asking for readers' opinions made them "feel part of the newspaper."

Managing editor David Yarnold had suggested the note to readers during a *Mercury News* editors' meeting that included Ceppos, the photo editor and a news editor. Ceppos decided to add the invitation for readers to comment.

"In this case the picture was so jarring and so different from what the *Mercury News* usually does that we felt we owed readers an explanation — on the front page, right under the picture," Ceppos said.

"The key issues were taste and whether this guy should be given such a prominent platform. In the end, we decided that this photograph told us even more than we already knew about the mindset of Richard Allen Davis."

Five other Bay Area newspapers published the photo of the obscene gesture on their front pages. The *Marin Independent Journal* ran the photo on its editorial page with an accompanying editorial. The *San Francisco Chronicle* published the photo on its front page but without an editor's note. The newspaper reported more than 130 negative phone calls, and several readers canceled their subscriptions. *The Sacramento Bee* decided not to publish the photo, allowing the text to convey Davis' message. *The Bee's* drop-head read: "Killer flips off camera after verdicts read." Reporter Patrick Hoge referred to the act in his third paragraph, writing, "Silently, menacingly, Davis winked, kissed the air and flashed an obscene gesture with both hands."

Bee executive editor Gregory Favre said that editors who said they published the photo to show "what type of person Davis really is" were looking for an excuse to run it.

"You run that picture for shock value only," Favre told *Editor & Publisher*. "There was no other redeeming value in it. We didn't run it to show that Davis is a despicable, disgusting contemptible human being. What he did spells that out thousands of times more than any picture could ever do."

Analysis

Sometimes reasonable individuals pursuing the same goal radically disagree on a course of action. Editors Ceppos and Favre both wanted to tell the story of what happened in the courtroom at a crucial moment in that celebrated trial. They landed on opposite ends of the decision-making spectrum, though both would argue they reported the truth of that story and properly served their readers. Ceppos, and editors at other papers, used the picture to carry the impact. Favre believed words alone would accomplish the task.

While Ceppos could talk himself blue in the face trying to defend Favre's challenge that he was just looking for an excuse to run the picture, the *Mercury News* editor took the best course of action to justify his decision. He held himself and his paper accountable by taking a public stance on why they ran the photo.

The principle of accountability says "Journalists should clarify and explain news coverage and invite dialogue with the public over journalistic conduct."

Ceppos tied his "Dear Reader" column to the photo to explain the paper's decision to run what many would term an offensive picture. This real-time explanation, used judiciously, is an excellent tool of accountability and a key element of the ethical decision-making process.

Additionally, when editors have to write down and publish the how and why of a decision, they are required to be reflective. They know their judgment and logic will be scrutinized in a very public forum. And, knowing that they will likely face dissent from some readers, they must anchor their decisions in a principle that at least will be respected, even if disagreed with.

Ceppos took the additional step of urging readers to give the paper feedback on the decision to publish the photo. The pro and con vote on the use of the picture is interesting, but not nearly as important as the fact that more than 1,200 readers made the effort to respond to Ceppos' invitation.

That invitation and the response to it speak loudly of the importance of news organizations creating an ongoing dialogue with those they serve. Such conversations, whether about dramatic photos or the coverage of complex and controversial issues, help news organizations better understand the communities they serve. Just as importantly, the conversations should help the public better understand the essential role journalism plays in a democratic society. To be sure, disagreements on course of action will continue, but that can be conducted out of mutual respect.

— from the Third Edition, Black, Steele and Barney

Photojournalism

What the Codes Say

The Denver Post

Denver Post news photography must be genuine in every way. Photographs must not be staged or posed. They must not be altered, barring exceptional circumstances, and then only with approval of the Managing Editor/Presentation, the Managing Editor/News and/or the Editor, and with full disclosure to readers.

Nothing should be added to or omitted from scenes, and only traditional adjustments (such as cropping, dodging, burning, contrast and saturation) are acceptable. If colorizing techniques are used, the practice should be disclosed.

The newspaper's intervention in a photograph, such as in an illustration, should be unmistakable to the reader. Readers should understand our role in arranging portraits, especially in fashion or home-design shots and other interpretive photography.

Photo captions must fully explain the picture's context. A caption for an environmental portrait, for instance, should indicate that the subject is posing for illustrative purposes, unless it is obvious to the reader. For example, "Bob Smith demonstrates the window cleaner device he invented." Is Bob Smith actually cleaning, or is he demonstrating for purposes of a photograph? Such distinctions should be honestly disclosed. Every effort should be made to preserve contextual information provided by the photographer in the final edited version of the caption.

Captions and credits should clearly label a photo illustration. If there is any doubt about whether to use a photo illustration, a photo editor and the Managing Editor/Presentation should be consulted. While it is possible to create images that appear real using a composite of photographs for an illustration (for instance, using a person's head on another's body), we should avoid using such images. Approval of composite images should come from a consensus of parties, including photo, section, design and graphics editors, and the Managing Editor/Presentation. If there is concern from any of the parties involved, it may be appropriate to find another visual solution.

The origin of the photo, whether produced by staff, freelancers or marketing sources, should be clearly labeled.

Sarasota Herald-Tribune (Florida)

The power of documentary photography is based on the fact that real moments are captured as they happen. Anything done to alter the process, before or after the image is recorded, diminishes that power and turns it into a lie. It has always been the policy of the *Herald-Tribune* that content alteration of documentary news photographs is unacceptable. We strive for fair and accurate visual reporting. While no protocol can anticipate every situation, common sense and good judgment will be our guiding principles. It should be noted that there is a clear difference between such documentary news photos and feature portraits and illustrations that are posed or created for a particular story. It is imperative that we keep one thing in mind — the credibility and integrity of the *Herald-Tribune* is at stake.

Manipulation of the subject

The same ethical standards that apply to written stories apply to documentary news photos, including spot and general news photos, sports photos and enterprise feature photos. *Herald-Tribune* photographers will not create scenes or direct events with the purpose of making them appear as if they were "found" moments. If a photojournalist is unable to record a natural moment as it occurs, it should not be recreated.

Portraits

Portraits shot by staff photographers must not mislead readers to believe the moment was captured spontaneously. Captions must also be written in a way that does not mislead. For example, we should not say Joe Smith works in his workshop when he is actually there for the purpose of being photographed.

Illustrations

When photo illustrations are used, they must clearly be fictional. All photo illustrations should be labeled as such.

Digital Manipulation

Manipulation of images electronically for the purpose of better reproduction is permitted. Any such alteration will only include techniques that have been traditionally accepted in chemical darkrooms. This includes dodging and burning in selected areas within a photograph so long as it does not change the content of the image. This may also include the correction of technical defects in a photograph such as dust spots or color shifts caused by mixed lighting. Objects within a photo may not be moved, added, deleted, combined or altered. No photographer, artist, designer, or image technician may change the actual color content of any documentary news photograph. Photographs may not be flipped, stretched or shrunk to fit a layout.

The Journal Times (Racine, Wisconsin)

The following protocol must be followed if there is any question about the accuracy of the color of a photo, or whether there are details that should be altered in consideration of acceptable community standards such as accidental inclusion of genitals or obscene gestures or language.

A newsroom consultation group shall discuss the question. The group shall include: the page editor; the photographer, when possible; the director of photography, when possible; the top newsroom editor available, the editor of the section where the photo will appear.

The editor of the newspaper shall have the final say. The group will reach a consensus decision if the editor is not available. Any members of this group who are not present for the discussion should be left a message about the question that arose, and how it was resolved.

San Jose Mercury News

In the interest of integrity and fairness, photographers and editors should exercise caution in the use of "set-up" photographs. In the same way that reporters do not make up quotes, photographers do not reconstruct scenes or events with the purpose of making them appear as if they were "found" moments.

However, photographers are often called upon to make environmental portraits or do illustrative photography. In no way should such photographs be approached or treated as anything but what they are. They are either portraits or are demonstrative of a situation. Both should be clearly labeled.

That means that care should be taken in writing captions so they do not suggest the picture is something it is not. For example, is Clark Kent working in his study or is he simply in his study (for purposes of a portrait)? Is Lois Lane actually practicing her technique of boomerang tossing or is she demonstrating her technique of boomerang tossing (for purposes of a photograph)? Such distinctions make a difference...

Ordinarily, consent is implied if a photographer approaches a subject, indicates that he/she is a newspaper photographer and asks for names and other facts. In some circumstances, written releases may be required (at mental health institutions or orphanages, for example).

The Virginian-Pilot (Norfolk, Virginia)
VISUAL ACCURACY
Documentary photo

This is a candid or unposed photo that records news, features or sports. The spirit of the documentary photo is to be honest and above board with readers. Any appearance or suspicion of manipulation of documentary photos strikes against our core values. Submitted photos should meet these same standards.

For questions about photo authenticity, check with a photo editor.

Posing or re-enacting a documentary photograph is unacceptable. Altering a documentary photo is also unacceptable. This includes eliminating or adding material to the photo.

Examples:

- Do not ask someone to repeat an action for a documentary photo. The photographer would not ask a wife to again hug her husband at a ship homecoming because he missed it the first time.
- Do not cut out a "live" news photo. Cutouts can make a news photo look like a feature photo. Let the reader have full information.
- A photographer, photo editor or designer should not eliminate a telephone line from a photo to "clean up" the scene. Clouds, sky, grass or other elements should not be added to make room for type or make the photo fit a hole.

Adding type to a documentary photo is permissible under "Type in Photo" guidelines, which are part of the design styleguide. See the DME for presentation or News Editor.

Portrait photo

This photo is usually posed and it should be obvious to the reader if it is. A mug shot, a group photo or an environmental portrait with the subject looking at the camera are examples. With candid portraits follow the guidelines of documentary photos. Portrait photos shouldn't be altered.

Photo-illustration

This type of photograph turns 180 degrees from documentary photojournalism and uses the medium as an artist uses colored chalk to illustrate a story. In a successful and ethical photoillustration, it is obvious to the reader that the photo is not a candid documentary photo. A photo-illustration credit line should reinforce the fact that the photo is not a real situation.

Icon photos

This category is much like the photo-illustration — almost anything goes. It includes simple photos that illustrate or label stories. Examples include photos of planes, ships, money, hockey sticks, hands, buildings, etc. Cutout photos would be included in this. It is not necessary to credit these photos.

To use or not to use

When in doubt, use common sense. Know privacy rules and laws. Shooting the photo usually is not the problem. Publishing the photo may be. Using sound judgment, the photographer should almost always shoot the picture. The editing process will determine whether the photo will be used. The photo editor, page editor and news editor will also help determine publication. Some photos should be approved by a deputy managing editor, managing editor or the editor. Some red flags:

- death
- nudity or sexual content
- exaggerated grief
- blood or other body fluids
- photo is too good to be true (it may be set up)
- vulgar words or gestures (these may be hidden in a photo)
- cheap shot (zipper open, food on the face)
- unflattering expression not related to the event or situation
- people performing dangerous acts
- violence
- racial stereotypes
- photos that may otherwise shock or appall readers

GUIDING QUESTIONS

Is the photo appropriate to the story?

Is the news value worth upsetting the reader?

Is the photo from this community or from far away?

What are the paper's general standards of taste?

Do you need to pass the photo through the top editor?

Does it pass the "breakfast table" test?

Obscenity

What the Codes Say

Specific codes of ethics don't cover the issue of lewd language as much as they once did. Most references to the question appear to be in stylebooks, rather than in codes of ethics. Perhaps it's because of changing mores, as *The Washington Post* refers to in its code.

Detroit Free Press

Our guiding standard is whether an important journalistic purpose is served by using objectionable language. The harsher the language, the more important our purpose should be. Only the broadest sort of guidelines can apply; a word or phrase that is newsworthy in one context may be entirely objectionable in another. The use of any obscene or tasteless language is limited to quoted material. The speaker and the audience are of primary importance in determining whether any obscenity will be reported. Generally, when an obscenity is deleted in a quotation, hyphens will stand for all but the first letter. Harsh obscenities may be used only with approval of a managing editor.

Reuters Handbook of Journalism
GRAPHIC DETAILS, OBSCENITIES AND BLASPHEMY

As journalists, we have an obligation to convey the reality of what we report accurately, yet a duty to be aware that such material can cause distress, damage the dignity of the individuals concerned or even in some cases so overpower the viewer or reader that a rational understanding of the facts is impaired. We do not sanitize violence, bowdlerise speech or euphemise sex. We should not, however, publish graphic details and obscene or blasphemous language gratuitously or with an intention to titillate or to shock. There must be a valid news reason for running such material and it will usually require a decision by a senior editor. In all cases, we need to consider whether the material is necessary to an understanding of the reality portrayed or described. We should also be mindful that our customers in different markets often have different thresholds and needs. All such stories should be sent ATTENTION EDITOR with an accompanying explanation of why the material has been used. Such material, if published, should be brought to the attention of readers in brackets at the top of the story e.g. (Note strong language in paragraph 6) or (This story contains graphic details in paragraphs 7, 9, 12-14). We spell out expletives. It is then the responsibility of online desks pushing news directly to consumers to deal with the copy appropriately.

The Denver Post

Out of respect for our readers, *The Denver Post* avoids prurience, profanity and obscenity.

That said, sometimes the use of graphic or inflammatory language is essential to the context of a story or photograph. In some cases, omitting the language might alter the story's meaning or render the story incomplete. The editor or Managing Editor/News must approve use of graphic or inflammatory language.

Slang, foreign languages and colloquialisms also can be minefields. Writers and editors should avoid the use of words or phrases if they might be offensive to some racial, religious, gender or ethnic groups, unless the language is essential to the story's meaning or completeness. A department head should be consulted when making such decisions, and the Editor or Managing Editor/News should be informed.

The Washington Post

The Washington Post as a newspaper respects taste and decency, understanding that society's concepts of taste and decency are constantly changing. A word offensive to the last generation can be part of the next generation's common vocabulary. But we shall avoid prurience. We shall avoid profanities and obscenities unless their use is so essential to a story of significance that its meaning is lost without them. In no case shall obscenities be used without the approval of the executive editor or the managing editor or his deputy.

The Associated Press

We do not use obscenities, racial epithets or other offensive slurs in stories unless they are part of direct quotations and there is a compelling reason for them.

If a story cannot be told without reference to them, we must first try to find a way to give the reader a sense of what was said without using the specific word or phrase. If a profanity, obscenity or vulgarity is used, the story must be flagged at the top, advising editors to note the contents.

A photo containing something that could be deemed offensive must carry an editor's note flagging it.

When a piece of video or audio contains something that might be deemed offensive, we flag it in the written description (rundown, billboard and/or script) so clients know what they are getting. Recognizing that standards differ around the world, we tailor our advisories and selection of video and audio according to customer needs.

We take great care not to refer readers to websites that are obscene, racist or otherwise offensive, and we must not directly link our stories to such sites.

In our online service, we link the least offensive image necessary to tell the story. For photo galleries and interactive presentations we alert readers to the nature of the material in the link and on the opening page of the gallery or interactive. If an obscene image is necessary to tell the story, we blur the portion of the image considered offensive after approval of the department manager, and flag the video.

11

Privacy

The public often has a need for information that others, for a variety of motives, would like to keep private. Citizens value knowing about certain activities of public officials, even though the officials may wish to restrict flow of that information. There also is value in the public's knowing about meaningful details of accidents, tragedies and crimes, even though the gathering and distribution of such details might invade someone's sense of privacy.

Such stories highlight the journalist's dilemma in balancing the competing ethical principles of telling the truth while minimizing the harm.

Public discussions that ultimately may bring some benefit often cannot begin without some invasive and harmful disclosure. A story about the spread of AIDS and the failure of society to respond may present this disease as just another abstract threat unless specific names are attached to the story.

Stories that make allegations of criminal activity or unethical behavior, ranging from government corruption to child abuse, are less accurate and potentially unfair if individuals go unidentified. To identify individuals is certain to cause some harm, however.

Crime stories are necessary to inform members of the public of both their own safety and to provide them with information on the performance of those responsible agencies of government. On the other hand, coverage of crime is bound to cause some invasion of privacy.

Harm from privacy invasion is almost certain, but it is more difficult for a journalist to fully identify benefits from an intrusion. Thus it is important to recognize the primary ethical obligation of journalism is to inform the public by seeking truth and reporting it as fully as possible. That obligation must then be balanced against the obligation to respect individuals and their privacy.

The challenge for journalists is to be courageous in seeking and reporting information, while being compassionate to those who are being covered.

Privacy Checklist

- How important is the information I am seeking? Does the public have a right to know? A need to know? Merely a desire to know?
- What level of protection do individuals involved in the story deserve? How much harm might they receive? Are they involved in the news event by choice or by chance?
- How would I feel if I were being subjected to the same scrutiny?
- Do I know the facts of the story well enough? What else do I need to know?
- What can I do to minimize the privacy invasion and the harm? Can I broaden the focus of the story by including more "victims," thereby minimizing harm to a select few? Can I postpone the story without significantly jeopardizing information important to the public?
- Do I need to include other individuals to gain more perspective in the decision-making process?
- Should I be focusing more on the system failure or the big-issue picture instead of focusing intensely on individuals?
- Can I clearly and fully justify my thinking and decision? To those directly affected? To the public?

CASE STUDY 37:

'Outing' Arthur Ashe

Summary

This is one of the earliest, and most notorious, cases of media naming a prominent person living with AIDS. In April 1992, a *USA Today* reporter called former professional tennis star Arthur Ashe and asked if Ashe had AIDS. Ashe would neither confirm nor deny the story, although he previously had confided in family and some friends, including at least two journalists, that he did indeed have AIDS. He had contracted the HIV virus from a heart surgery blood transfusion in the mid-1980s, and he had known for more than three years that he had AIDS.

Editors at *USA Today* told Ashe that the paper would not report his AIDS without on-the-record sources. They also said they were pursuing the matter despite his objection. Their position was that a prominent, although retired, sports figure with AIDS was important news.

The next day, Ashe called a news conference to announce he had the disease. His announcement alluded to rumors and half-truths

> Arthur Ashe's anguish and the pain to his family caused reporters and editors to question again why they are willing to inflict such trauma.

about his condition and expressed anger at what he felt was intrusion by the media into his privacy. Of particular concern was the effect of disclosure on his young daughter in light of public attitudes toward AIDS. Ashe became the first celebrity to disclose he had contracted the disease from something other than sex or drug abuse.

"I am angry that I was put in the position of having to lie if I wanted to protect my privacy," he said.

Ashe, who was 48 at the time of his announcement, was the most prominent African-American male tennis player in history. He had won three grand slam titles, the U.S. Open in 1968, the Australian Open in 1968, and Wimbledon in 1975. He retired from professional tennis in 1980 but continued to maintain public visibility through his television commentaries on tennis, his involvement with the apartheid struggle in South Africa, and his public comments on the exploitation of college and high school athletes. He died in 1993.

Analysis

While public disclosure that a person has any of hundreds of diseases may not raise questions of privacy invasion, such volatile topics as AIDS and rape generate emotionally protective public responses. Some argue that the disclosure of information about those who have AIDS or those who have been raped has a unique stigma attached. Others question whether the stigma will dissipate without more public, specific discussion on the topic, including the use of names of prominent victims.

Arthur Ashe's anguish and the pain to his family caused reporters and editors to question again why they are willing to inflict such trauma. Decisions should come from a balance of arguments for both sides, however.

It is not adequate to argue "newsworthiness" about a public figure without some supporting list of social benefits. For example, Ashe's case may confirm to some people for the first time that the disease is not solely a sex-and-drugs product, creating a very different example of a celebrity victim for audiences to observe. Such a disclosure adds a dimension that may affect attitudes people bring to contacts and relationships with AIDS victims. Perhaps disclosure of Ashe's affliction may not change attitudes toward the disease, but the principle of an open society suggests that more will change from publishing important stories than from keeping such stories under wraps.

The Arthur Ashe case exemplifies the precarious balance between the principles of maximizing truth-telling and minimizing harm. This case speaks to the continuing challenge journalists face in weighing the harm of reporting certain information against the benefits of revealing that information.

Those who would argue that journalists should not have pushed Arthur Ashe into a corner, essentially forcing him to go public, place the most weight on the minimize-harm principle. They believe that the harm caused to Ashe and his family was tremendous, recognizing that such revelations could have a serious impact on him, his family or his career.

They would argue that having AIDS is a private matter and one should retain the choice over when and how it would be revealed. They would argue that compassion necessitated honoring Ashe's privacy. They would argue that revealing Ashe's medical situation was merely using him as a means to a journalistic end.

On the other hand, those who argue in favor of publishing such information and reporting it place the most weight on the principle of maximizing truth-telling. They believe that this information was significant and its significance benefited the public. They would argue that AIDS is a major health, social and public-policy issue — perhaps the top such issue of the time, especially in the '90s. They would argue that revealing how Arthur Ashe contracted AIDS through a blood transfusion years earlier added to the pressure to make blood supplies safer. They would argue that Ashe's continued high public profile made what happened to him meaningful to a great number of people, including those who might find inspiration from him or those who might financially invest in him in some way.

They would argue, too, that Ashe's position as a member of the board of directors of a major insurance company made him part of the public debate over AIDS, given the controversy over how insurance companies treat people with the disease. Finally, they would argue that while Ashe clearly suffered from the pressure of the revelation, the harm to him or his family was not nearly that great, given the way in which he contracted AIDS. While some still would shun him, most people would be more likely to feel sympathy and empathy rather than revulsion or disdain.

Whether the benefits outweigh the anguish is still the decision of the individual reporter or editor. At least two journalist friends who knew of Ashe's illness chose not to tell. Such a choice, while an acceptable exercise of independence, inevitably raises questions of consistency. How far would the journalists go in refusing to disclose information about friends, when they would routinely publish that same information about others?

To those journalists who would reveal that Ashe had AIDS, there is an additional responsibility. They should publicly justify their action, explaining how and why they decided as they did.

— from the Third Edition, Black, Steel and Barney

CASE STUDY 38:

Covering, or Covering Up, Suicide?

WHAT: The death of Jeff Smith (names have been changed) resonated through-out Red Wing, Minnesota. The 19-year-old hanged himself. The pain was ex-acerbated by the fact that five years earlier his brother, George, was killed in a car accident. Jeff was survived by his parents and sister.

His death occurred on a Sunday evening in August. I was editor of *The Red Wing Republican Eagle* at the time, and when the newspaper's staff arrived Monday morning, word already had spread throughout the community as friends connected on the Internet. *The Republican Eagle* had a longstanding policy of identifying deaths that are the result of other than natural causes.

The policy understandably was not welcomed by all on the premise that sui-cide often is the result of depression — a sickness. In one case, a family pointed out that the person who took his life was on medication that created a chemical imbalance. Depression was a significant factor in this suicide. Smith had never gotten over his brother's death and was undergoing treat-ment for depression.

> It's equally important, the newspaper believed, to be a partner in presenting information that may prevent copycat occurrences.

By Monday morning, friends already had organized a meeting at the church for family and friends to share stories and console each other. The newspaper re-ported the suicide in Monday's edition and included a notice of the gathering.

This story carried extra sensitivity due to the circumstances. A friend of the family, who also was on staff at Goodhue County Mental Health Center, contacted the editor to discuss a way to share with readers — primarily friends of Smith — signs of depression and suicide. It's fairly routine for schools to bring in grief counselors to talk with students in the aftermath of a tragedy. But this death occurred during the summer with no organized opportunity to meet with Smith's peers. Counselors were available Monday afternoon for a brief period at the church, but the need was evident for broader distribution of the message.

It's equally important, the newspaper believed, to be a partner in present-ing information that may prevent copycat occurrences. The mental health cen-ter specifically requested a story on the signs of depression that may forewarn a suicide. We were sensitive to the fact that we could not write such a story without referring to Smith's death, and we did not want to run the story with-out the family's awareness — even blessing.

The timing of the story played a role, too. We deemed it important to publish the story before the funeral with the thought that it would help friends visiting the family understand the illness — depression — that led to his death.

Question: As an overall policy, should newspapers identify suicides? In this specific case, should the newspaper detail the circumstances of depression that led to the individual's suicide?

WHO: The final decision of what to publish ultimately rests with the top newsroom editor. But in this case, as with so many stories that deal with challenging and sensitive circumstances, many individuals will be affected. In that regard, it's important to involve as many people — within the newspaper family as well as the community at large — in the decision-making process.

Deadlines often present obstacles to reaching as many people as you'd like. That's why it's instructive for newsrooms to methodically brainstorm — away from the pressure of deadlines — and frame policies for some of the tough decisions that increasingly face newsrooms. For example, what information and photos do you publish from the scenes of fatal accidents? Should you identify high school students who have been suspended from extracurricular activities for violating local school district or state high school league rules? Having a general policy will make it much easier to evaluate these stories as circumstances arise. Policies always should be subject to revisiting and revision based on specific circumstances.

The family was the primary consideration in the pursuit of this story. The newspaper intended to identify suicide as the cause of death, per its policy. But the additional consideration was the broader coverage linking the youth's death to his struggle with depression caused by the death of his older brother.

This story had a clear impact on the community, too. Smith was an involved and popular high school student. His father worked in retail, and his mother worked in the school district. Grieving is inherent in all deaths, but this one was abuzz throughout the community as people started their work week.

The story could be educational, too, to help readers recognize other individuals who may be suffering depression and susceptible to causing them personal harm.

The newsroom also was under a microscope for how it would handle such a sensitive story. How it approached individuals in gathering the information and how it told the story would likely have an impact on its credibility and ability to collect information for other sensitive stories. The fact that the "cause of death" was a public record took a back seat to how the newspaper dealt with such a challenging story.

WHY: "Is this story news? How should we report it?" These two questions are among the basic five Ws and H for evaluating and writing any news item, and they require extra consideration when dealing with challenging events. In this case, the suicide was being talked about in the community. It had an impact on people beyond the immediate family. It was news.

Untimely deaths typically generate conversation in a community, and suicides stir even greater emotions. It's standard procedure at most schools to call in counselors in the wake of an untimely death of a classmate, whatever the cause. School was not in session due to summer recess, but that did not stop the buzz. It was the talk of the town among people at work, at the coffee shops and at dinner tables.

We had to determine the most sensitive way to approach the family. If we approached them for a broader story on their son and brother's depression that led to the suicide, they suddenly were thrust into a broader public discussion beyond what would have occurred with just a short notice on the death. But this untimely death clearly tugged at the community's emotions as evidenced by the decision by friends and mental health advocates to convene a special meeting at the church the day after the death to share memories and help people work through their feelings.

Many in the health care community regard suicide as a national epidemic. The latest statistics identify suicide as the No. 3 cause of death among youths and young adults ages 15 to 24 in the United States. Shedding light on the causes of suicide can be regarded a true public service.

Grieving with death — especially suicide — is difficult enough for immediate family. It can be equally discomforting for friends and co-workers who do not feel comfortable in approaching the family. Publishing the facts can put to rest rumors and make it easier for individuals to approach a family.

HOW: *The Republican Eagle* pursued and published a front-page story complete with family photo on Smith's struggle with depression that led to his suicide. In the same edition, at the request of the family, we published a column from their pastor on suicide. Primary credit for the story went to the Smiths who were willing to share their story and to the staff at Goodhue County Mental Health Center who helped us connect with the family. I also wrote a column so readers understood the sensitivity with which we approached this story.

The story had both immediate and long-term impacts. The interview with the family was published the afternoon of the visitation. The lengthy line of people waiting to visit the family was expected, but the story likely played a role. More than one person told us that they initially did not intend to go to the funeral home but changed their minds after the story appeared. That was not the end of the story, however.

The interview was the start of a broader community response. The family worked with a mental health center to sponsor a forum to help people understand the dynamics of depression and suicide. An overflow crowd filled the municipal theater to hear personal stories from panelists, including local residents. Crisis hotlines were immediately flooded with calls.

A local bank took note of the response and decided to take the discussion to another level as a community service project. A steering committee was formed with representatives from school, youth and health care professionals. Within a few months, the bank, assisted by a private foundation, brought the founders of the Light for Life Foundation International-Yellow Ribbon Suicide Prevention Program to the community.

Parents of a suicide victim in Westminster, Colorado, started the national project. The steering committee, working with mental-health professionals, conducted school assemblies for each of grades 7–12. Counselors were available to talk. Between the middle school and high school, approximately 60 kids came forward for immediate counseling. Nearly 150 kids volunteered to work on creating a youth board. The steering committee also succeeded in getting the school to include discussion of depression and suicide in the health curriculum beginning in eighth grade.

Not all suicides will have such an impact. Not all families of victims will be so sharing of a tragedy. The underlying lesson, however, is that even issues as sensitive as suicide can become a positive force in communities if newspapers treat the subject with respect and care.

— *Jim Pumarlo, SPJ Ethics Committee*
former editor, Red Wing *(Minnesota)* Republican Eagle, *1982–2003*

CASE STUDY 39:

Public and Private Jewell

Summary

For a few months after the bombing at Centennial Park during the 1996 Olympic Games in Atlanta, few figures were as public as Richard Jewell.

A 33-year-old security guard on duty in the park in the early morning hours of July 27, 1996, Jewell had discovered an abandoned knapsack containing a bomb and quickly moved people away minutes before it exploded. Two people died as a result of the bombing, and Jewell, a young man seeking a career in law enforcement, was hailed as a hero who had saved perhaps many more lives.

Three days later, in its Olympics special edition, the afternoon *Atlanta Journal* reported that Jewell was under surveillance and was the focus of the federal investigation into the bombing. Suddenly, the would-be hero, lauded for his ambitions, was painted in a dramatically different light. "Jewell ... fits the profile of the lone bomber," the *Journal* wrote. The story, which did not attribute the information to any source, was news to Jewell.

> Journalists, perceiving a frenzied public interest, continued on their own to dig up facts about Jewell. He lived with his mother, they reported. His apartment was tiny, they reported. He wore a baseball cap and was overweight, they reported.

That afternoon, a CNN anchor read the *Journal* story on air. Soon, CNN confirmed through its own unnamed sources that Jewell was a suspect. Wire services, network news operations and most newspapers picked up the story as the big news of the day. "Hero or villain?" questioned a *Boston Herald* headline. "Hero now bomb suspect," declared *USA Today*.

Dallas Morning News national editor Pam Maples told *American Journalism Review* that readers who had seen Jewell's story "all over TV" expected to read more about it in the morning paper. *Seattle Times* national editor Greg Rassa told *AJR*: "Won't we appear foolish for being the only medium in the country not to name Jewell?"

Other news outlets, such as *The New York Times*, played down the information, noting that Jewell had not been named on the record as a suspect.

For the next two months Richard Jewell was in the news almost daily. Law-enforcement officials, pressured to resolve the case, held frequent news conferences but were unable to pin anything substantive on Jewell. Journalists, perceiving a frenzied public interest, continued on their own to dig up facts about Jewell. He lived with his mother, they reported. His apartment was tiny, they reported. He wore a baseball cap and was overweight, they reported.

On October 26, the FBI exonerated Jewell, stating that, barring any new evidence, Jewell was no longer a target of the Olympic bombing investigation.

On October 28, Jewell spoke at a news conference. He said he had endured "88 days in hell" and said the news media "cared nothing for my feelings as a human being."

Under threat of a libel suit, NBC and CNN moved quickly to settle with Jewell before a claim was ever filed. The Atlanta *Journal-Constitution* stood by its coverage, maintaining it had done nothing wrong by merely reporting on various law-enforcement investigations and by reporting details about someone who was thrust into the spotlight by those investigations. On November 8, the newspaper said, "It was not illegal, immoral or unethical to publish the story about the FBI's investigation of Richard Jewell."

Testifying before the Senate Committee on the Judiciary Subcommitee on Terrorism, Technology and Government Information in December 1996, Steve Geimann, then president of the Society of Professional Journalists, said: "We, the media, blew it in July. Our coverage of the bombing and the search for a suspect was, in hindsight, excessive, overblown and unnecessarily intruded into the life of Mr. Jewell."

Analysis

Hindsight does offer us a different lens to view our actions, and it's not surprising that many journalists offered *mea culpas* when the Justice Department cleared Jewell. This case, however, offers us lessons far beyond what played out in Atlanta that summer of the Olympic Games. The lessons speak to how we honor the principles of truth-telling, independence and minimizing harm, and how news organizations can be more accountable in their professional duty.

Joann Byrd, who retired after a 47-year journalism career that included stints as editorial page editor of the *Seattle Post-Intelligencer,* ombudsman at *The Washington Post* and chair of the Ethics Committee of the American Society of Newspaper Editors, suggested that the main lesson journalists should have drawn from the Jewell case "is that law enforcement people may be wrong. This is only one of the recent cases where journalists went even further than law enforcement in our presumption that police suspicions were right."

Byrd said the media coverage would have been very different if "journalists had presumed from the start that the FBI's focus on Jewell was wrong. We would have pressed the FBI about other suspects every day. We would have gone to sources — including previous employers — who had good experiences with Jewell. We would have done our best to reconstruct his alibi, and to give attention to his lawyers and his mother and anyone else who would provide a different picture of him."

Byrd argued that journalists should not presume that law enforcement is wrong in such situations, but should recognize that the "law enforcement work is preliminary — more preliminary than all of our disclaimers made it sound this time."

The quest for truth in a high-profile, developing story requires journalists to be at their very best. In this case, too many journalists were overzealous in pursuing Jewell and exhuming his background. Too few journalists were aggressive in examining the law enforcement officials and investigating the strength of the case against Jewell.

It probably was inevitable that news reports at some point would tie Richard Jewell's name to the FBI investigation. He was already at the center of the case, given his role as a security guard at the scene of the bombing. It would have been difficult if not impossible to report merely that the investigation was focusing on a security guard. Some people would assume it was Jewell, given his central role in the incident. Some might point fingers at other Centennial Park security guards, causing harm to their reputations.

Keith Woods, former dean of the faculty at The Poynter Institute, said it was not improper to name Jewell as the man law enforcement was investigating. Woods said the ethical failures occurred in the choices journalists made *after* identifying Jewell as a suspect. Woods referred to "the placement of a story, the tone of the storyteller, the framing of the story. Declaring that Jewell 'fit the profile' of a bomber went beyond the media mandate. Describing him as all but a maladjusted mama's boy, as one print story did, is not what the First Amendment demands of journalists."

Indeed, the intense coverage of Jewell often painted him as a trapped man. Over and over networks played slow-motion video of Jewell walking away from his truck in the parking lot of his home. Over and over he was pictured at the center of a swarm of photographers and reporters. Over and over the story of the crash of his police car into another squad car during a previous job was retold. The tone of the video and the words in many of the stories often portrayed him as a loser at best, a killer at worst.

In writing about the case after Jewell was cleared by the Justice Department, Woods said "this new pseudo-psychology journalism that we have seen emerge in the past decade is anathema to informed, reasoned public discourse. It is sophisticated rumor-mongering. It encourages quick judgment and mob mentality. Worst of all, it happens every day in smaller, less dramatic ways, when the lives of 'suspects' are investigated and explicated by journalists single-mindedly seeking facts to validate the accusations.

"We gnash our teeth and wring our hands over Richard Jewell, but I worry about those many less-public people who are bitten each day by rabid watchdogs."

— from the Third Edition, Black Steele and Barney

POSTSCRIPT: Richard Jewell died in August 2007 at the age of 44. *The New York Times* reported he had serious medical problems, including diabetes. Eric Robert Rudolph confessed to the Centennial Park bombing in 2005.

CASE STUDY 40:

'Naming' a Dilemma

Summary

In July 1994, 7-year-old Megan Kanka of Hamilton Township, New Jersey, was kidnapped, raped and murdered, allegedly by a neighbor who, unbeknown to the community, was a twice-convicted sex offender.

Less than two weeks after her body was found, New Jersey lawmakers pushed through an emergency measure requiring police to notify communities when certain sex offenders move into a neighborhood. It was called Megan's Law, and it sparked a national drive, fueled by presidential politics, to pass a federal law bearing the same name and intent.

The case also renewed debate among news organizations trying to identify the line that separates their responsibility to the public and their responsibility to vulnerable individuals.

That debate came to focus on the case of E.B., an Englewood, New Jersey man who successfully petitioned a federal appeals court in 1996 to prevent authorities from carrying out Megan's Law, which requires police to notify neighbors, day care centers and schools whenever convicted sex offenders move into a community.

> The fact that E.B. was trying to derail a law of such national prominence and statewide popularity gave the story all the news value it needed to propel his real identity into the newspaper, Oswald said.

E.B. confessed to the 1969 rapes and gruesome murders of two Virginia boys, one of whom he buried alive. He admitted those crimes in 1976 while in prison and undergoing therapy after molesting three boys in New Jersey. He served his sentence and was released in 1989. He and his wife bought a house and lived in Englewood for more than six years without notice.

Then came Megan's Law and the lawsuit. And then came the Guardian Angels and their leader, Curtis Sliwa.

Unhappy and impatient with the legal processes preventing the wholesale dissemination of names and information, Sliwa's group printed fliers bearing the man's identity and declaring, "E.B., we know who you are." They handed out the fliers in the neighborhood where he lived. A political activist broadcast the man's name on Sliwa's radio show.

At the *North Jersey Herald & News*, a copy editor noted that a story about those events bore E.B's full name. "The copy editor said, 'We've got a story here with a name in it. Do we want to run this?' ," *Herald & News* editor Ian Shearn said. "That story was barreling right toward the press. We pulled it."

One news organization in the area confronted the ethical dilemma of choosing between public information and individual privacy. The involvement of community activists such as the Guardian Angels challenged the media to make independent decisions about identifying E.B. as public support of Megan's Law grew.

From the moment the lawsuit was filed, E.B.'s true identity was available and legally could have been printed and broadcast. It took little research to figure out he was the man who confessed to choking and raping a 14-year-old Petersburg, Virginia, boy and burying him alive, then stabbing a 13-year-old boy 21 times after raping him. The boys lived a block apart.

State Associated Press reporters tracked down the name quickly, and then had to decide what to do with it. They decided to withhold the name until the courts ruled. "We had the full range of discussion with good arguments on both sides," said Mark Mittelstadt, AP New Jersey bureau chief. "We tried to act responsibly without contributing to the problem. This was a tough one."

John Oswald, managing editor for *The Jersey Journal*, had no trouble figuring out his newspaper would become the first in the state to run E.B.'s real name. With a local peg for the story (the politician who named E.B. on the radio lived in the *Journal*'s coverage area), the newspaper's leadership came to a deadline decision. "It seems like a really basic point of information," Oswald said. "We run the names of shoplifters in [nearby] Bayonne. We're not going to run the name of a man who killed two kids — tortured and raped them? I don't see the point of that." E.B.'s decision to challenge Megan's Law in court made him a public person, Oswald said. The fact that E.B. was trying to derail a law of such national prominence and statewide popularity gave the story all the news value it needed to propel his real identity into the newspaper, Oswald said. "There weren't great hours of debate going on about it" at the *Journal*, he said, inasmuch as the issue first surfaced on deadline after a television station broadcast E.B.'s name. A small group of *Journal* editors debated the question "for about an hour," Oswald said.

By contrast the Bergen County *Record* convened more than 20 people — editors, reporters, even a former prosecutor now writing about legal affairs — in a meeting that Editor Glenn Ritt said "eventually turned into a seminar." The discussion lasted about three hours, Ritt said, and yielded a decision to wait until the courts had ruled before deciding whether to release E.B.'s name. "We didn't want to make an ad hoc policy that we would have to revisit the next time this kind of case came up," Ritt said.

The *Record* did have an opinion, though. In its editorial, "Why we're not naming E.B.," the newspaper said his crimes "were monstrous, and we believe the community has a right to know who he is. But we also believe that in a nation of law, the court should be given time to rule on the case."

For the news organizations involved, the case prompted great soul-searching and few clear answers. "I don't know if there's a right or wrong answer, only the one we came to," AP's Middelstadt said.

Analysis

Even the most difficult of ethical dilemmas *do* have right or wrong answers to them. That's the nature of ethics. But few cases have two clear choices.

To publish E.B.'s name strictly for competitive reasons would be ethically unsupportable, since it does not rely on a moral principle. To publish E.B.'s name by caving in to pressure from authorities also would be ethically questionable, since it violates the principle of independence. To make an immediate decision about publishing without considering one's professional duty or the significant consequences of the action is ethically indefensible.

At the same time, there are several possible *right* answers to this dilemma, although they may be grounded in different ethical principles.

Most of the newsroom decision-makers worried about the potential consequences of publishing E.B.'s name in such a charged environment, where the threat of violent vigilantism was thought to be high. They also worried about the swamp they might walk into by journalistically embracing the legislative and legal movement to get more and more information about crime and criminals out to the public. Those papers that held back on naming E.B. gave strongest weight to the principles of independence and minimizing harm.

Using a different principle, *The Jersey Journal*'s John Oswald saw his paper's responsibility as clear: to tell the truth and name E.B. Oswald found no reason to hold back, believing the public benefit of disclosure outweighed any potential of harm.

No matter how courts rule in this and similar cases, news organizations will continue to face similar tough calls when the public's right to know clashes with an individual's right to privacy.

"Where do you stop?" asked Shearn of the *Herald & News*. "Do you print the name and address? Do you print the model of the car? The license plate number? His picture? Do you tell people where he works? Where he drinks? And is the newspaper the venue to do that?"

The difficulty in answering such questions must not deter the effort to make good ethical decisions. News organizations can use the guiding principles of truth-telling, independence and minimizing harm as a moral compass in that decision-making process. And, once a decision has been reached, it is also morally appropriate to go public with your thought process, letting the readers know that the tough calls were not made capriciously. These principles help you recognize and resolve conflicting loyalties to different stakeholders.

Good decisions require some reflection and reasoning. We must not be trapped by our gut reactions when an ethical issue clearly strikes a strong emotional chord. A high-stakes issue deserves attention. To borrow from a time-honored warning: *Stop* your reaction; *look* at what you know and what you don't know; and *listen* to what others have to say.

Good ethical decisions are a product of collaborative decision-making, even on deadline. Different voices will raise legitimate concerns and potential alternative actions. A decision must be made. Make it a justifiable one.

— This case study originally was written by Keith Woods for The Poynter Institute website.

Privacy

What the Codes Say

San Jose Mercury News

The *Mercury News* is sensitive to the privacy of victims of rape and child molestation, and of subjects who clearly would be in physical danger by publication of their names and addresses. There may be circumstances in which we would nevertheless publish such names, but they must be approved by the Executive Editor or Managing Editor.

Ordinarily, consent is implied if a photographer approaches a subject, indicates that he/she is a newspaper photographer and asks for names and other facts. In some circumstances, written releases may be required (at mental-health institutions or orphanages, for example).

The Virginian-Pilot (Norfolk, Virginia)

CRIME REPORTING

- We identify criminal suspects only after arrest warrants have been issued, they have been arrested or they have been formally charged. When we write about people accused of wrongdoing, we provide them an opportunity to respond. That effort should include seeking comments from defense attorneys, family members and friends.

- As a rule, we do not name juvenile suspects. We do identify suspects 14 or older who are charged with committing crimes serious enough to warrant their prosecution as adults. We name suspects younger than 14 when the act is public, particularly brutal or of legitimate concern to the community.

- We use sparingly such phrases as "unavailable for comment'" or "could not be reached.'" We do so only after we have worked hard to reach suspects, their attorneys and others with a stake in the story.

- We report a suicide only when the incident occurred in public or involved a public figure.

- Using "allegedly" does not protect us from libel. Instead, cite multiple official sources, court records and testimony to make stories credible.

- Generally we try to name everyone involved in a crime serious enough to warrant a story. Names of victims or witnesses may be withheld if there's a legitimate concern for their safety. We do not name victims of sexual crimes unless they request it. Decisions to publish or withhold a name should be approved by a deputy managing editor.

- When we identify suspects, we use differentiating details, such as full name, middle initial, age, street and occupation. Providing these details helps ensure accuracy and prevents innocent people with the same name from being implicated.

- Reporting bomb threats and similar hoaxes may lead to "copycat" threats. We generally avoid reporting these, except when many lives are disrupted for extended periods or when the threat attracts considerable community attention.

- When a public safety incident involves a public figure, we should apply our usual standards for determining whether a story is warranted. Ask this question: Does the incident conflict with the person's public role? For example, we would write about a politician with a long record of opposing drugs who is arrested for cocaine use.

- When a public safety incident involves someone closely connected to a public figure, we should apply our usual standards for determining whether a story is warranted. Ask this question: Is the public figure involved in the incident? When in doubt, do not implicate the public figure. For example, a school principal's name probably would not be included in a story about a spouse's drug arrest.

The Associated Press

We do not generally identify those who say they have been sexually assaulted or pre-teenage children who are accused of crimes or who are witnesses to them, except in unusual circumstances. Nor do we transmit photos or video that identify such persons. An exception would occur when an adult victim publicly identifies him/herself.

Senior editors/managers must be consulted about exceptions.

Philadelphia Inquirer

Privacy. Many of the people mentioned in the news columns are public officials, who expect their activities to be the subject of scrutiny, or public figures, who often seek out publicity. However, private citizens who have not sought public notice are frequently surprised, and sometimes upset, when they are approached by reporters or find themselves written about. This is especially true in tragic situations. Staff members should approach stories with both a desire to inform the public and compassion for the individuals involved.

A private citizen who is thrust unwittingly and unwillingly into a public situation is likely to be unfamiliar with newsgathering practices. Staff members should clearly identify themselves when approaching such inexperienced people and treat them with courtesy.

Relatives of public officials and public figures are sometimes newsworthy solely because of their family position. Articles about such people should be handled thoughtfully and not be simply voyeuristic.

When it is decided that a person in a news story should not be named, such as a rape victim or a witness in possible danger, thought should be given to other information, such as home address, place of work or school attended, which might tend to identify the person.

A person's mental or physical infirmities, sexual orientation or the like generally should not be referred to unless relevant to the story.

12

Source-Reporter Relationships

Sources are the foundation of a journalist's success, developed and nurtured and often protected for the future. The reputation a reporter or newspaper or television station has for protecting sources who provide sensitive information is a part of the continuing dynamic of successful journalism.

At the same time, audiences and conventional wisdom expect sources to be fully identified as a way of assessing and assigning media credibility. Audiences generally have a right to detailed information held by reporters and editors. Only an argument of seeking a greater good, or trying to avoid grievous harm, can justify not identifying the sources of information.

Use of anonymous sources is a decision demanding careful consideration. When an editor decides to keep sources confidential, the editor should recognize that doing so places the reputation of the newspaper, station or website on the line, asking audiences to accept the information on faith.

Confidentiality is not the only ethical concern journalists face when dealing with sources. Indeed, the fundamental relationship between journalists and their sources has been subjected to moral scrutiny because it is, by nature, a "use and be used" relationship. Writer Janet Malcolm, in a two-part *New Yorker* series and a subsequent book titled *The Journalist and the Murderer*, wrote:

> Every journalist who is not too stupid or too full of himself to notice what is going on knows that what he does is morally indefensible. He is a kind of confidence man, preying on people's vanity, ignorance, or loneliness, gaining their trust and betraying them without remorse. ... On reading the article or book in question [the source] has to face the fact that the journalist — who seemed so friendly and sympathetic, so keen to understand him fully, so remarkably attuned to his vision of things — never had the slightest intention of collaborating with him on his story but always intended to

write a story of his own. The disparity between what seems to be the intention of an interview as it is taking place and what it actually turns out to have been in aid of always comes as a shock to the subject.*

Journalists by and large disagreed with Malcolm's strident point of view. Her charges did cause some healthy soul-searching within the industry, however. If nothing else, Malcolm caused journalists to recognize the tenuous nature of the reporter-source relationship. The bottom line is a warning to keep a professional distance or to behave so honorably during the interviewing and the writing that sources are not deceived.

Source/Reporter Relationships Checklist

- All else being equal, provide full identity of your news sources. The story is more credible, and future sources will recognize your basic ground rules. Generally, confidentiality should be granted only to protect someone who is relatively powerless or who is in a position to lose the capacity to continue as a solid source of information. In addition, the story should be of overriding public importance.
- Make sure sources understand the basic ground rules concerning on the record, off the record, not for attribution, etc. Make those conditions clear before you begin the conversation under those rules.
- Do not abuse naïve news sources, and don't be abused by sophisticated ones. Don't put words in their mouths, but at the same time don't let them dictate to you only the story they want to tell. You're a journalist, not a flack.
- Before promising confidentiality, try to obtain the same information from sources willing to be quoted.
- Do not permit "after the fact" requests for confidentiality.
- Don't let anonymous sources use the cloak of anonymity to attack other individuals or organizations.
- Make sure you understand your newsroom's policy on confidentiality before promising it to sources. You may need the consent of your editors, and/or you may have to share the source's identity with your supervisor. Professional burdens of trust must expand to include the reporter, editor and sources, always with an eye to the needs of the public.
- Once you promise confidentiality, keep your promise. Ask yourself how far you and your news organization are willing to go to keep that promise. Are you willing to tell your source that he/she and you are likely to be

---

* Source: Janet Malcolm, *The Journalist and the Murderer*. New York: Vintage Books, 1990, pp. 3–4.

subpoenaed in case of a libel or invasion of privacy suit? Are you willing to go to jail?

- Always bear in mind the power of the press when dealing with sources. You are in a position to cause harm or benefit. Use that power with great discretion. Do your sources know you are a reporter? Do you and they assume that everything they reveal is fair game for publication?

- Are you willing to spell out in your news stories the methods you used to gain information from sources and why you may be protecting confidentiality?

CASE STUDY 41:

A Self-Serving Leak

WHAT: *San Francisco Chronicle* reporters Mark Fainaru-Wada and Lance Williams were widely praised for their stories about sports figures involved with steroids. They turned their investigation into a very successful book, *Game of Shadows*. And they won the admiration of fellow journalists because they were willing to go to prison to protect the source who had leaked testimony to them from the grand jury investigating the BALCO sports and steroids scandal.

Their source, however, was not quite so noble. Attorney Troy Ellerman was using them. He leaked the information, then tried to get a major case against his clients dismissed on the grounds that grand jury information had been leaked.

> Different journalists will have different answers to the question of if it's ever permissible to break a promise to a source.

Ellerman, former commissioner of the Colorado-based Professional Rodeo Cowboys Association, represented two major figures in the BALCO investigation. He had sworn under oath that he was not the source of the leaks that were reported in the *Chronicle* beginning in late 2004.

But he kept quiet for two years after a federal judge ordered the two reporters jailed for refusing to identify their source for the leaked information. They never did go to jail because that condition was part of the plea deal that Ellerman agreed to when he finally admitted that he was the source — that he had allowed the two reporters to see transcripts of the grand jury testimony of San Francisco Giants slugger Barry Bonds and other high-profile figures in the case.

It was February 2007 when Ellerman finally admitted his role as the leaker, but Williams and Fainaru-Wada still declined to discuss the case.

Question: Should the two reporters have continued to protect this key source even after he admitted to lying? Should they have promised confidentiality in the first place?

WHO: The decision-makers in this case, the moral agents, are Mark Fainaru-Wada and Lance Williams, the two reporters and authors.

The editors who supervised them also have a moral role in this case and in the decisions that were made. That makes them and their newspaper, the *San Francisco Chronicle*, major stakeholders.

Of course, Bonds and the other star athletes who were implicated have a high investment in the consequences of this case. Ellerman's stake is especially high. Others who could be considered stakeholders include Major League Baseball; the U.S. Attorney's office in San Francisco, which for a time was thought to be the source of the leaks; the rodeo association for cowboys, which fired Ellerman as commissioner after this came to light, and which already had been facing complaints about the way it was run; Ellerman's other clients; and *Chronicle* readers.

WHY: The overriding principle here is a reporter's obligation to keep a promise — and a promise of confidentiality to a source has the legal effect of a contract, the U.S. Supreme Court has said.

On the other hand, a journalist's first obligation is to tell the truth, and concealing a source requires concealing part of the truth. Here, as in the Judith Miller case, where the former *New York Times* reporter was protecting a source who was manipulating her by giving her questionable information, the reporters knew the identity of someone who was breaking the law. They could have identified someone whose identity is a major news story. But they did not. Tim Rutten of the *Los Angeles Times* had this to say:

> To assert any form of journalistic privilege in a situation like that is something far worse than moral obtuseness. Conspiring with somebody you know is actively perverting the administration of justice to your mutual advantage is a betrayal of the public whose protection is the only basis on which journalistic privilege of any sort has a right to assert itself.

Others, though, continued to see the two reporters as First Amendment role models. After the federal court dropped its subpoena intended to force the reporters to reveal their source, Peter Scheer, executive director of the California First Amendment Coalition, told the Associated Press it was one of the best possible outcomes for journalism.

"Ultimately, the reporters did not have to go to jail and they did not have to compromise on ethics," Scheer said, "and that's a good thing. All the press can promise, and it's not a lot, is that we're not going to give you up."

HOW: Different journalists will have different answers to the question of if it's ever permissible to break a promise to a source. Most would say it's never all right. The public may be intensely curious to find out the name of the leaker, but let other reporters go to work on that.

Others, though, would say (in hindsight) that the problem is being too free with unconditional promises of anonymity. In fact, more and more mainstream media outlets are adopting strict rules about confidential sources; more and more are trying to discourage it. And some are saying also that reporters should warn sources that, depending on the situation, there may come a time when it's necessary to reconsider the promise, or to renegotiate it.

One of those times may be when it becomes apparent that a source has lied or has cynically attempted to manipulate a reporter. It's a lesson in why a compact of confidentiality should not be entered into casually. Promising to protect a source should be a last resort, not a way to break the conversational ice.

— SPJ Ethics Committee

CASE STUDY 42:

Crossing the Border

Summary

A Copley News Service reporter, S. Lynne Walker, and photographer Jeffrey Brown accompanied a 21-year-old Mexican immigrant from central Mexico to Chicago, a 3,500-mile, 13-day journey that included illegally crossing into the United States. Walker and Brown also witnessed Luis Muñoz purchase a fake green card in Los Angeles before hopping on a flight with him to Chicago.

The story ran as a 14-part series in Copley's flagship newspaper, *The San Diego Union-Tribune*, and was picked up on the wire by several other newspapers throughout the country. Copley-owned newspapers in Illinois, which initiated the series because of an influx of illegal immigrants in the Chicago area, published the account of Muñoz's journey in a special section called "A Journey to the Promised Land."

Readers raised questions about the ethics of reporting such a story. Some called for Walker and Brown to be prosecuted for aiding and abetting an illegal act. Others charged that Walker and Brown had glorified Muñoz and illegal immigration. Readers accused the newspaper of providing a blueprint for immigrants on how to cross the border illegally.

> "We never misled anybody," Walker said. "Our problem was convincing everyone that we were journalists."

Walker and Brown said they merely played the role of reporter-observer. They said they paid none of Muñoz's expenses during the trip and never aided and abetted him in a crime. Instead, they wanted to put a face on illegal immigration, to help people understand why anyone would undertake such a treacherous and dangerous journey.

"We knew there would be criticism," Walker said. "We wanted to give people an inside look at why people cross the border (illegally) every day, and why it's impossible to stop it."

The journey started in Muñoz's hometown north of Mexico City. Walker and Brown, a photographer with the Copley-owned Waukegan *News-Sun* in Illinois, rode a bus with Muñoz to Tijuana, then struck a deal with smugglers to sneak them across the border.

Walker and Brown said they told the smugglers they were journalists. The smugglers were skeptical, suspecting that Walker and Brown were American authorities, but eventually agreed to shepherd them across the border with Muñoz. The smugglers planned to charge Muñoz $450, while charging Walker and Brown half that amount because they were Americans.

"We never misled anybody," Walker said. "Our problem was convincing everyone that we were journalists."

Walker and Brown previously had discussed with Copley editors their plan to cross into the United States without passing through a legal port of entry — a misdemeanor offense. Walker and Brown said the story was compelling enough to warrant breaking the law.

"There was no other way to do the story," Walker said.

In a mountainous area east of Tijuana, Mexican authorities apprehended the smugglers, along with Muñoz, Walker and Brown, and drove them to jail.

Walker and Brown identified themselves as journalists. The Mexican authorities asked them to testify against the smugglers, but Walker and Brown refused, after calling the U.S. consulate in Tijuana. The Mexican police eventually released Walker, Brown and Muñoz, and they returned to Tijuana.

They found another smuggler who was successful in shuttling them across the border into San Diego, then on to north San Diego County where they were put in a safe house. Another smuggler drove them to Los Angeles.

After Muñoz purchased the fake documents, the three flew on to Chicago. There, Muñoz secured a job as a dishwasher, where he earned almost 10 times his salary in Mexico.

Brown was a finalist for the 1997 Pulitzer Prize in feature photography for his work chronicling the journey.

Analysis

Can you report accurately on someone with whom you have broken laws, whom you have watched violate a number of laws, with whom you have been arrested (and against whom you have refused to testify), and with whom you have shared a 3,500-mile journey?

This reporter and photographer said they could; the two parties remained largely independent of each other. They wrote a series to chronicle the odyssey and shed some light on the problems of illegal immigration in the United States.

Neither critics nor Pulitzer jurors seemed to think the shared experience affected the reporting. Critics concentrated on the lawbreaking and the message the stories sent to the world.

Clearly, the journalists tried to be nonintrusive flies on the wall to the Mexican immigrant's journey, but they were necessarily involved to the extent they were arrested with him in Mexico, committed the misdemeanor of illegal entry themselves and watched him violate numerous U.S. immigration laws. The journalists must be trusted on this, but it is difficult to see how the emotional bond of shared experiences would have affected the ultimate story. They did the immigrant no favors and probably will never see him again. The power of the immigrant, in short, is negligible.

Balancing those concrete actions are the abstract benefits of readers informed in detail about the experiences (and presumably the mindset) of one alien determined to find a better life for himself in a country whose laws do not welcome him.

The role of information is often underrated by critics of the media. At least some of the critics, however, recognized the power of the information to upset the status quo of immigration laws and practices (glorifying immigration and providing a blueprint for illegal immigrants.)

It is difficult to see how Muñoz himself affected the ultimate story of the journey, but the reporter's and photographer's presence through those 3,500 miles could not have helped but color the story, probably to its benefit. Presumably, experiencing the trip shaped the journalists' attitudes toward the system, toward immigrants and toward other elements they would have encountered.

Virtually any experience journalists have, however, will affect their outlook and influence their writing and photography. The question is whether the experience creates a bias that would result in an unrealistic image projected by the ultimate story.

These journalists, and their project, suggested they were looking to experience what illegal immigrants experienced and to project that experience as accurately as they could for readers.

The Pulitzer nomination suggested they were able to do that.

One who has a commitment to the distribution of information must conclude that the information gathered and distributed more than offsets in social value the damage done by law violations and observations of violations. Information is a critical commodity, and the test is whether the image created by the journalists in the aftermath of their journey was an accurate recounting of the experience of an immigrant.

Critics of the Copley News Service project would do well to consider the nature of the source-reporter relationship in this project and the potential benefits and costs of the project to the source, to U.S. immigration policies and to the readers. In addition, they should ask what makes any story compelling enough to break a law — and, if journalists do decide to break laws, what degree of accountability do they and their employers owe "the system"?

— from the Third Edition, Black, Steele and Barney

CASE STUDY 43:

Connie Chung and Newt's Mom

Summary

The veteran CBS news personality and host of "Eye-to-Eye with Connie Chung" was interviewing the parents of Newt Gingrich, perhaps the second most powerful politician in the world and soon to become speaker of the U.S. House of Representatives. In the course of the interview, which was conducted in December 1994 and aired the next month, Kathleen Gingrich let on that her son held no high regard for the wife of perhaps the most powerful politician in the world.

With cameras recording in the comfortable surroundings of the Gingrich home, and urging Kathleen Gingrich to disclose her son's private comments about Hillary Rodham Clinton, Chung said:

> Deception in the search for information may be more justifiable in the reporter-source war when the source is a seasoned veteran determined to hang on to the information being sought.

"Why don't you just whisper it to me, just between you and me?"

Mrs. Gingrich replied: "She's a bitch. About the only thing he ever said about her."

Hardly said in a whisper, the response spoke volumes — if not about the Gingrich-Clinton relationship, then about relationships between journalists and their sources.

Promoting the interview, CBS released the quote two days before the January 4, 1995, broadcast. Kathleen — and, by extension, Newt — Gingrich's words became front-page news in many papers and a top story on the evening network telecasts.

Newt Gingrich reacted swiftly and vociferously, implying that his mother — a star-struck innocent — had been victimized by an unethical reporter. He described Chung's question and the very act of asking it as "despicable."

"I think Connie Chung owes Mrs. Clinton an apology, and she owes my mother an apology," he said, adding that the question and the broadcast of the answer were ploys designed to drive up ratings.

Chung denied she had taken advantage of Kathleen Gingrich. She said Mrs. Gingrich was in a "playful mood" and "knew exactly what she was doing as three cameras were videotaping her."

In the flurry of media criticism that followed, there were few heroes to be found among the players in this case.

Chung was roundly criticized. "Connie Chung lied," wrote syndicated columnist Colman McCarthy. " 'Between you and me' ought to mean exactly that." Wrote Gina Lubrano, reader representative at *The San Diego Union-Tribune*, "In her duplicity, Chung displayed an appalling lack of ethics that should be of concern to all journalists."

CBS, too, was taken to task for exploiting — "marketing" — the quote, which was never explained in fuller context.

Others defended Chung and CBS for merely doing their jobs — reporting what was said — and for recognizing that, despite the way Chung set the ground rules for the question, Kathleen Gingrich's quote was newsworthy enough to transcend that agreement and to weather whatever storm of outrage resulted.

For his part, Newt Gingrich was able to make political hay out of the whole affair, attacking the media while defending his mother, while a vulgar comment involving his biggest political nemesis echoed around the country for weeks.

And even Kathleen Gingrich was held up to criticism for not maintaining her son's confidence. "I can't tell you what he said," she had playfully told Chung. And then, Kathleen Gingrich did just that.

Analysis

Chung's primary responsibility was to generate information for her audience. In this case, in a comfortable, homey, benign setting, she was teasing out from a source a bit of information about two of the most politically powerful people in the United States, the speaker of the U.S. House and the activist wife of the nation's president.

At the same time, deception is a corrosive, socially destructive device that victimizes the target by causing that person to believe something the deceiver herself does not believe. Such actions tear at a society's social fabric.

Deception in the search for information may be more justifiable in the reporter-source war when the source is a seasoned veteran determined to hang on to the information being sought. In such a case the contest between reporter and source may be a fairly equitable battle of wits with able opponents playing a well-established game. In-game deception is an honorable part of American gamesmanship — witness feints and fakes in football, basketball and baseball to throw opponents off balance.

Now, was Mrs. Gingrich the innocent Newt said she was (in which case one wonders why he let her into the cage with Chung in the first place), or was she a seasoned warrior engaging in the normal battle of wits between reporter and source? Different people will answer that question differently, and therein lies an emotional discussion with few objective answers.

Nevertheless, give CBS credit for allowing itself to be held accountable by leaving Chung's whispered assurance in the final presentation. Keep in mind the "just between you and me" phrase could have been edited out, and subsequent Gingrich outrage would have been merely speculative.

It is difficult to see the harm of the quote, except for an inevitable, immeasurable reduction in media credibility and a rise in suspicion among innocent sources who are confirmed in their notion that reporters are mad bombers lying in wait to lay waste to hard-earned reputations. Seasoned sources, on the other hand, are aware that deceptions — whether for good or ill — are always a stick of dynamite in the vigorous reporter's tool box as the reporter mines for elusive information.

— from the Third Edition, Black, Steele and Barney

CASE STUDY 44:

Deep Throat, and His Motive

WHAT: The Watergate story is considered perhaps American journalism's defining accomplishment. Two intrepid young reporters for *The Washington Post*, carefully verifying and expanding upon information given to them by sources they went to great lengths to protect, revealed brutally damaging information about one of the most powerful figures on Earth, the American president. They worked diligently on a story others were too indifferent, or too lazy, to pursue, and their reporting eventually forced Richard Nixon to resign, winning them a Pulitzer Prize as well.

The reporters, Bob Woodward and Carl Bernstein, became icons. After their stories broke in the mid-1970s, enrollment increased at journalism schools. They continue to be celebrated decades later for their integrity in never revealing the name of their principal source, "Deep Throat." It was not until that source broke his silence in 2005 that anyone knew "Deep Throat" was Mark Felt, a high-ranking official at the Federal Bureau of Investigation at the time he was talking to *The Post*. And, for some critics, that raised questions.

Question: Is protecting a source more important than revealing all the relevant information about a news story?

WHO: Woodward and Bernstein's promise to protect "Deep Throat's" identity was fully supported by their executive editor, Ben Bradlee. Together, the three are the major decision-making moral agents in this case.

It was a decision that ultimately affected many stakeholders, most notably Mark "Deep Throat" Felt himself, and of course Woodward and Bernstein, who had made a promise that journalists treat with the highest reverence. Nixon clearly was a stakeholder, as were others in his administration.

And in this case it also can be argued that the public had a higher stake than it does in many news stories because of the importance of the information revealed by a source who would not have revealed it had his identity not been kept secret.

WHY: Two major ethical principles are at issue in this very famous case. First is the journalistic credo that granting anonymity to a source is a vow that never should be broken. The other principle, at odds with the first, is that a journalist's primary duty is to reveal information, not conceal it, and often the source of that information is an important part of the story, suggesting a motive or agenda for the leak.

In this case, some critics have held that Felt, who died in late 2008 at age 95,

was manipulating *The Post* because he wanted to get even with the president for having passed him over for promotion to FBI director after the death of the legendary J. Edgar Hoover.

One analyst, George Friedman, wrote this for an intelligence and strategic consulting firm called stratfor.com: "This was not a lone whistle-blower being protected by a courageous news organization; rather, it was a news organization being used by the FBI against the president, and a news organization that knew perfectly well that it was being used against the president. Protecting Deep Throat concealed not only an individual, but also the story of the FBI's role in destroying Nixon."

HOW: Most journalists consider *The Washington Post*'s decision to protect Deep Throat an example of journalism at its finest. Working so hard for so long to keep the promise of anonymity allowed information to be revealed that was critically important to the survival of democracy and its need to correct its flaws. The role of a free press is to reveal those shortcomings, after which a responsive government can — or should — make the needed changes. In this case, the cover-up was perhaps more important than the crime itself because it uncovered flaws in the presidential character. Nixon's resignation became inevitable — a cathartic moment for the country.

And yet reporters must continue to be very careful about promising anonymity. In some settings — Washington, D.C., in particular — it's almost impossible to get anyone to talk without making such a promise. But in other areas of the country, where bureaucracy and politics are not so entrenched, news executives insist that promising anonymity should be used only as a last resort, not to break the ice at the beginning of an interview. The source of a leak sometimes is even more interesting than the leaked information because it may reveal a motive that is less than the epitome of integrity.

— Fred Brown, SPJ Ethics Committee

CASE STUDY 45:

Keeping a Promise to a Source

Summary

Political campaigns can be full of pitfalls for journalists caught between candidates under stress. In a case in Minnesota, editors of the *Minneapolis Star Tribune* and *St. Paul Pioneer Press Dispatch*, acting under traditional prerogatives, overrode a reporter's promise to a source and disclosed the source's name.

On condition he not be identified, the source, an employee of an ad agency working for the Republican lieutenant governor candidate in Minnesota, had given reporters embarrassing information about the other lieutenant governor candidate in the closing days of the campaign. The hot tip was that the candidate had been arrested nearly 20 years earlier on a shoplifting charge.

Believing the campaign tactic of disclosing information of questionable relevance was a bigger story than the long-ago shoplifting charge, editors at both the *Star Tribune* and the *Pioneer Press Dispatch* independently disclosed the source of the information.

> The key ethical question may lie in editors' motives.

The reporters' source was fired from the agency, took legal action against the newspapers and won a U.S. Supreme Court ruling in 1991 that promises of confidentiality may be legally enforceable under state law.

Despite the court decision, a question still exists about whether the newspaper may not morally justify disclosure of the source's name, despite the promise of its agent (the reporter), and despite legal rulings to the contrary. Editors generally have assumed that even though reporters' assurances to their sources are important, circumstances can justify an overriding of the reporters' judgment. The question of overriding legal consideration when making an ethical call is also important.

Analysis

A number of significant questions are raised in this case:

- Is it reasonable for a reporter to be able to assure a source of confidentiality and expect the news organization to support the promise?

- Should a reporter be required to consult with editors before offering source confidentiality?

- How important should a story be to risk discrediting the reporter and damaging the news organization's credibility?

- What kind of discussion should take place in the newsroom before a reporter's promise is violated? What weight should the reporter's input have in the discussion?
- Would other stakeholders, particularly the news audiences and the sources, feel the breaking of a promise was justifiable?

The ethical conflict in this case is between two virtues: (1) the right of the source to expect a promise to be kept and (2) the feeling of the editors that the audience needed the information about the source. Audiences' need for that information should be so great that damage done by the breaking of a reporter's (and, hence, the newspaper's) promise is acceptable.

The key ethical question may lie in editors' motives. If their intent was to inform readers about a campaign tactic they considered questionable, justification comes fairly easily. If, however, editors were even subconsciously trying to embarrass a candidate by trying to expose the candidate's agent, ethical justification becomes prohibitively difficult. Generally, any good that may come from embarrassing the candidate will be more than offset by damage to the newspaper's reputation among sources, and probably among readers. Violations of promises have a heavy burden to produce some greater good. In this case, that "good" would be a fully informed readership presumably better able to make a voting decision.

As in other ethics issues, editors are obliged to search their own minds for motives. In their social role, editors can most easily defend an action that places audience interest first and can be justified to the audience. Editors should acknowledge to their readers or listeners that publication of the source's name was not a matter taken lightly, recognizing that future coverage may be at risk because other sources will be reluctant to confide in reporters.

— from the Third Edition, Black, Steele and Barney

CASE STUDY 46:

To Love and Work in Denver

When reporter Lesley Dahlkemper and Mike Feeley, a state senator from a Denver suburb, started dating in the early 1990s, she gave up covering politics for Colorado Public Radio in favor of covering education, hoping to pre-empt potential conflicts of interest. But when Feeley decided in 1997 to run for governor, and the couple decided to marry, Dahlkemper — a widely respected eight-year veteran at KCFR — soon found herself out of a job.

That unpleasant resolution resulted after months of debate and hand-wringing at KCFR. Initially, Dahlkemper and station news director Kelley Griffin said the talk had been tentative and hypothetical. "For a year and a half, the subject was broached, batted around, but never seriously discussed," Dahlkemper said. Although discussions preceded Griffin's appointment as news director, "I would say the station didn't walk it all the way through," Griffin said. "We've never said, 'If you were this, then this.' I did find, in an old file folder, on yellowed paper, our ethics policy. It was actually

> The news director and her reporter still disagree over two key points: a possible distinction between a conflict of interest and the appearance of such conflict, and whether KCFR ultimately chose the best option when it lost a solid journalist.

pretty sound, but it had not been distributed for some time."

The situation escalated in May 1997 when Feeley officially announced he would explore a run for governor. The press release announcing that decision also mentioned he would marry Dahlkemper, whom the release identified as a Colorado Public Radio reporter, on May 25.

The once-blurry dividing line on the issue became clearer: Station managers believed Dahlkemper could not continue to cover the news without creating at least the appearance of conflict of interest; she did not believe her credibility could be compromised. "I had stated clearly that I would have no role in his campaign — which made his political consultants nuts," Dahlkemper said.

While seeking advice from media ethicists and researching examples of similar situations at other media outlets, Griffin sought to balance the station's desire to retain Dahlkemper while not appearing to compromise the news staff, which included three full-time reporters, two hosts, a news researcher and a news director.

"I started talking to people about what this would mean to the newsroom," Griffin said. "Nobody said it wouldn't matter at all. Some people would say she could cover some things — but would (her reporting) work covering some things and not others? And with our staff size, could we afford that?

"The political reporter already was ... talking to all the prospective candidates, and we felt we could easily be charged with favoring one candidate, or ignoring something to overcompensate, or saying something negative about another candidate."

While Dahlkemper was preparing to return to work after her wedding, the station considered alternative roles for her and granted her time off to consider reassignment. One idea was to establish an arts beat and put Dahlkemper on it. "We thought about adding it," Griffin said, "but again, one of the issues here is a tax for funding the arts."

The perception of a conflict of interest was a nagging issue that wouldn't go away. "There was this whole question of, 'What if the *Denver Post* ran a big story about (Feeley's) campaign? Why didn't Colorado Public Radio do that?" Griffin said.

And so "we determined we would create a position outside the newsroom for the duration of the campaign," Griffin said. The job may entail fund-raising, a music research project, producing prototype programs, "even doing some outside reporting for National Public Radio," Griffin said.

But Dahlkemper held fast to her conviction that "there was no direct conflict, no immediate impact," and resigned rather than accept reassignment, which she felt would have meant admitting that her professional credibility could be compromised by her marriage to a possible gubernatorial candidate.

"What became lost in the mix was the station's reputation and my track record for integrity," Dahlkemper said. She wanted the opportunity, at least, to prove her impartiality through her performance.

Two local newspaper columnists at least partly agreed with her after her resignation.

The *Denver Post*'s Fred Brown, then national president-elect of the Society of Professional Journalists and former chair of its ethics committee, wrote, "(P)erformance is more important than perception. And there is much more to behaving ethically than merely avoiding conflicts of interest. There's hard work, respect, objectivity, fairness, compassion, thoroughness, a healthy skepticism. Dahlkemper didn't lose those qualities when she became Mrs. Candidate."

Sue O'Brien, the *Post*'s editorial page editor, wrote in her column: "Why not see if common-sense guidelines could work? Share the problem with KCFR listeners — probably one of the most thoughtful and articulate groups of media consumers anywhere — and let them make their own judgments about spin."

The news director and her reporter still disagreed over two key points: a possible distinction between a conflict of interest and the appearance of such conflict, and whether KCFR ultimately chose the best option when it lost a solid journalist.

"Appearance can undermine your credibility," Griffin said. "We rely on public perception that we don't have anything more to do than to report the truth."

Said Dahlkemper, "I think the perception of conflict of interest became all-consuming."

Griffin: "Part of what we were trying to do, in doing things ethically, was to be sure we've built the proper walls the proper height. And if we removed her from the newsroom, that would show we had done what we could."

Dahlkemper: "The question remains, Can a reporter continue as a reporter if her spouse is elected to political office? I had hoped Colorado Public Radio would've broken new ground on this."

Colorado Public Radio has updated its ethics code since this episode, and every staffer is given a copy. Griffin said she also was considering that staffers sign a form consenting to the code.

"In creating the policy and talking about it, we created a climate where people understand that you have to tread lightly and you have to disclose," Griffin said. "It's the framework that reporters need to bring to everything. To have people think of it whenever the potential arises.

"In Lesley's case, the conflict was there even before the marriage, during her relationship with Mike Feeley. I don't think we looked hard enough at that."

— from the Third Edition, Black, Steele and Barney

Source Relationships

What the Codes Say

Many publications have adopted much more specific language in this area in recent years, especially as it pertains to policies on use of anonymous sources. Here are some examples, edited to eliminate repetitiveness.

The Associated Press

Transparency is critical to our credibility with the public and our subscribers. Whenever possible, we pursue information on the record. When a newsmaker insists on background or off-the-record ground rules, we must adhere to a strict set of guidelines, enforced by AP news managers.

Under AP's rules, material from anonymous sources may be used only if:

1. The material is information and not opinion or speculation, and is vital to the news report.
2. The information is not available except under the conditions of anonymity imposed by the source.
3. The source is reliable, and in a position to have accurate information.

Reporters who intend to use material from anonymous sources must get approval from their news manager before sending the story to the desk. The manager is responsible for vetting the material and making sure it meets AP guidelines. The manager must know the identity of the source, and is obligated, like the reporter, to keep the source's identity confidential. Only after they are assured that the source material has been vetted should editors allow it to be transmitted.

Reporters should proceed with interviews on the assumption they are on the record. If the source wants to set conditions, these should be negotiated at the start of the interview. At the end of the interview, the reporter should try once again to move some or all of the information back on the record.

Before agreeing to use anonymous source material, the reporter should ask how the source knows the information is accurate, ensuring that the source has direct knowledge. Reporters may not agree to a source's request that AP not pursue additional comment or information.

The AP routinely seeks and requires more than one source. Stories should be held while attempts are made to reach additional sources for confirmation or elaboration. In rare cases, one source will be sufficient — when material comes from an authoritative figure who provides information so detailed that there is no question of its accuracy.

We must explain in the story why the source requested anonymity. And, when it's relevant, we must describe the source's motive for disclosing the information. If the story hinges on documents, as opposed to interviews, the reporter must describe how the documents were obtained, at least to the extent possible.

The story also must provide attribution that establishes the source's credibility; simply quoting "a source" is not allowed. We should be as descriptive as possible: "according to top White House aides" or "a senior official in the British Foreign Office." The description of a source must never be altered without consulting the reporter.

We must not say that a person declined comment when he or she is already quoted anonymously. And we should not attribute information to anonymous sources when it is obvious or well known. We should just state the information as fact.

Stories that use anonymous sources must carry a reporter's byline. If a reporter other than the bylined staffer contributes anonymous material to a story, that reporter should be given credit as a contributor to the story.

And all complaints and questions about the authenticity or veracity of anonymous material — from inside or outside the AP — must be promptly brought to the news manager's attention.

Not everyone understands "off the record" or "on background" to mean the same things. Before any interview in which any degree of anonymity is expected, there should be a discussion in which the ground rules are set explicitly.

These are the AP's definitions:

On the record. The information can be used with no caveats, quoting the source by name.

Off the record. The information cannot be used for publication.

Background. The information can be published but only under conditions negotiated with the source. Generally, the sources do not want their names published but will agree to a description of their position. AP reporters should object vigorously when a source wants to brief a group of reporters on background and try to persuade the source to put the briefing on the record. These background briefings have become routine in many venues, especially with government officials.

Deep background. The information can be used but without attribution. The source does not want to be identified in any way, even on condition of anonymity.

In general, information obtained under any of these circumstances can be pursued with other sources to be placed on the record.

The Virginian-Pilot (Norfolk, Virginia)

Treat every source fairly and with respect. Always identify yourself as a journalist so sources know their comments could be published. For exceptions, talk to an editor.

Anonymity

Anonymous sources should be rare and reasoned. Editors have the right and duty to know the identity of unnamed sources before publication. If a source's identity cannot be revealed by a reporter to an editor, the information will not be published. Any exception must be approved by the publisher.

We will not permit an unnamed source to demean, attack or vilify a named person or institution unless the publisher expressly approves on the basis of carefully considered and compelling reasons.

GUIDING QUESTIONS

- Can someone else provide the information you're looking for?
- Can an on-the-record source confirm the anonymous source's information?
- Is the information crucial to public understanding of an important matter?
- Does the source have a legitimate reason for wanting to be shielded? Will identification put the source in physical danger or jeopardize his/her career or result in some other serious form of retribution?
- Have you skeptically analyzed the source's motives? Is the information merely a character attack?

- When we decide a source should be shielded, we must tell the reader as much as possible about the unnamed source short of revealing identity, including the reason for anonymity.
- We will avoid attributions like "key officials said" and "informed sources said." Instead, as an example, an unnamed source giving us information about a closed legislative meeting might be described as "a participant and a supporter of the bill."
- When you agree to shield a source, make sure he/she clearly understands the ground rules. For example, if the source is lying will you keep the promise of anonymity? Will you go to jail for the source? Will the source come forward if you or the newspaper is subpoenaed? What if the source later discloses the information publicly?
- If you make a promise to shield a source, you must keep it.
- We also want to avoid the use of anonymous people in routine stories. As a general rule, such attributions as "an onlooker said" do not belong in our newspaper. If someone refuses to be identified, don't use the quote. This

means interviewing more people, but the result will be a more believable story.

Pre-publication review

We encourage reporters to call sources to verify quotes or information. For accuracy's sake, you may read back passages of a story. However, we do not allow sources to approve stories for publication.

Radio Television Digital News Association

Identify sources whenever possible. Confidential sources should be used only when it is clearly in the public interest to gather or convey important information or when a person providing information might be harmed. Journalists should keep all commitments to protect a confidential source.

San Jose Mercury News

We will avoid the use of unnamed sources. We will make every attempt to get sources to speak on the record in every instance.

We will not allow the use of unnamed sources in the case of personal attacks and we will avoid letting them be the sole basis for any story.

In all cases, we will attempt to get independent, corroborating sources for every assertion in a story.

We will attribute information to unnamed sources only when news value warrants and it cannot be obtained any other way.

When a story arises where the reporter and editor together believe that the use of an unnamed source may be necessary, the following guidelines apply:
1. The editor and reporter need to ask each other: why does this person need to remain unnamed? There must be a thorough discussion between reporter and assigning editor of whether there is any other way to get the story and the ramifications of using the unnamed source, considering the option of not running the story at all if the source cannot be identified. We recognize that some people may be risking their livelihood by speaking out for a story and need to be protected.
2. If both reporter and editor agree that the use of an unnamed source is necessary, the source must be described in as much detail as possible to indicate the source's credibility. Simply attributing a comment to "a source" is inadequate.

    We should try to be as specific as possible. We should use the source's job title or general job description or say how they know the information if possible. We should use the word "person" or an equivalent rather than the word "source" in most cases; the word "source" is journalistic jargon and is vague. And we should be precise about the number of sources we have for any piece of information; saying "sources close to the investigation" when there is only one source is not acceptable.

Some examples of phrasing that works in describing an unnamed source: "a city employee" or "a person present at the meeting"' or "a university administrator" or "someone who has seen the affidavit."

3. While it is important to protect the identity of our unnamed sources, we should not mislead our readers in order to provide this protection. So we should not say that a key source "could not be reached for comment" if we reached them and had a not-for-attribution interview. Likewise, if an unnamed source in a story is quoted on the record elsewhere in the same story, we should not allow the source to use the on-the-record quote to make contradictory assertions or distort the facts.

4. The reporter must identify the source to his or her editor and the editor must ask for the identity of any unnamed source used in the story. Editors who learn the identity of the source will be bound by the same confidentiality agreement reached between the reporter and the source, and the source's identity will not be made known to anyone outside of the *Mercury News*.

5. In cases where the assigning editor judges the story to be of great importance, of a highly sensitive nature or has any questions about using the unnamed source, that editor needs to bring the story to a department head for discussion and approval. In all cases where a story is based largely on unnamed sources, the matter should be discussed with a department head. Department heads should discuss any sensitive issues with their supervisors.

6. Every story that includes an unnamed source must include a notation indicating that the use of the source has been discussed with an assigning editor (Sources OK - Luis). In cases where the use of the source has been brought to the attention of a department head, there should also be a notation indicating the department head's approval (Sources OK — Elisabeth).

Wire stories: Carefully consider whether to allow the use of unnamed sources in stories produced by other newspapers or wire services, particularly from Washington, D.C., where the practice is common. Since we cannot check the credibility of unnamed sources in wire stories the way we can with staff-produced stories, the following guidelines should apply:

1. Wire stories should be held up to as many of the standards required of staff-produced stories as possible. These include not allowing the use of unnamed sources in the case of personal attacks and using unnamed sources only when news warrants and it cannot be obtained any other way.

2. Whenever possible, consult any in-house experts who may be knowledgeable on the topic discussed by an unnamed source: does it ring true? Are any red flags raised?

3. Consider the source: is the news organization offering the story credible? Is the story on a topic on which that news organization would have expertise? You wouldn't expect *Sports Illustrated* to break a big story with unnamed sources on politics, for example.

4. Carefully examine how the story is written and any circumstantial evidence that would point to the story being true or not: does it all add up?

5. Spell out clearly in the wire story that the unnamed source is "an unnamed source in *The Washington Post*" so that readers are clear it is not a source of a reporter at the *Mercury News*.

6. In cases where there are significant conflicts between the attribution of information in the wire story and the *Mercury News* policy on unattributed sources, an effort should be made to contact the originating news agency for more information. This should be done especially when the information comes from another Knight Ridder newspaper.

7. Any doubts about the story, about questionable sourcing or insufficient attribution should be brought to the attention of an editor.

Philadelphia Inquirer

The *Inquirer* recognizes that readers are concerned about the use of unnamed sources for reasons including:

- That an unnamed source makes it difficult for them to judge the worth of the information.

- That anonymous sources may offer speculative or incorrect information, knowing they will not be held accountable for it.

These and other problems can contribute to the public distrust of newspapers. Thus, The *Inquirer* discourages the use of unnamed sources and wishes to confine them to occasional circumstances. Still, this needs to be balanced with the need to present vital information to the reader that cannot be obtained by other means.

The Denver Post

Pre-publication Review

Stories should not be shown to sources or people outside the newsroom prior to publication.

However, it is sometimes acceptable to allow a source to review portions of stories for purposes of accuracy. For example, an engineer might be sought to review a technically descriptive passage in an environmental story that details how sewer piping allows toxic chemicals to flow into public waters.

Such exceptions should be approved beforehand by the Managing Editor/News.

Personal Relationships

At its core, *The Denver Post*'s ethics policy attempts to eliminate conflicts of interest and even the appearance of conflicts of interest. The engine for that policy is honesty, full disclosure and willingness to discuss issues that arise.

The Post recognizes that staff members are held to a high standard, and it also recognizes that the same standard cannot govern the lives of spouses, loved ones, close friends or associates.

Some guidelines:

- Staff members should not write about, photograph, illustrate or make news judgments about family members, friends or close associates. Columns or a writer's story being told in the first person would be an obvious exception.

- Staff members should notify a department head about friendships or relationships that could be a conflict of interest. The intent is not to limit an employee's personal life but to resolve potential conflicts.

- When in doubt — and whenever situations arise — consult with a department head.

The Washington Post

The Washington Post is pledged to disclose the source of all information when at all possible. When we agree to protect a source's identity, that identity will not be made known to anyone outside the *Post*.

Before any information is accepted without full attribution, reporters must make every reasonable effort to get it on the record. If that is not possible, reporters should consider seeking the information elsewhere. If that in turn is not possible, reporters should request an on-the-record reason for concealing the source's identity and should include the reason in the story.

In any case, some kind of identification is almost always possible — by department or by position, for example — and should be reported.

No pseudonyms are to be used.

13

Being Accountable

Journalists are accountable to their readers, listeners, viewers and each other. That statement from the SPJ Code of Ethics seems innocuous enough. On its face it is perfectly logical. After all, why shouldn't journalists be accountable to their audiences and to each other?

The principle is reasonable, but its execution is problematic.

The code of the nation's largest organization of news professionals says journalists should:

- Clarify and explain news coverage and invite dialogue with the public over journalistic conduct.
- Encourage the public to voice grievances against the news media.
- Admit mistakes and correct them promptly.
- Expose unethical practices of journalists and the news media.
- Abide by the same high standards to which they hold others.

These are the standards and practices that fall under the code's accountability principle. They define the construct. They make clear that journalism does not exist in a self-interested vacuum but in an environment of reciprocity. They list the stakeholders, those who have the right to call journalists into account for meeting or falling short of their own and their audiences' expectations. They follow — but do not contradict — the code's principle of independence, suggesting that while seeking independence from the forces of corruption that journalists remain inexorably connected to others.

There's a problem, however. Based in part on the existence of a Constitutional amendment that says "Congress shall make no law," American journalism has a long history of cantankerous independence, a resistance to criticism from others and even from within its own ranks. The battles to sustain First Amendment freedoms are instructive. In general, they have resulted in the sense that government can hold journalists accountable for their behaviors — in matters of libel, privacy, copyright, obscenity and the like — only after the fact. Prior restraint is another matter altogether. Some journalists have taken this relationship with government to another, more problematic level, arguing that calls for accountability by members of the public and even by other journalists somehow violate the news media's First Amendment privileges.

For nearly three-quarters of a century, journalism organizations have struggled with ways to build accountability and/or enforcement into their codes of ethics. The Society of Professional Journalists is no exception. For a variety of reasons, it has never had an effective enforcement mechanism. Its present code, framed primarily by "ideal expectation" guiding principles and positive rather than minimalistic standards and practices, does not lend itself to rigid enforcement. It does, however, address the core issue of accountability by reminding journalists that they can and should be called to judgment by the public and by other professional journalists. (The code wisely avoids issues of accountability to government; after all, it is a code of ethics, not a body of law.)

If journalists decide to hold themselves accountable to the public and peers, what forms does that accountability take? The most obvious may be several journalism reviews (*American Journalism Review, Columbia Journalism Review, St. Louis Journalism Review*); journals put out by professional organizations (*Quill, IRE Journal, Nieman Reports, The American Editor, Masthead*, etc.); trade and academic publications (*News Photographer, Newspaper Research Journal, Media Studies Journal, Journal of Mass Media Ethics*, etc.). The struggling ombudsman movement (a few dozen of the nation's 1,500 daily newspapers) and the stagger-step press council movement come to mind. So do the op-ed pages, the talk shows and the media review sections of the daily press and, of course, the nation's hundreds of journalism schools, in which press criticism is flourishing.

All in all, however, the "calling journalists to judgment" business is of questionable impact on an industry more committed to independence than to accountability.

Going public with our decision-making processes is not always a panacea. Sometimes when audiences better understand why we did what we did, they empathize with our dilemma and lower their lances. On other occasions, our attempts at accountability merely confirm audiences' worst suspicions about how news is made.

It has been said that journalism is not thin-skinned, but that it has no skin at all. If the industry has a serious claim on professionalism, and if it seeks to build and sustain bonds with audiences, and if it hopes to retain independence from government control, it will do well to carefully address the notion of accountability. The fourth leg of the SPJ Code of Ethics acknowledges the importance of balancing accountability with the other three principles: seeking and reporting truth, minimizing harm and acting independently.

Celebrity Coverage: When Is It Time to Say Enough?

The death of Princess Diana in 1997 was a legitimate news story. After a while, the coverage got a bit overwrought, but the princess was more than just a celebrity. The murder trial of O.J. Simpson, starting much earlier with that bizarre slow-speed police chase, deserved coverage, too — probably not as much as it ended up getting, but he had been a star in football and film and had also been a role model.

Then came February 2007, with the death of Anna Nicole Smith and the antics of Britney Spears. The cable television news shows lost their moorings.

Maybe it was because it was February, when winter is old and gray and has worn out its welcome in the major media capitals, when the snow is spattered with grime and reporters are getting cabin fever. But is there really any excuse for serious, responsible media to devote so much attention to people who are famous mainly for being famous?

This pursuit of celebrity is a form of addiction. We know it's not good for us — or for our audiences — but we can't seem to help ourselves. We justify it by saying we're only giving readers what they crave.

Celebrity news: When is it time to say "enough"?

Consider the nature of your audience.

Cover only significant developments.

Look for substance and cultural context.

Sideline the publicity hounds.

Polls in fact show that the public thinks there's too much media attention paid to celebrities. But ratings, circulation figures and visits to websites suggest that the public, despite its protestations to pollsters, does indeed pay attention.

At some point, though, enough is enough. How do you tell when you've reached the saturation point? I asked my communication ethics students at the University of Denver what they thought and how they would structure a policy for handling celebrity news.

The first thing they mentioned was audience. It depends on the demographics of your readers and viewers. Obviously, *The Wall Street Journal* will have a different philosophy about celebrity news than will, say, the *New York Post* because of who their readers are.

Part of the analysis of audience, therefore, involves competition. The voracious appetite of 24/7 news channels seems to demand that all of them drop everything to cover the same dubious events. But was it really necessary for every one of them to broadcast every moment of the judicial determination of what to do with Anna Nicole's earthly remains? Judge Larry Seidlin was a sideshow who muscled his way into the spotlight. Critics suggested he was looking to become the next Judge Judy.

Responsible media should sideline the Seidlins of the world; do not give them the attention they seek so blatantly. Yes, they're hard to ignore. But don't give them more exposure than is absolutely necessary.

There's some hypocrisy in the way the "responsible" media managed to get these stories before the public; they did it while tsk-tsking at the way other media had gone overboard in their coverage.

One may argue that that approach has a certain validity; excessive coverage can be a news story itself. And it's legitimate to look for broader substance and cultural context in these fluffy stories. My University of Denver students thought it would be worthwhile to seek comments from experts in sociology and mental health about the implications of Britney Spears' decision to shave her head and seek late-night tattoos.

Other possible legitimate stories: What should parents tell their children about these bizarre personalities? Why do they command so much attention? Who are today's legitimate role models, if any?

Cover only the significant developments: The final disposition of Smith's remains; the determination of the paternity of her newborn. Perhaps short stories on Spears' repeated returns to rehabilitation are worthwhile for the moral lessons they may contain. The nature of "significant" should be a newsroom discussion.

Ethical decision-making involves, first, recognition of an ethical problem — and excessive celebrity coverage is a problem — and, second, thorough discussion of how to deal with the problem. Different organizations and individuals will have different answers and different policies. The important thing is to have something in place so you're ready to stand up for your principles and not be swept away in the tide.

— Fred Brown, SPJ Ethics Committee

CASE STUDY 47:

You Don't Know Jack

WHAT: In 2004, a prize-winning journalist at an extremely well-read publication resigned after allegations were brought against him that he fabricated several of his stories, including one that won him a Pulitzer Prize. Jack Kelley made up people who didn't exist, said he witnessed events that he actually never saw and put others' reputations on the line while doing so. *USA Today*, his employer of 21 years, nominated him for a Pulitzer Prize five times, and it was later determined that he fabricated at least part of a story that won him the honor.

When *USA Today* published its exposé on the situation, the newspaper reported that Kelley fabricated substantial portions of at least eight major stories, lifted nearly two dozen quotes or other material from competing publications, falsely represented what was happening in photographs he ran with his stories, lied in speeches he gave for the newspaper and conspired to mislead those investigating his work. The investigation later found that he had been fabricating stories since 1991.

Kelley quit in January 2004 after admitting to misleading those investigating his work, and a team was formed to investigate all of his stories because the

> Legal action would be another possibility for the paper to consider because the employee falsely represented the company by submitting stories he knew weren't true.

company feared he had plagiarized other pieces. The group reviewed 720 articles, each looked over by two members of the nine-member team. According to the *USA Today* article, Kelley lied about the following:

- Spending a night with Egyptian terrorists in 1997.
- Meeting a vigilante Jewish settler named Avi Shapiro in 2001.
- Watching a Pakistani student unfold a picture of the Sears Tower and say, "This one is mine," in 2001.
- Visiting a suspected terrorist crossing point on the Pakistan-Afghanistan border in 2002.
- Interviewing the daughter of an Iraqi general in 2003.
- Going on a high-speed hunt for Osama bin Laden in 2003.
- Observing the bomber in the 2001 story that won him a Pulitzer Prize.

Question: How does the newspaper rectify the situation?

WHO: The perpetrator: Jack Kelley, a Pulitzer Prize-winning author who had worked at *USA Today* for his entire 21-year career.

The decision-makers: *USA Today* publisher Craig Moon was ultimately responsible for what was published in his paper. The nine-member investigative team was headed by three former newspaper editors, including Bill Hilliard (ex-president of the American Society of Newspaper Editors), Bill Kovach (co-founder of the Committee of Concerned Journalists and former editor of the *Atlanta Journal-Constitution*) and John Seigenthaler (*USA Today*'s founding editorial director).

The stakeholders: the public who had read and respected Jack Kelley's stories for many years, the advertisers who trusted that they were investing in a reputable publication and, of course, Kelley himself.

WHY: Principles at issue include Kelley made up stories and then presented them to the public as factual news. Deception and dishonesty are just two of the terms that can describe his actions.

There were several issues to consider when *USA Today* discovered his deceit. First, what should the paper do with the offending reporter? Second, what kind of damage control do you conduct in a situation such as this? Third, what will be the effect on the public perception of the newspaper? Last, how do you go about preventing a similar situation in the future?

If you were *USA Today*, how would you go about handling this reporter's actions? Would you place him on probation while you investigated? How far into the investigation would you fire him? At what point would you let the public know of his indiscretions? Would you make a public apology? What would you say?

HOW: In a situation such as this, it is important to have an emergency communication plan in place to avoid public confusion. Only specified people should communicate with the public or media on the matter, and the employees of the company should be informed on the investigation. To keep credibility, it would be imperative for a comprehensive investigation with severe consequences for the reporter in question to be launched.

Legal action would be another possibility for the paper to consider because the employee falsely represented the company by submitting stories he knew weren't true. This would show the public that the newspaper prides itself on news values and takes any breach seriously.

DECISION: *USA Today* asked three journalists with impeccable credentials to head an investigative team that spent weeks reviewing Kelley's work. The three team leaders spent more than 20 hours interviewing Kelley. *USA Today* published the panel's findings in PDF form on the Internet and issued a public apology to its readers and the profession. Kelley was dismissed, and Hal Ritter, the managing editor of the news section, and Karen Jurgensen, editor, both resigned after the scandal.

— Laura Barth and Sara Stone, Baylor University

CASE STUDY 48:

The Times and Jayson Blair

WHAT: Jayson Blair advanced quickly during his tenure at *The New York Times*, where he was hired as a full-time staff writer after his internship there and others at *The Boston Globe* and *The Washington Post*. Even accusations of inaccuracy and a series of corrections to his reports on Washington, D.C.-area sniper attacks did not stop Blair from moving on to national coverage of the war in Iraq. But when suspicions arose over his reports on military families, an internal review found that he was fabricating material and communicating with editors from his Brooklyn apartment — or within *The Times* building — rather than from outside New York.

> The consequences of Blair's actions are so broad that it is important to have representatives from all staff levels, as well as journalists outside *The Times* staff, weigh in on corrective steps.

Some *Times* staffers, opposed to what they viewed as favoritism by Executive Editor Howell Raines, blamed a star system that allowed Blair to advance unusually fast in an extremely competitive, mostly veteran environment. Blair's former boss, Jonathan Landman, said race played a large part in the African-American writer's ascendancy.

The findings of a 25-member committee headed by Allan Siegal, an assistant managing editor, led to the appointment of a public editor and stricter editorial policies. But staffing changes and higher standards could not change what happened: *The Times*' reputation was deeply tarnished. Raines and Managing Editor Gerald Boyd resigned in a cloud of mismanagement. Journalism, in general, suffered perhaps the biggest blow to its credibility in U.S. history.

Question: How does *The Times* investigate problems and correct policies that allowed the Blair scandal to happen?

WHO: The consequences of Blair's actions are so broad that it is important to have representatives from all staff levels, as well as journalists outside *The Times* staff, weigh in on corrective steps. Leading this group should be one or several highly ethical consensus-builders who can solicit and synthesize ideas from throughout the profession.

In the case of *The Times*, stakeholders range from the humble retiree who simply reads his paper in the morning to the power-wielding diplomat who relies on foreign policy reports to inform her decisions. Journalists, too, lose ground when a colleague lowers the public's value of their work. As a group, the biggest stakeholders are citizens of democracies, which depend on journalists to grow trust in readers with accurate reporting.

WHY: The Blair case raises questions about hiring, management and overall editorial policy.

First, there is the issue of relative inexperience in a super-high-stakes newsroom. Is it fair to senior staffers to allow a fresh-out-of-college writer to step into the ranks? More important, is it fair to expect such an inexperienced writer, however talented, to produce reporting as sharp as that of a decorated correspondent? While a pure meritocracy allows an individual of any experience level to fill any role, talent in the absence of experience could lead to diminished professionalism: Blair's ability to impress editors with his writing may have led to him feeling that facts are less important than prose.

Second, there is the question of who is responsible for letting Blair go so far. Is it the editor who hired him straight from the University of Maryland? How about successive editors, who, despite their mediocre evaluations, did not object loudly enough to Blair's promotions? Could the executive and managing editors, with their big-picture roles and busy days, truly be responsible for one staffer's malfeasance?

Third, there must be a better way. Is it enough to know what went wrong and tighten the reins on practices such as anonymous sources? Or does *The Times* need an auditor, someone it pays for a scolding? Why should an outsider be allowed to make recommendations on better internal practices? Then again, how could an insider, in earshot of the mess itself, lead the committee to fix things?

HOW: *The Times* decided that to remedy the nasty ramifications of the Blair scandal, it would commission an insider, along with others inside and outside *The Times* newsroom, to investigate problems and suggest changes. The insider, Siegal, decided *The Times* should hire an outsider (who would be former *Life* magazine editor Daniel Okrent) to suggest further improvements. And *Times* editorial policy changed to reflect a much more cautious, conservative atmosphere concerning staff promotions and, especially, verification of reporting. A notable example of the latter aspect regards anonymous sources. In terms of staffing, *The Times* went so far as to require written evaluations for any candidates transferring between posts.

A particularly difficult aspect of the fallout, although one welcomed by staffers who felt marginalized, was the dual resignation of Raines and Boyd. That development, at least in the view of Publisher Arthur Sulzberger, was for the greater good of *The Times*. Symbolically, their departures made it possible for observers to view *The Times* as a reformed institution.

— *Adrian Uribarri, SPJ Ethics Committee*

CASE STUDY 49:

And the Winner Is ...

WHAT: The 2000 presidential election was riddled with controversy. Mistakes were made on both sides of the political spectrum, from indiscretions to straight-up unlawfulness. But the biggest offenders on Election Day itself were not the candidates, George W. Bush and Al Gore, or their supporters. The biggest offenders were the members of the media.

Before Election Day, the race was tight, with Bush in the lead in the state-by-state race and Gore an extremely close second. Every vote counted, at least in the "trifecta." That's what the three states were called that hung the election in the balance: Pennsylvania, Michigan and Florida. If the trailing Gore could win these three, he could take the lead and the Oval Office. But if Bush could retain even one of these states, the presidency was his.

Did the news media's early and erroneous release of the Bush v. Gore presidential race affect voters before the polls closed?

As time ticked on, it became clear that everything would come down to the Sunshine State. Gore decided to end his 18-month campaign in Florida, where Gov. Jeb Bush, brother of George W. Bush, was busy making calls to his fellow Republicans throughout the state. The stakes were unbelievably high, while the voting differentials were low. Numbers were close, and it became clear that the voters in Florida would decide the presidency.

At 7 p.m. Eastern Time on Election Day, the portion of Florida lying in the Eastern Time Zone closed its polls. The VNS, or Voter News Service, had gathered information in exit polls at precincts throughout the Eastern Time Zone and used it to arrive at its prediction that Al Gore had won Florida. The portion of the Florida population residing in the Central Time Zone still had another hour of voting. But VNS did not wait for those Central Time exit polls to close before submitting their projected winner to the TV networks. Their rush to get the information on air turned out to be a mistake that would cost the media a lot of credibility.

At 6:49 p.m. Central Time, the radio crackled the false message over the airwaves that Al Gore was the projected winner of the state of Florida. In the ensuing minutes, seconds even, other networks picked up this news flash and ran with it. And within the next 11 minutes, two-thirds of all voters in Florida's western panhandle heard about it.

Before the incorrect information could be retracted, the voting lines closed at 7 p.m. Central Time. People only had to arrive by 7 p.m. to be allowed to vote. They could wait in line for as long as it took. So the polls themselves wouldn't have closed until every person who arrived had been allowed to vote. But when last-minute voters on the way to their voting stations heard the news, their feeling of ineffectiveness was overwhelming. Many voters reported that they turned around and went home.

Some 187,000 registered voters in the Florida Central Time Zone didn't vote in the Bush v. Gore election. Perhaps a number of them chose not to vote out of pure disinterest. But many didn't vote due to the false "winner announcement" heard over the radio. A Yale University study estimates a loss of 10,000 votes for Bush due to the blunder. Another study, done by a Washington, D.C.-based firm, puts the loss at about 11,500 votes. It estimates that 28,050 voters were discouraged from voting due to the premature announcement and that 64 percent of those voters were planning on voting for Bush.

The VNS, as well as various news networks, later apologized for their enormous error. But hardly any of the network heads were willing to accept the terrible impact their mistake had made on the integrity of the presidential election. ABC News President David Westin said, "There was no point during the evening when it was likely or even possible that voters would decide not to vote simply because of the erroneous projection of the presidential race in Florida." Clearly Westin underestimated the power of the media because, as one dissuaded Florida voter put it, "You know, a lot of people take the news as gospel."

Question: Did the news media's early and erroneous release of the Bush v. Gore presidential race affect voters before the polls closed? And, on a larger scale, does the race to beat competitors affect the trustworthiness of news networks? Does the race to be first result in guesswork journalism?

WHO: NBC was the first network to announce the false report of Gore's Florida victory. What would you have done as a reporter for another news network? Would you have borrowed the story and run with it, even though you knew the Central Time polls wouldn't close for at least another 11 minutes?

Pretend you're a Florida voter on your way to the polls. Traffic is jammed, you're tired from a long day of work and the lines at the polls will undoubtedly be long. You hear over your car radio that Gore has already won Florida. Would you continue to the polls to cast your vote anyway? Or would you take the news for truth, turn your car around and head on home for dinner?

WHY: A similar situation occurred in the 1980 election in the race between Ronald Reagan and Jimmy Carter. President Carter's approval ratings had been so low that, come November, he didn't appear to stand a chance. When projections showed Reagan's incredible advantage, Carter chose to concede before many West Coast voters ever made it to the polls.

The erroneous VNS projections caused a similar effect in 2000. Many voters on the West Coast, operating on a later schedule than their fellow Americans in the East, voted, or opted not to vote, based on false information.

Thus, because of technology and our incredible ability to communicate over entire continents, the integrity of the presidential election has greatly suffered.

HOW: Why would the VNS report false information? Do you think the error was malicious? Or do you think it was simply a case of competitive journalism gone awry?

Think of ways that this situation could have been avoided. Possible examples may include better fact checking or a wider range of sources.

Also, consider large and small effects that the news media can have on individuals. How can you, as a journalist, work to avoid involvement in rapacious reporting? Does news need to be confirmed as 100 percent accurate before being reported?

Since the 2000 election, the news media have made strides to avoid repeating their blunder. They no longer will rely on the VNS. In fact, the VNS has disbanded. News networks now take their own polls, and they are much more careful about estimating races that are too close to call. But the news business is still a race against time. As CBS News Vice President Linda Mason said, "If we hit 270, if anybody gets to 270, we're certainly going to estimate the president."

ANALYSIS: The VNS made a big mistake by failing to include absentee voters and in relying on antiquated computer software programs to create inaccurate information. Complete accuracy is needed before information is presented to the public. And that's simply not the case here. News and truth must be synonymous.

In spite of tabloids, blogs and other non-reliable sources, people still look to the media for their news, their truth. As a practitioner of journalism, you have a duty to report the truth. Of course, you have a duty — not to mention a financial urgency — to report it in a timely manner. Old news doesn't sell papers. But if timeliness and the urge to beat out competitors come at the cost of telling the truth, it's not worth it. Your career can end over mistakes like that. Entire nations can be jeopardized with mistakes like that.

— Elizabeth Suggs and Sara Stone, Baylor University

CASE STUDY 50:

CIA Crack Contra-versy

Summary

The reprint of the *San Jose Mercury News* series "Dark Alliance" hit the desks of newspapers across America in the summer of 1996 with an unusual greeting from executive editor Jerry Ceppos. His letter began, "Dear Editor: At first I found the story too preposterous to take seriously."

Ceppos, it turned out, wasn't alone.

Several of the nation's largest newspapers criticized the *Mercury News'* three-part series, challenging its findings and questioning the motives and skills of its author, investigative reporter Gary Webb.

The series alleged that two Nicaraguan drug dealers with connections to the CIA-backed Contra army — along with a Los Angeles drug dealer — had "opened the first pipeline between Colombia's cocaine cartels and the black neighborhoods of Los Angeles, a city now known as the crack capital of the world." (The series called one of the Nicaraguans "the Johnny Appleseed of crack cocaine.") The drug dealers funneled "millions in drug profits" to the Contras, the newspaper reported, adding that the ring "helped spark a crack explosion in urban America." All this took place at the same time the guerrilla army was being funded and advised by the CIA, the series reported. The *Mercury News* never flatly asserted that the CIA was behind any drug dealing or was even aware of it.

In his letter to editors Ceppos wrote, "A drug ring virtually introduced crack cocaine in the United States and sent the profits of the drug sales to the U.S.-government supported Contras in Nicaragua. All the while, our government failed to stop the drug sales. ... In quiet, reasoned articles, Webb proved the case."

The *Los Angeles Times* didn't think so. Nor did *The Washington Post* and *The New York Times*, among other newspapers, which debunked the series. In October 1996, the *Mercury News* responded by publishing its own analysis of the series and its criticism. The lengthy piece was written by a reporter not connected to the original series.

Numerous issues surfaced regarding the series: the conduct of the reporter and editors, the role of the Internet and reaction from other media outlets.

Consider:

The series did not establish a firm link between the CIA and drugs. Yet a logo that ran on the *Mercury News'* website — and in the reprints — depicted a man smoking a crack pipe superimposed over the CIA seal. The logo did not appear in the newspaper. The logo was removed from the website only after a critical story appeared in *The Washington Post*. Ceppos told *American Journalism Review* that the logo was the newspaper's "main regret."

The stories ignited anger and outrage, particularly in the African-American community. At first, when the series received a muted response, many black leaders suggested that if these sorts of suspicions had been raised concerning any other community, there would be widespread calls for congressional investigations and demands for government action. "People in high places were winking and blinking, and our children were dying," said U.S. Rep. Maxine Waters, a Los Angeles Democrat.

According to *American Journalism Review*, Ceppos didn't read the entire series before it ran.

Critics of the series argued that the *Mercury News* had irresponsibly fanned suspicions about a government conspiracy to destroy black neighborhoods. Supporters, meanwhile, said that although some aspects of the newspaper series may have been hyped, the general thesis—that drug dealers associated with the Contras sold cocaine in South Central Los Angeles at about the time the crack explosion began—should not have been brushed aside.

> Two keys to judging this story lie in the motives and competency of both the reporter and the *Mercury News* editors.

The Washington Post, L.A. *Times* and *New York Times* led the charge in dismantling the series, though not all media reaction was unfavorable.

The L.A. *Times'* three-part condemnation of the series covered six and a half pages—more than the *Mercury News'* original pieces. In its 5,000-word attack, *The Washington Post* called the series "weak on evidence." *Post* ombudsman Geneva Overholser wrote that the *Mercury News* series was "seriously flawed ... reported by a seemingly hotheaded fellow willing to have people leap to conclusions his reporting couldn't back up." Overholser also called the *Post*'s attack a "case of misdirected zeal," however, and concluded that "the *Post* (and others) showed more passion for sniffing out the flaws in San Jose's answer than for sniffing out a better answer themselves."

After re-examining "Dark Alliance" with seven *Mercury News* reporters and editors, Ceppos acknowledged in a May 1997 column that the series had "shortcomings," was "oversimplified" and fell short of his journalistic standards.

"We fell short at every step of our process, in the writing, editing and production of our work," Ceppos wrote in the column, which appeared on the front page of the *Mercury News'* Sunday opinion section. "Several people here share that burden .... But ultimately, the responsibility was, and is, mine."

Ceppos wrote that the *Mercury News* presented only one interpretation of complicated, sometimes conflicting evidence; oversimplified the complex issue of how the crack epidemic in America grew; created impressions, through imprecise graphics and language, that were open to misinterpretation; and failed to label the amount of money involved in the drug ring as an estimate.

The reporter, Gary Webb, who was reassigned to a *Mercury News* bureau in Cupertino, California, and instructed not to report further on the case, stood by his story. In an interview with *The Washington Post*, Webb called Ceppos' column "very bizarre" and in some cases "misleading." He added: "I'm not happy about it at all. It's rather nauseating." Webb resigned from the *Mercury News* in December 1997 and took a state government job. His book, also titled *Dark Alliance*, was published in fall 1998. Unable to find another job in daily journalism, Webb committed suicide in December 2004.

Analysis

Two keys to judging this story lie in the motives and competency of both the reporter and the *Mercury News* editors. If Webb's purpose was to attract readers and draw attention to himself with only sketchily supported declarations, the story would be difficult to defend because a reporter's conviction that the truth is being told is a bedrock necessity of journalism. Similarly, then, the conviction must be supported by solid reporting.

Assuming his sincerity and some substantive competence, the arena in which Webb was operating is a particularly secretive one, meaning that an intense search for story information is only the first step in the truth-telling process. Others must come forward with their information once the first step is taken. If, after conducting serious, professional fact-gathering, Webb had a high level of confidence in his thesis about the drug explosion and its victims, his only course was to start the public discussion. If the story as far as he could take it had merit, it could attain a life of its own as more information was disclosed.

Webb certainly started the discussion, but its direction may be questioned. It would appear the media critics cited above looked more at his methods and information than at either confirming or discrediting the story per se. This could certainly raise the question of whether journalists are not sometimes more conditioned to protect icons — often their sources — than to provide information the public needs. While it is important to ask publicly whether the story was solid, the emphases of the critics suggest they were more intent on disciplining a rogue colleague than on seeking truth themselves. Nevertheless, journalists calling colleagues to account is a healthy practice.

Because of the secretive nature of both drug dealers and the Central Intelligence Agency and because the minority community portrayed as victims of the drug explosion sees itself as neglected by the media, the agenda raised by Webb has inherent value. Partial repudiation of its own story and reporting, however, suggests the *Mercury News* was not as persuaded as Webb that his information and conclusions were sound. It is interesting to note that the newspaper waited until external criticism reached a crescendo before conducting its own self-examination; a bit more front-end editing and soul searching probably would have been more productive than the post hoc scrambling Ceppos and others engaged in. That said, public accountability remains a valuable component of the entire journalistic enterprise.

As is often the case, perhaps the whole truth of the "Dark Alliance" will never be told. Yet the story ran, seeking to illuminate dark corners, and the reporter's own newspaper and other media called the account into question.

Some questions that could be asked in the production of this and related news stories:

What standards of fairness should apply to public discussion about government agencies? Does their power to control information about themselves (particularly the more secretive agencies, such as the CIA) require a different standard of fairness as we engage the public in an open discussion?

Is there any justification, such as marketing, for including elements in your promotional material that were not fully supported by the story itself (the CIA logo on the Web page and in reprints)? Should newsrooms and marketing departments be held to the same standards of truth-telling, fairness and accuracy?

How morally defensible is it to present a united front (the newspaper defending its reporter) against outside criticism when members of your own staff may agree with some of the critics?

What level of proof should a reporter have before drawing conclusions about such matters as a vague connection between the CIA and a drug explosion in a minority neighborhood?

What level of proof would justify inciting an African-American (or any other) neighborhood's anger against a government agency, as was done in this case? Can discussion born of public anger be considered healthy?

— from the Third Edition, Black, Barney and Steele
updated and revised by Elizabeth K. Hansen

Accountability

What the Codes Say

The New York Times

Corrections. Because our voice is loud and far-reaching, *The Times* recognizes an ethical responsibility to correct all its factual errors, large and small. The paper regrets every error, but it applauds the integrity of a writer who volunteers a correction of his or her own published story. Whatever the origin, though, any complaint should be relayed to a responsible supervising editor and investigated quickly. If a correction is warranted, fairness demands that it be published immediately. In case of reasonable doubt or disagreement about the facts, we can acknowledge that a statement was "imprecise" or "incomplete" even if we are not sure it was wrong.

Rebuttals. Few writers need to be reminded that we seek and publish a response from anyone criticized in our pages. But when the criticism is serious, we have a special obligation to describe the scope of the accusation and let the subject respond in detail. No subject should be taken by surprise when the paper appears, or feel that there was no chance to respond.

Radio Television Digital News Association

Professional electronic journalists should recognize that they are accountable for their actions to the public, the profession, and themselves.

Professional electronic journalists should:

- Actively encourage adherence to these standards by all journalists and their employers.
- Respond to public concerns. Investigate complaints and correct errors promptly and with as much prominence as the original report.
- Explain journalistic processes to the public, especially when practices spark questions or controversy.
- Recognize that professional electronic journalists are duty-bound to conduct themselves ethically.
- Refrain from ordering or encouraging courses of action that would force employees to commit an unethical act.
- Carefully listen to employees who raise ethical objections and create environments in which such objections and discussions are encouraged.
- Seek support for and provide opportunities to train employees in ethical decision-making.

San Jose Mercury News

Errors, whether made by the reporter, editor or source, shall be acknowledged. This includes all matters of fact, including the misspelling of proper names. When an error has been made, it shall be acknowledged in a straightforward correction, not disguised or glossed over in a follow-up story. Corrections and clarifications shall appear in a consistent location under the heading "Setting the Record Straight."

The Virginian-Pilot (Norfolk, Virginia)

We will publish our code of ethics on our website and Pilot's Intranet.

We will use a regular box on the editorial page or Public Editor's A2 box referring readers to the ethics policy on the website.

The editor or public editor will introduce to the public the Pilot's adoption of an updated code of ethics and professionalism. The editor or public editor also may write subsequent columns that revisit the code and give examples of how it was used.

Cyberjournalist.net

Be Accountable

Bloggers should:

- Admit mistakes and correct them promptly.
- Explain each weblog's mission and invite dialogue with the public over its content and the bloggers' conduct.
- Disclose conflicts of interest, affiliations, activities and personal agendas.
- Deny favored treatment to advertisers and special interests and resist their pressure to influence content. When exceptions are made, disclose them fully to readers.
- Be wary of sources offering information for favors. When accepting such information, disclose the favor.
- Expose unethical practices of other bloggers.
- Abide by the same high standards to which they hold others.

Public Broadcasting Service

Responsiveness to the Public

Producers must work with PBS to respond to and interact with the public. This may include providing an outlet for public feedback about content and helping to create material for the Web that allows audiences to learn more, seek background information, access documents alluded to in a program, answer questions that a program might not have been able to address, and even customize information.

Accountability is a goal, including answering audience questions and responding to criticisms about programs or content. When public feedback is published by PBS it should be labeled as such, and standards for publication — such as those relating to obscenity or personal attacks — should be clearly communicated.

Detroit Free Press
Acting with integrity

- We will act honorably and ethically in dealing with news sources, the public and our colleagues.
- We will obey the law.
- We will observe common standards of decency.
- We will take responsibility for our decisions and consider the possible consequences of our actions.
- We will be conscientious in observing these Principles.
- We will always try to do the right thing.

Blogging by Reporters

San Jose Mercury News

Generally, freelancing for online sites shall follow the guidelines for print. However, online is developing so rapidly and business alliances are so fluid, it is difficult to draw a definite line between what *Mercury News* staffers can and cannot do.

Because the "Friend or Foe" distinction is often blurred online, freelance decisions are best made on a case-by-case basis. For example, in most cases a cross-link can be established from a competing site to MercuryNews.com. ("Mark Schwanhausser covers Personal Finance for the *San Jose Mercury News*. For more of the *Mercury News*' award-winning business coverage, go to ...") The value in spreading the word about the paper may override the fact that the site competes with MercuryNews.com.

In general, staffers will need to notify a supervisor to freelance for online publications that compete directly with the *Mercury News* or Knight Ridder digital sites. When making "Yes or No" decisions, supervisors must take the marketplace into consideration. (For example, if a staffer is offered $1,000 to do freelance work for an online site and Mercury Center can only offer $100, the supervisor must take the disparity in pay into account.)

When freelancing online, the staffer, when appropriate, is to be identified with the *Mercury News*. Whenever possible, a cross-link between the site and MercuryNews.com will be established.

The Denver Post

All blogs on Denverpost.com or its related sites (i.e., PoliticsWest.com) must first be approved by a supervisor and by the Managing Editor/News or the Editor.

Nothing may be published under the *Denver Post* name, or on its Internet sites, unless it has gone through an editing and/or approval process. While blogs are more often written in an informal and personal style, everything that is posted to a blog must be factual and fair. Maliciously and inaccurately attacking private citizens or public officials is prohibited, and any criticism of public officials needs to meet the same standards of fairness as in print.

Blogging about people or institutions with which you have a personal relationship is a conflict of interest. The same standards you would adhere to in the paper apply to blogs.

A staff member of *The Denver Post* who publishes a blog on a website outside of the *Denver Post*'s control should first alert a supervisor or the Managing Editor/News. This requirement is similar to the freelancing guidelines in our ethics policy. A staff member should not write or blog for a site operated by a *Denver Post* competitor without approval of a supervisor and the Managing Editor/News. Any questions about what may constitute a competitor should be discussed with the Managing Editor/News or the Editor.

A staff member who writes a personal blog or who writes for a non-*Denver Post* Internet site should generally avoid writing about topics, institutions or organizations they cover for *The Denver Post*. This helps to prevent any confusion between professional and personal activities. No personal blog should imply the endorsement of *The Denver Post*, and no *Denver Post* photograph, video, text or audio may be used on a personal blog without permission from *The Denver Post*.

Staff members who post comments on Internet chat sites, Web pages or the blogs of others should use their names and avoid using pseudonyms. We do not publish stories anonymously in the paper, and we should not blog or post online anonymously.

Post reporters who are not columnists, and editors, should avoid posting opinions on blogs, chat sites or Web pages that would raise questions about their objectivity as a reporter or editor. Failure to observe this guideline could result in being removed from a beat, barred from reporting certain subjects or other disciplinary action.

Postings on outside blogs, whether they are your blog or another's, should be written in a temperate tone. They should not attack, humiliate or defame others. The line between a strong blogging "voice" and opinion is often a thin one that is not easily discerned by others. Staff members should also take great care in writing posts that might otherwise violate our ethics policy. Taking a strong position on a political issue, for instance, can raise the same questions of fairness and objectivity as marching in a political protest. When in doubt, consult a supervisor.

Referring to personal blogs and websites in the paper is forbidden unless authorized by the Managing Editor/News or Editor.

The private Web pages and blogs of staff members should be free of advertising or sponsorships from organizations or individuals who may fall into your area of coverage or expertise.

Staff members who blog should disclose any potential conflicts of interest due to memberships, affiliations or personal agendas, and resist pressure from any special interest that seeks favored treatment.

Bloggers should admit mistakes and correct them quickly.

APPENDIX

A

Ethics as a
Dynamic Dialogue

When the Society of Professional Journalists set out to revise its code of ethics in 1995, journalism was facing one of its many crises. Circulation and audience numbers were declining. Polls showed the public was losing confidence in the news media's accuracy and fairness, and that people felt the media were too negative. That hasn't changed, but the challenge has been exacerbated by the emergence of competition from new, smaller, more individualized media.

The new media, Web-based and more personal, provide a wealth of information, down to the most specialized of details. They allow the seeker of facts to conduct a precise search for rare and arcane subjects. They permit a provider of information virtually limitless opportunities to hold forth on any number of topics. Delivery systems — "platforms," some call them, or even (ugh) "mediums" (traditionalists have been brought up to think that mediums speak to the dead; media should endeavor to speak to the living) — are constantly evolving.

But even as the technologies change, the principles don't. A responsible journalist still owes the highest allegiance to being as reliably accurate as humanly possible. He or she should strive to be fair, even when delivering opinions, should be independent of undue or undisclosed influences, and must be accountable for what he or she puts forward for public consumption.

The 1996 revision of the code of ethics included new language intended to encourage more media responsiveness and awareness of how reporting can affect people's lives. Two of the four sections — Minimize Harm and Be Accountable — reflect this concern. The other two sections — Seek Truth and Report It, and Act Independently — are more in the traditional, assertive, unimpeded, influence-free ideal of a free press.

The first three principles are based on the Poynter Institute's teaching concept of media ethics. The 1995-96 SPJ ethics committee added Be Accountable as a sort of enforcement clause. Unlike licensed professions, such as law and medicine, journalism cannot impose sanctions or penalties on those who violate its principles. It must rely on disclosure, a free exchange of viewpoints on what some consider to be unethical behaviors.

This appendix, written by members of the SPJ Ethics Committee, is an effort to explain how the code of ethics relates to emerging trends in journalism. It is not possible to anticipate what specific ethical dilemmas may arise in a changing media environment. But it is possible to apply the code's general principles to a broad range of issues. For example:

Seeking truth: It's easier with the Web to find truths at the micro level, where many knowledgeable and prolific providers of information increasingly hold forth. But those "truths" may not be reliable until they have been aggregated and filtered, tested by other information also originating at the micro level. Everyone on the informational tree, from bloggers and sources up to top editors, needs to consider the advantages and perils of seeking truths online. E-mail interviews are convenient for journalists at all levels, and e-mail is a good way to check facts with sources. Weblogs are an effective way to gauge opinion, but journalists should be skeptical of accepting them as fact. Hyperlinking (online linking to other sources of information) helps in verifying sources and collecting and organizing data, a process akin to editing but more accurately (and recently) called aggregation; it's a new tool for seeking and reporting truth. Information, or raw data, is more available at the basic, micro level, often aggregated through crowdsourcing, or what amounts to an open call to the participating public to produce solutions to the problems presented.

Minimizing harm: The dangers of rumor, error, misleading emphasis and deceit are heightened when information flows so easily from online sources directly to the consumer. Although hyperlinking can give added depth to news reports, it also increases the risk of perpetuating others' errors. There are fewer filters or editors online and many amateur informational sources; we see a need and responsibility to acquaint bloggers and other nonprofessional informational sources with traditional journalism ethics.

Independence: By definition, there is more independence when "everybody is his own publisher." But the need for the independent blogger to make a living creates new temptations and alliances that challenge the traditional notions of the impartial journalist. And it increases the obligation to emphasize the balancing principle of accountability.

Accountability: It's a more important principle than ever in the world of digital journalism, and in fact hyperlinking, blogging and other new techniques facilitate accountability in ways that letters to the editor and other traditional forms of feedback and criticism couldn't hope to duplicate. Accountability is easier because there's less distance between the stately trees of mainstream journalism and their informational roots, which are now traceable. With more news sources and more potential for error, there's more of an obligation at all levels and in all media to hold each other accountable.

The ethics committee is one of SPJ's larger and most active committees. It is constantly discussing, e-mailing and blogging about ethical questions, and considering the application of ethical principles to a seemingly inexhaustible stream of new ethical issues. Members of the committee don't always agree on everything, as will be apparent from some of the subsequent entries in this appendix. But that's the nature of ethics — there are few, if any, hard and fast answers. The key is to ask the right questions. Readers of this book may join the discussion at www.ethicalreporting.com.

— Fred Brown and Peter Sussman, SPJ Ethics Committee

Seek Truth and Report It

Seek Truth and Report It is the first principle in SPJ's Code of Ethics, and comprises nearly half of the entire document. There is a good reason for that. Truth — or accuracy, which is easier to define and measure — is a journalist's No. 1 obligation. It makes no difference what medium is used to deliver the information. From the briefest of tweets to the longest magazine articles and fact-based books, responsible reporting is critical to a journalist's reputation, reliability and even competitiveness.

The introduction to the section on truth reads: *Journalists should be honest, fair and courageous in gathering, reporting and interpreting information.* Those three traits — honesty, fairness and courage — apply at all levels of reporting and to all media. Honesty includes dealing openly with sources as well as telling the story factually and fully, and fairness requires covering all relevant points of view on an issue. Courage means that while journalists should respect their sources, they should not be afraid of the people they report on.

The individual provisions of this section say that journalists should:

- *Test the accuracy of information from all sources and exercise care to avoid inadvertent error. Deliberate distortion is never permissible.*

- *Diligently seek out subjects of news stories to give them the opportunity to respond to allegations of wrongdoing.*

- *Identify sources whenever feasible. The public is entitled to as much information as possible on sources' reliability.*

- *Always question sources' motives before promising anonymity. Clarify conditions attached to any promise made in exchange for information. Keep promises.*

People may have different "truths" based on what they believe, but accuracy is a more tangible thing. Accuracy includes being precisely correct in quoting what people say about their beliefs, their take on the facts. A responsible journalist should be highly confident that the statements presented as fact are attributed, documented and accurate.

Double-check spellings of names; be sure of your identification of streets and neighborhoods. Unless an online aggregator is fully confident in the sources to which he or she links, there should be independent verification of facts. Accuracy is more important than journalistic independence. If you're uncertain you've got a fact right, you might e-mail your proposed phrasing of that bit of information to the source to see if you have understood it correctly. Remember that a single story rarely tells the full truth. New facts emerge over time, and stories may develop in new directions. Truth emerges from accurate reporting, and accurate reporting comes from journalists committed to these fundamental principles of fairness and accuracy.

- *Make certain that headlines, news teases and promotional material, photos, video, audio, graphics, sound bites and quotations do not misrepresent. They should not oversimplify or highlight incidents out of context.*
- *Never distort the context of news photos or video. Image enhancement for technical clarity is always permissible. Label montages and photo illustrations.*
- *Avoid misleading re-enactments or staged news events. If re-enactment is necessary to tell a story, label it.*

These are among the more specific provisions of the code, designed to address particular media. They apply, for instance, to "Photoshopping" images to make them appear more dramatic, adding or subtracting elements to make a bolder statement. Newsmagazines in particular have been criticized for altering images; SPJ has issued several statements denouncing the practice. The image-shifters usually apologize and promise to do better, but somehow the occasional "photo-illustration" continues to show up without proper labeling. Note that the guideline says *never* distort.

- *Avoid undercover or other surreptitious methods of gathering information except when traditional open methods will not yield information vital to the public. Use of such methods should be explained as part of the story.*

This principle is related to the first set. The use of anonymous sources is discouraged in more and more professional media, even in Washington, D.C., where anonymity has been almost a given in dealing with government officials. Ideally, though, anonymous sources should be used only as a last resort. And even then, the nature of the source should be clarified in some way that explains why anonymity was granted.

- *Never plagiarize.*

This is only the second principle in the code that uses the absolute "never." Some members of the committee that drafted the code felt "plagiarize" should have been defined. Others felt that journalists understood the meaning almost instinctively. It means that you shouldn't use someone else's words or images without giving the original author credit. It's something Internet providers of information need to be especially mindful of, because it's so easy to copy and paste. And sometimes the use of another's product is inadvertent — something seen while researching a story (formerly known as "reading the clips") stays in the mind, and the writer isn't fully aware of recalling and reusing a pithy phrase. So it's a good idea to recheck your sources to make sure your version isn't the same as theirs.

- *Tell the story of the diversity and magnitude of the human experience boldly, even when it is unpopular to do so.*

- *(Journalists should) Examine their own cultural values and avoid imposing those values on others.*
- *Avoid stereotyping by race, gender, age, religion, ethnicity, geography, sexual orientation, disability, physical appearance or social status.*
- *(Journalists should) Support the open exchange of views, even views they find repugnant.*
- *Give voice to the voiceless; official and unofficial sources of information can be equally valid.*

These, too, are related. Accurate, fair coverage may challenge traditional definitions of news to shine a light on new issues and groups of people who have been under-reported in the past. It requires keeping an open mind and avoiding stereotypes, bias and unverifiable allegations. Perhaps the best advice journalists can follow in living up to these principles is to seek out people who aren't like you. That includes using sources you may disagree with politically and personally. Be aware of your own prejudices and try to behave as a judge tells a jury to behave — make your judgments in the context of the information presented to you that is relevant to the case, or the story. Use your judgment, too, in deciding which points of view carry more weight than others. Your personal background is valuable and cannot, nor should it, be ignored. It may guide you in directions different from your colleagues. But that is a matter of a different perspective, one you can articulate energetically and factually while avoiding favoritism, self-interest or prejudice.

- *Distinguish between advocacy and news reporting. Analysis and commentary should be labeled and not misrepresent fact or context.*
- *Distinguish news from advertising and shun hybrids that blur the lines between the two.*

These are important principles for the new media in particular to keep in mind. There is increasing pressure in all media to be more analytical, to interpret instead of merely observe. But in analyzing and even editorializing, no matter what medium you're operating in, you must be accurate. As the late Senator Daniel Patrick Moynihan is credited with saying, you are entitled to your own opinion, but not your own facts.

The Internet also creates new opportunities for individuals to express themselves, and even to make money doing it. But there are potential pitfalls. There are producers of marketable wares who are willing to pay bloggers or other online content providers to review or merely mention their products. Traditional journalists would say this is unacceptable. Some newer journalists may say it's a legitimate way to make a living. At a minimum, such arrangements should be disclosed whenever a paid review appears. The reader is entitled to know about that potential conflict of interest.

- *Recognize a special obligation to ensure that the public's business is conducted in the open and that government records are open to inspection.*

Journalists should acquaint themselves with the federal Freedom of Information Act and with whatever open meetings and open records laws apply in the states, counties and municipalities that they cover. It's entirely justifiable to challenge government officials when they don't follow these laws; if you've done your homework you'll often find you know more about the laws than they do. Larger media organizations, of course, usually have their own attorneys to back up their reporters when conflicts arise. But even individual freelancers, bloggers and other journalists can consult the resources of organizations such as the Society of Professional Journalists, the Reporters Committee for Freedom of the Press or local press and broadcast associations.

— Fred Brown, SPJ Ethics Committee

Minimize Harm

An old saw says truth hurts. And Will Rogers said, "A remark generally hurts in proportion to its truth." So how do journalists reconcile an ethics code that encourages seeking and reporting truth and minimizing harm?

Compassion is the key.

The four sections of the Society of Professional Journalists Code of Ethics are the pillars of press freedom — Seek Truth and Report It, Minimize Harm, Act Independently, and Be Accountable. All are essential in a democratic and free society. But without compassion — minimizing harm — the pillars would crumble. Journalists are society's watchdogs — enlightening the public and exposing wrongdoing. Journalists may have sympathy for the public official caught taking bribes, but they cannot ignore the act. Journalists must consider the greater good. Exposing wrongdoing harms the offender but benefits society. When truth is sought and reported, overall harm is minimized. The SPJ code says:

- *Ethical journalists treat sources, subjects and colleagues as human beings deserving of respect.*

That introduction to the Minimize Harm segment of the SPJ code has roots in the Golden Rule — do unto others as you would have them do unto you — ancient ethics noted in the Bible and by philosophers of Greece, China, India and other early civilizations. Compassion is ancient. It's in our genes. But it's not automatic. And journalists more than others must consider the effects of the words and images they publish. Such consideration is especially significant today when technology sends information around the globe in seconds on the Internet. It's impossible in such electronic immediacy to call back harm. Thus, it's imperative to think before acting. The code says:

- *Show compassion for those who may be affected adversely by news coverage. Use special sensitivity when dealing with children and inexperienced sources or subjects.*

- *Be sensitive when seeking or using interviews or photographs of those affected by tragedy or grief.*

Journalists must recognize the difference between public figures and those who are thrust into the public eye because they are victims or witnesses. Politicians, entertainers and athletes are accustomed to being questioned and they know how to handle tough and aggressive questions. Parents grieving over a child killed in a traffic accident are usually not public figures. They are not accustomed to public scrutiny, and they warrant sensitive treatment. Such situations require compassion rather than aggression. Journalists must get the complete accident story, but they also must respect privacy and grief. A patient and compassionate journalist will find a way to get information and minimize harm. Often victims and victims' relatives want to tell their story. A mother wants everyone to know that the child killed in the accident was loved, intelligent, fun to be with, and special. Compassionate journalists will listen and let the parents talk. They don't push. Journalists should imagine themselves in the parents' or other victims' situations, and treat them as they themselves would wish to be treated.

Journalists can write words carefully and compassionately, minimizing harm. Pictures, however, can be raw and shocking. Images of tragedies often require tough journalistic decisions. Again the journalist must wrestle with truth vs. compassion. Shock effect is sometimes an argument for publishing gruesome images. Bodies sprawled across a traffic accident scene can be a vivid warning to motorists — drive sober and carefully. But such visuals are an emotional kick in the stomach to family and friends of the victims and to those who have lost family and friends in similar tragedies. Exclusivity or being first with a picture is sometimes an argument, although a weak one, for portraying violence and tragedy. Compassion has no deadline. And once harm is done, it can't be undone. Deadlines demand quick decisions, but thorough discussion and consideration are necessary before any sensitive material is published.

Journalists should weigh the public right to know vs. the individual right to privacy. Consider these factors:

- What does the public need to know?
- What harm may come to some?
- How can the full story be told compassionately?

The answers to those questions will come from weighing journalistic values (the ethics code) along with personal and social values.

- *Recognize that gathering and reporting information may cause harm or discomfort. Pursuit of the news is not a license for arrogance.*
- *Recognize that private people have a greater right to control information about themselves than do public officials and others who seek power, influence or attention. Only an overriding public need can justify intrusion into anyone's privacy.*

Public records are public property and thus available to anyone. The fact that information is public is not a license to publish, however. Consider, for example, police information. The public has a right to information in a police report, but reckless use of that information could harm individuals. Here's an example: A volunteer clerk in a hospital gift shop is the victim of an armed robbery. The robber loots the cash drawer, flees and is at large. Police records identify the clerk. Do you publish the clerk's name? Consider: Is the clerk's name essential to the story? Is there a danger to the clerk? She could identify a criminal who is at large. Not publishing the clerk's name, generally, would not diminish the story's value. The important elements concern the act — armed robber, cash taken, robber at large, a description of the robber, no one harmed, etc. The greater good may be served by not publishing the victim's name. The public is informed of the robbery and the victim is protected.

- *Show good taste. Avoid pandering to lurid curiosity.*

Consider the accident pictures mentioned above. Drivers always slow and gawk at accident scenes. It's natural curiosity. Today, when everyone with a cell phone can take still and video pictures, journalists have greater access to early scenes of tragedy. In fact, news media encourage such public participation in newsgathering. Those "citizen" pictures may be exclusive and there is a great temptation to publish them, but journalists must ask: Are pictures of bodies on the highway necessary to the story? Perhaps sensitive cropping of the scene to remove the bodies and sensitive text can tell the story effectively and with compassion. Sometimes, gruesome pictures have an afterlife, especially in broadcast. They can appear again as promotion for future newscasts. That's not compassion. And it's not news. It's arrogance, and it's indifference, and it damages and demeans not just victims or the public, but the institution of journalism itself.

- *Be cautious about identifying juvenile suspects or victims of sex crimes.*
- *Be judicious about naming criminal suspects before the formal filing of charges.*
- *Balance a criminal suspect's fair trial rights with the public's right to be informed.*

In most cases, the names of juvenile offenders are not made public so as to encourage rehabilitation. Reporters may obtain juvenile identities, however, through other than public sources. Again journalists must weigh the public's right to know against the harm publication of the name may cause. The possibility of rehabilitation could be diminished by the stigma of public identification.

In sex crimes, too, publishing victims' names could add to the stigma and mental anguish that the victims have already suffered. Some prominent journalists, though, have argued that withholding the name of sex crime victims perpetuates the stigma. They also hold that because the suspect is named, the accuser should also be named. And in some cases, the victim has asked to be identified. The big question again is: Is the name important? Is publication worth the risks of harm?

Also, consider the criminal suspect. Police do not always arrest the right person. A rush to publish the name of a suspect before formal charges are filed can needlessly damage a person. Rushing to publication can cause harm. And when a suspect is charged and faces trial, journalists must take special care not to publish material that would diminish the suspect's right to a fair trial or in any other way impede justice. For example, speculation regarding the suspect's guilt is fodder for further journalistic investigation, but not for undocumented publication. Similarly, publication of past criminal records not germane to current charges could harm a suspect's chance of a fair trial.

Journalists walk an ethics tightrope when seeking and reporting truth while trying to minimize harm. Minimizing harm is not easy. It takes good sense as well as courage and compassion. It's therefore important that ethical decisions not be made in haste. Consult. Discuss. Weigh values and consequences. Think. And then act compassionately.

— Paul LaRocque, SPJ Ethics Committee

Act Independently

The First Amendment guarantees press freedom. The Founders included the press because they were concerned about interference by government, or by one church, with freedom of expression. They had lived with such oppression and believed an independent press could monitor what the three branches of government were doing and report that news to the public. From this came the concept of the Fourth Estate, the idea that the press could act as a watchdog on government. Without a free and independent press a democratic government cannot work effectively.

For roughly the first hundred years of our Union the press was highly partisan. It often spoke for particular parties or interests and most newspapers reflected a political point of view. Following the Civil War the press began to publish stories that were less partisan and more "objective." One reason was the creation of cooperatives, like The Associated Press, to share news. If you needed to share stories with other papers, news slanted toward a different political view would not be used by partisan press outlets. Newspapers also figured out they could sell to more people, not just those who agreed with a political stance, if their news was more accurate and fairly reported. A more independent and neutral press evolved and became the dominant model in the 20th century. University journalism programs were created that began to teach this model. Eventually, the public came to generally expect journalists to report the news, as *New York Times* publisher, Adolph Ochs wrote, "without fear or favor." Most papers had a political slant on the editorial pages but the bulk of the news section was reported in a more balanced fashion.

U.S. news outlets in recent years have become more obviously partisan again, particularly bloggers and cable news channels. The concentration of ownership of U.S. news media has brought more attention to the independence of news. So have major corporations who pay for large public relations and advertising staffs to mold the message about their interests in the press. But surveys show most Americans still want a neutral and fair press. How do journalists work to achieve that goal? One essential element is independence. Good journalism, no matter the platform, is free of taint from special interests or commercial causes.

The average person has a hard time trusting a judge who received large campaign donations from a business about which the judge makes decisions. We are concerned when we discover that a doctor's research, which concludes that a company's drug is superior, has been funded by that company. We question when a politician's relatives just happen to get plum jobs in government. Most of us have a hard time finding a way to restore our trust in a spouse who has cheated on us.

Journalists are not different. What we have to offer is our own credibility. If we can't be trusted, why should the public rely on us to seek truth and report it? The SPJ Ethics Code deals directly with this issue. The introduction to the section titled "Act Independently" reads: *Journalists should be free of obligation to any interest other than the public's right to know.* It goes on to say that journalists should:

- *Avoid conflicts of interest, real or perceived.*

If a local political reporter also serves on the Democratic County Committee, the public has a right to question the credibility of the stories he or she writes. Even if the reporter is very cautious about fairness, the average person will and should question the quality of the reporting. How can you be considered fair if you have active allegiance to a particular point of view? Journalists are usually some of the most informed members of society and of course we have opinions. But we must be careful about letting those opinions bleed into our stories. This is one area where editors are particularly important. Good editors can and should filter out unfair or opinionated work by reporters. Much of what is online today has no professional editing and that leads to excessive rumor-mongering and false information. Individual reporters have the highest obligation to monitor themselves. They should take themselves off stories about which they have an interest or can't be fair.

- *Remain free of associations and activities that may compromise integrity or damage credibility.*

A reporter who belongs to an environmental group and reports on issues that group is for or against has an obvious conflict. This is true for all journalists who choose to become involved with a particular cause. The objective reporter should not join such organizations and continue to report news about whatever that group espouses. Individual journalists who are by the nature of their work clearly and openly advocates for a particular organization or point of view should make that clear in their reporting — and they must still be accurate and fair. Does this mean isolating yourself from the community around you? No, but overt support of anything — even worthy charities like food drives or coat drives or Race for the Cure — must be recognized as an erosion of cold, hard objectivity.

- *Refuse gifts, favors, fees, free travel and special treatment, and shun secondary employment, political involvement, public office and service in community organizations if they compromise journalistic integrity.*

Several years ago a major resort offered reporters from around the country a free trip to cover its grand opening. Many news organizations sent people on the trip. Do you suppose very much negative was said about the resort in the stories written about it? No, the bulk of the coverage was cream-puff, positive coverage about how wonderful the place was. The labor problems, the potential dangers of the rides, or the environmental impacts required to build the resort were not mentioned. That's human nature. We tend to be nice to people who are nice to us. But good journalism should be dispassionately fair and complete. Ignoring parts of a story, because sources are nice, or will hire our spouse, or make sure we get front row seats, is not acceptable. We should recuse ourselves from stories in which there is real or perceived conflict.

Some bloggers have been revealed recently to be writing reviews of products or service for which they have been paid by the producer of the product. Clearly, this is a conflict.

- *Disclose unavoidable conflicts.*

Occasionally, a journalist will end up having to cover a story in which he or she does have a conflict. This is particularly true in smaller towns where people often know each other and have business, church or other dealings together. It is the responsibility of each journalist to reveal these conflicts in the story. For example: A zoning story has become news and it must be covered. A note should be attached to the story: "The developer is the reporter's cousin." Or, in a story that erupts about a sponsor or foundation that gives grants to a station, "WXXX receives funding from YYY Corporation" should be appended to the story. Disclosure does not solve every problem. But it can help with maintaining the trust of the audience. If disclosure is embarrassing to you or your news operation, that should send a clear message that you are treading on shifting ground.

- *Be vigilant and courageous about holding those with power accountable.*

Journalists should always consider the whole story, including possible victims of a government or private action. Political or financial prominence does not give the person who wields it a pass. In fact, those with power have perhaps an even greater obligation to the public than those without. Their actions can make a real difference in others' lives. Journalists should attempt to find and report on the actions of those in power, whether it's the local football coach or the CEO of the biggest employer in town. This kind of reporting can bring criticism and sometimes intimidation to a news operation. But it's important for democracy, and the public has a right to know what the power structure in a community, state or nation is actually doing. It is essential if we are to be the "watchdogs" the First Amendment envisions.

- *Deny favored treatment to advertisers and special interests and resist their pressure to influence news coverage.*

It is common for an advertiser, who spends dollars with a newspaper, online website or broadcaster, to expect to be treated well by that organization. When bad news happens to advertisers they would, of course, prefer that it not be covered. But fraud allegations, the arrest of the owner or a requested controversial zoning change are news. Journalists should cover those stories just as they would any other story. Advertisers may threaten to cancel their ads. Sometimes they do, and that means less money for the news outlet to pay for reporters, editors or the overhead. Most news media in the U.S. are privately owned and reliant on ad dollars. So there's an obvious conflict.

For many years good journalism operations have erected a "wall" between the editorial content and sales. The sales staffs and the news staff have little or no interaction. The news side reports, the sales staff sells ads. This wall is very important. What does a journalism operation have to offer its audience? Accurate, well-reported stories that can be trusted by that audience. In a word: Credibility. If the news is tainted by favoritism to sponsors, political parties, unions or any special interests, we have little reason to continue using this kind of source. The short-term impulse to take the money and ignore or distort news is detrimental to the very concept of independence and undermines the business model that has served us well for so long.By the way, this model is also best for most advertisers. They want their ads to be placed where they will garner the most trust. Why would a sponsor wish to place lots of money with a news organization that can't be relied on to carry accurate and fair news coverage? It's not in their best interests either.

- *Be wary of sources offering information for favors or money; avoid bidding for news.*

"Let's make a deal." says the source to the reporter. "I'll tell you what I know if you...." Fill in the blank. Give me cash. Give me tickets to the ball game. Buy me a six-pack. Write good things about me. Criticize my competition. It's not rare for a source to make this sort of request. And American businesses often make such deals with each other. You scratch my back, I'll scratch yours. Money and favors distort the market place.

Paying sources for information calls into question the value of that information. Is the source talking only because he is being paid? SPJ has taken several TV networks to task for paying for travel or other costs to gain exclusive rights to sources. This prevents other journalists from asking independent questions and building a broader, more complete story. It also calls into question the veracity of what a paid source claims.

It has become common for celebrities and their press agents to demand questions in advance and to control the time and access reporters have to their star. They imply they are doing the reporter a favor by granting face time with their client. The real intention is to make sure no reporter goes "off the reservation" and asks questions that might embarrass the star.

These practices should be rejected by ethical journalists. Press independence is a core principle of good journalism enshrined in the First Amendment. Without accurate news our democracy cannot thrive.

— Jerry Dunklee, SPJ Ethics Committee

Be Accountable

Accountability is the bottom line in journalism today. News and information pours down like a storm, every minute, every second. Making sense of it has never been more important, and being answerable for it never more vital, or more difficult.

Technologically, journalism has gone light years in a short time. Think about it. Many journalists working today started their careers by writing stories on typewriters. Now there's a new digital world of 24/7 bloggers, tweeters, Facebook, MyPage, YouTube, social media, texting, sexting, crowd-sourcing, hyperlinking, mainstream outlets and more. Some of these sources did not even exist, or were still fairly new, when the Society of Professional Journalists Code of Ethics was adopted in 1996.

The Internet adds another layer to the complexity of journalism as it takes it place alongside traditional journalism — print, broadcasting and cable. It's not just a matter of new technology shaking journalism to its core. That's happened before; the news business keeps reinventing itself.

Old journalism and new journalism have this in common: To be effective, they must be credible and trusted. Accountability can make that happen, but it will be a struggle. Journalism not only is in an economic slump, it's in a credibility slump, too. In its annual report on the state of the news media, the Pew Project for Excellence in Journalism reported that in early 2009, only 8 percent of Americans told an NBC *Wall Street Journal* poll that they had a "great deal" of confidence in the national news media while 18 percent said they had "no confidence at all." That was similar to results in 2002.

Online journalism fared worse. The Pew report said that online news outlets "are viewed with more skepticism than their print, broadcast and cable counterparts. Of seven organizations evaluated, none is viewed as highly credible by even a quarter of online users able to rate them." The survey included *Google News, Yahoo News, AOL News, Drudge Report, Salon, Huffington Post* and *Slate.*

That is a dismal showing for an industry trying to gain public trust. Making matters worse, professional journalists have as low opinion of online journalism as does the public. At the 2009 SPJ convention in Indianapolis, a speaker said people monitoring the Internet said 80 percent of what they find is hateful crap. He added that it was more diatribe than dialogue.

Bloggers say they operate under an informal code of ethics that tolerates certain types of rumor and poorly sourced information, as long as it's clearly labeled as such. And if information proves to be bad or false, under this dictum, it must be removed or replaced as soon as possible in a prominent way.

In that way, say bloggers, the Internet is self-correcting to a far greater extent than mainstream media. It would not serve journalism, however, if the Internet became a shooting gallery of questionable information, followed by challenges, corrections or denials. All journalists, regardless of medium, should try getting it right the first time, a longtime goal in professional journalism.

Traditional journalists once called themselves "gatekeepers," people who decided what gets reported in newspapers or on the air. A writer for *Kosmos* magazine had this to say about the changing roles of journalists: "Journalists are no longer gatekeepers to the stories that matter, though many have been so busy guarding the gate that they have not noticed the fence is gone."

Even the names for journalism are changing. Some people call it journalism, others call it an online conversation, while others call it a news ecology. This backdrop of journalism in transition, and sometimes turmoil, brings us to accountability as one of the answers to paving the way to the future. By definition, accountability means being answerable or capable of being explained. Accountability makes it clear where you stand, and how credible you are. This battle, as always, is fought on two fronts. The public is a partner in news coverage. We ask the public to trust us every time we publish or broadcast a news report. We should trust the public to take a close look at what we do and how we do it.

The SPJ Code of Ethics clearly states that "*journalists are accountable to their readers, listeners, viewers and each other.*" Note the "are," not "should be," as in other introductory sections of the code. The code also says:

- *Clarify and explain news coverage and invite dialogue with the public over journalist conduct.*
- *Encourage the public to voice grievances against the news media.*

We're getting better at that. Newspapers, in particular, now regularly print corrections and clarifications, admitting mistakes and oversights. As simple as that sounds, it was a long time in coming and is relatively recent. Though journalists can dish it out, they are notoriously thin-skinned about criticism. Not so long ago, people who called the news desk with a complaint about the coverage — because they thought a story was inaccurate — were given a few minutes to state their case, then forgotten as soon as the conversation ended. Sometimes it was a polite conversation, sometimes not. Today, some news organizations have ombudsmen and public editors who spend their days listening to public complaints and doing something about them, rather than ignoring them. They question news staffs about accuracy and report their findings.

- *Admit mistakes and correct them promptly.*

Journalists have learned to be polite to their customers and take them seriously, and admit when they are wrong. That's the upside. Here's the downside:

Journalists often treat other journalists with great deference — one that could be described as see no evil, speak no evil and hear no evil. But in the interests of accountability, journalists should not tolerate bad journalism, or bad journalists. They should call attention to abuses in journalism. Being ethical means taking a stand. They should not tolerate dishonest, corrupt or unethical journalists. Journalists should not lie, cheat or steal in the pursuit of news.

- *Expose unethical practices of journalists and the news media.*

The code is intended to be voluntary, but freedom of the press and freedom of speech do not give journalists permission to act unprofessionally or like ill-mannered jerks. When journalists go over the line, other journalists — like those on the SPJ Ethics Committee — should call them to account for it. The committee regularly releases statements criticizing news organizations for unethical conduct. One statement condemned "checkbook journalism," paying for interviews or paying to transport people for exclusive coverage. Another involved hiring experts to comment on issues without disclosing that the experts have conflicts of interest because of ties to the industries involved in the story. Journalists have an obligation to make journalism a better place to work, leaving it better than they found it. As tough as that may be at a time of budget cuts and layoffs, the future of journalism must be considered.

- *(Journalists should) Abide by the same high standards to which they hold others.*

Some journalists say they don't want to be journalism ethics cops, that any criticism of other journalists is an infringement of the First Amendment. But journalists gladly hold everyone else to high standards — government officials, the medical and legal professions, among others. It's a double standard, and one that has cost journalism dearly in credibility. Accountability means being tough on ourselves, as well as others. Other professions, licensed professions, have ways of disciplining their unethical practitioners. But journalists do not have licenses, nor should they. Still, one of the ongoing debates in SPJ is whether to insist on adherence to the code. As one of the advocates of that view, I have held that a code of ethics that does not require action becomes mere words on paper. The debate shouldn't be considered closed. As journalism changes, the views of SPJ members on this issue may also have changed.

Journalism depends on what we do each day as reporters, writers, editors and management, not just by the work we do, but by the way we do it. Being an ethical journalist leaves a legacy that we create, for others to follow. That's accountability.

— *Casey Bukro, SPJ Ethics Committee*

B

The Code through the Years

Note: *Older versions of the Code contain original parenthetical material. It can be identified by standard parentheses (...). Newer material inserted during the editing of this book is surrounded by brackets [...].*

1926 version

(Editors' Note [original]: These Canons of Journalism were drawn up and adopted by The American Society of Newspaper Editors in their annual conventions of 1924 and 1925. The 1926 convention of Sigma Delta Chi, sitting at Madison, Wisconsin, in November, officially adopted the Canons in behalf of the fraternity.)

The primary function of newspapers is to communicate to the human race what its members do, feel and think. Journalism, therefore, demands of its practitioners the widest range of intelligence, of knowledge, and of experience, as well as natural and trained powers of observation and reasoning. To its opportunities as a chronicle are indissolubly linked its obligations as teacher and interpreter.

To the end of finding some means of edifying sound practice and just aspirations of American journalism, these canons are set forth:

I. Responsibility — The right of a newspaper to attract and hold readers is restricted by nothing but considerations of public welfare. The use a newspaper makes of the share of public attention it gains serves to determine its sense of responsibility, which it shares with every member of its staff. A journalist who uses his power for any selfish or otherwise unworthy purpose is faithless to a high trust.

II. Freedom of the Press — Freedom of the press is to be guarded as a vital right of mankind. It is the unquestionable right to discuss whatever is not explicitly forbidden by law, including the wisdom of any restrictive statute.

III. Independence — Freedom from all obligations except that of fidelity to the public interest is vital.

1. Promotion of any private interest contrary to the general welfare, for whatever reason, is not compatible with honest journalism. So-called news communications from private sources should not be published without notice of their source or else substantiation of their claims to value as news, both in form and substance.
2. Partisanship, in editorial comment which knowingly departs from the truth, does violence to the best spirit of American journalism; in the news columns it is subversive of a fundamental principle of the profession.

IV. Sincerity, Truthfulness, Accuracy — Good faith with the reader is the foundation of all journalism worth of the name.

1. By every consideration of good faith a newspaper is constrained to be truthful. It is not to be excused for lack of thoroughness or accuracy within its control or failure to obtain command of these essential qualities.
2. Headlines should be fully warranted by the contents of the articles which they surmount.

V. Impartiality — Sound practice makes clear distinction between news reports and expressions of opinion. News reports should be free from opinion or bias of any kind.

1. This rule does not apply to so-called special articles unmistakably devoted to advocacy, or characterized by a signature authorizing the writer's own conclusions and interpretation.

VI. Fair Play — A newspaper should not publish unofficial charges affecting reputation or moral character without opportunity given to the accused to be heard; right practice demands the giving of such opportunity in all cases of serious accusation outside judicial proceedings.

1. A newspaper should not invade private rights or feeling without sure warrant of public right as distinguished from public curiosity.
2. It is the privilege, as it is the duty, of a newspaper to make prompt and complete correction of its own serious mistakes of fact of opinion, whatever their origin.

VII. Decency — A newspaper cannot escape conviction of insincerity if while professing high moral purpose it supplies incentives to base conduct, such as are to be found in details of crime or vice, publication of which is not demonstrably for the general good. Lacking authority to enforce its canons, the journalism here represented can but express the hope that deliberate pandering to vicious instincts will encounter effective public disapproval or yield to the influence of a preponderant professional condemnation.

(Editors' Note [original]: The A.S.N.E. adopted the above Canons of Journalism at their 1924 convention, and their 1925 convention voted to add the following paragraph):

To its privileges under the freedom of American Institutions are inseparably joined its responsibilities for an intelligent fidelity to the Constitution of the United States.

1973 version

[First revision since 1926; adopted by the 1973 national convention of The Society of Professional Journalists, Sigma Delta Chi. References to "newspapers" are replaced by "media" or "mass media." Much of the language is similar to 1926; Casey Bukro of the Chicago Headline Club wrote this version.]

The Society of Professional Journalists, Sigma Delta Chi, believes the duty of journalists is to serve the truth.

We believe the agencies of mass communication are carriers of public discussion and information, acting on their Constitutional mandate and freedom to learn and report the facts.

We believe in public enlightenment as the forerunner of justice, and in our Constitutional role to seek the truth as part of the public's right to know the truth.

We believe those responsibilities carry obligations that require journalists to perform with intelligence, objectivity, accuracy and fairness.

To these ends, we declare acceptance of the standards of practice here set forth:

RESPONSIBILITY: The public's right to know of events of public importance and interest is the overriding mission of the mass media. The purpose of distributing news and enlightened opinion is to serve the general welfare. Journalists who use their professional status as representatives of the public for selfish or other unworthy motives violate a high trust.

FREEDOM OF THE PRESS: Freedom of the press is to be guarded as an inalienable right of people in a free society. It carries with it the freedom and the responsibility to discuss, question and challenge actions and utterances of our government and of our public and private institutions. Journalists uphold the right to speak unpopular opinions and the privilege to agree with the majority.

ETHICS: Journalists must be free of obligation to any interest other than the public's right to know the truth.
1. Gifts, favors, free travel, special treatment or privileges can compromise the integrity of journalists and their employers. Nothing of value should be accepted.

2. Secondary employment, political involvement, holding public office, and service in community organizations should be avoided if it compromises the integrity of journalists and their employers. Journalists and their employers should conduct their personal lives in a manner that protects them from conflict of interest, real or apparent. Their responsibilities to the public are paramount. That is the nature of their profession.

3. So-called news communications from private sources should not be published or broadcast without substantiation of their claims to news value.

4. Journalists will seek news that serves the public interest despite the obstacles. They will make constant efforts to assure that the public's business is conducted in public and that public records are open to public inspection.

5. Journalists acknowledge the newsman's ethic of protecting confidential sources of information.

ACCURACY AND OBJECTIVITY: Good faith with the public is the foundation of all worthy journalism.

1. Truth is our ultimate goal.

2. Objectivity in reporting the news is another goal, which serves as the mark of an experienced professional. It is a standard of performance toward which we strive. We honor those who achieve it.

3. There is no excuse for inaccuracies or lack of thoroughness.

4. Newspaper headlines should be fully warranted by the contents of the articles they accompany. Photographs and telecasts should give an accurate picture of an event and not highlight a minor incident of out context.

5. Sound practice makes clear distinction between news reports and expressions of opinion. News reports should be free of opinion or bias and represent all sides of an issue.

6. Partisanship in editorial comment that knowingly departs from the truth violates the spirit of American journalism.

7. Journalists recognize their responsibility for offering informed analysis, comment and editorial opinion on public events and issues. They accept the obligation to present such material by individuals whose competence, experience and judgment qualify them for it.

8. Special articles or presentations devoted to advocacy or the writer's own conclusions and interpretations should be labeled as such.

FAIR PLAY: Journalists at all times will show respect for the dignity, privacy, rights and well-being of people encountered in the course of gathering and presenting the news.

1. The news media should not communicate unofficial charges affecting reputation or moral character without giving the accused a chance to reply.

2. The news media must guard against invading a person's right to privacy.

3. The media should not pander to morbid curiosity about details of vice and crime.
4. It is the duty of news media to make prompt and complete correction of their errors.
5. Journalists should be accountable to the public for their reports, and the public should be encouraged to voice its grievances against the media. Open dialogue with our readers, viewers and listeners should be fostered.

PLEDGE: Journalists should actively censure and try to prevent violations of these standards, and they should encourage their observance by all newspeople. Adherence to this code of ethics is intended to preserve the bond of mutual trust and respect between American journalists and the American people.

1987 version

[Incorporates changes made in 1984 and 1987; they are indicated by italics. The pledge, in particular, is new and eliminates the admonition that journalists should "actively censure" breaches of the code.]

The SOCIETY of Professional Journalists, Sigma Delta Chi, believes the duty of journalists is to serve the truth.

We BELIEVE the agencies of mass communication are carriers of public discussion and information, acting on their Constitutional mandate and freedom to learn and report the facts.

We BELIEVE in public enlightenment as the forerunner of justice, and in our Constitutional role to seek the truth as part of the public's right to know the truth.

We BELIEVE those responsibilities carry obligations that require journalists to perform with intelligence, objectivity, accuracy and fairness.

To these ends, we declare acceptance of the standards of practice here set forth:

RESPONSIBILITY: The public's right to know of events of public importance and interest is the overriding mission of the mass media. The purpose of distributing news and enlightened opinion is to serve the general welfare. Journalists who use their professional status as representatives of the public for selfish or other unworthy motives violate a high trust.

FREEDOM OF THE PRESS: Freedom of the press is to be guarded as an inalienable right of people in a free society. It carries with it the freedom and the responsibility to discuss, question and challenge actions and utterances of our government and of our public and private institutions. Journalists uphold the right to speak unpopular opinions and the privilege to agree with the majority.

ETHICS: Journalists must be free of obligation to any interest other than the public's right to know the truth.

1. Gifts, favors, free travel, special treatment or privileges can compromise the integrity of journalists and their employers. Nothing of value should be accepted.
2. Secondary employment, political involvement, holding public office, and service in community organizations should be avoided if it compromises the integrity of journalists and their employers. Journalists and their employers should conduct their personal lives in a manner that protects them from conflict of interest, real or apparent. Their responsibilities to the public are paramount. That is the nature of their profession.
3. So-called news communications from private sources should not be published or broadcast without substantiation of their claims to news values.
4. Journalists will seek news that serves the public interest despite the obstacles. They will make constant efforts to assure that the public's business is conducted in public and that public records are open to public inspection.
5. Journalists acknowledge the newsman's ethic of protecting confidential sources of information.
6. *Plagiarism is dishonest and is unacceptable. [added in 1984]*

ACCURACY AND OBJECTIVITY: Good faith with the public is the foundation of all worthy journalism.
1. Truth is our ultimate goal.
2. Objectivity in reporting the news is another goal *which* serves as the mark of an experienced professional. It is a standard of performance toward which we strive. We honor those who achieve it.
3. There is no excuse for inaccuracies or lack of thoroughness.
4. Newspaper headlines should be fully warranted by the contents of the articles they accompany. Photographs and telecasts should give an accurate picture of an event and not highlight a minor incident of out context.
5. Sound practice makes clear distinction between news reports and expressions of opinion. News reports should be free of opinion or bias and represent all sides of an issue.
6. Partisanship in editorial comment that knowingly departs from the truth violates the spirit of American journalism.
7. Journalists recognize their responsibility for offering informed analysis, comment and editorial opinion on public events and issues. They accept the obligation to present such material by individuals whose competence, experience and judgment qualify them for it.
8. Special articles or presentations devoted to advocacy or the writer's own conclusions and interpretations should be labeled as such.

FAIR PLAY: Journalists at all times will show respect for the dignity, privacy, rights and well-being of people encountered in the course of gathering and presenting the news.

1. The news media should not communicate unofficial charges affecting reputation or moral character without giving the accused a chance to reply.
2. The news media must guard against invading a person's right to privacy.
3. The media should not pander to morbid curiosity about details of vice and crime.
4. It is the duty of news media to make prompt and complete correction of their errors.
5. Journalists should be accountable to the public for their reports, and the public should be encouraged to voice its grievances against the media. Open dialogue with our readers, viewers and listeners should be fostered.

PLEDGE: *Adherence to this code is intended to preserve the bond of mutual trust and respect between American journalists and the American people.*

The Society shall — by programs of education and other means — encourage individual journalists to adhere to these tenets, and shall encourage journalistic publications and broadcasters to recognize their responsibility to frame codes of ethics in concert with their employees to serve as guidelines in furthering these goals [amended in 1987].

1996 Version

For the current version, please see page 8 or visit http://www.spj.org/pdf/ethicscode.pdf.

Bibliography

Online Resources

Accuracy in Media (AIM)
http://www.aim.org/

American Journalism Review
http://www.ajr.org/

American Society of News Editors
http://asne.org/
ASNE links to other ethics codes: http://asne.org/key_initiatives/ethics/ethics_codes.aspx

Asian American Journalists Association
http://aaja.org/

Associated Press Managing Editors
http://www.apme.com/

Association for Education in Journalism and Mass Communications
http://www.aejmc.com/

Columbia Journalism Review
http://www.cjr.org/

Cyberjournalist.net
http://www.cyberjournalist.net/category/resources/ethics-and-credibility/

Ethics AdviceLine for Journalists
http://www.ethicsadvicelineforjournalists.org/

European journalism codes of ethics
http://ethicnet.uta.fi/

Fairness & Accuracy in Reporting (FAIR)
http://www.fair.org/index.php

Freedom Forum
http://www.freedomforum.org/

Investigative Reporters and Editors (IRE)
http://www.ire.org/

J-Lab: The Institute for Interactive Journalism
http://www.j-lab.org/

Knight Media Digital Center
http://www.knightdigitalmediacenter.org/

Minnesota News Council
http://news-council.org/

National Association of Black Journalists
http://www.nabj.org/

National Association of Hispanic Journalists
http://www.nahj.org/

National Institute for Computer Assisted Reporting
http://data.nicar.org/

National Press Photographers Association
http://www.nppa.org/

Newspaper Association of America
http://www.naa.org/

Online News Association
http://journalists.org/

Organization of News Ombudsmen
http://newsombudsmen.org/

Poynter Institute
http://www.poynter.org/

Quill magazine
http://www.spj.org/quill.asp

Radio Television Digital News Association
http://www.rtnda.org/

Reporters Committee for Freedom of the Press
http://www.rcfp.org/index.php

Society of Professional Journalists
http://www.spj.org/
SPJ Ethics Hotline: http://www.spj.org/ethicshotline.asp

Washington News Council
http://wanewscouncil.org/

Useful Books and References

Auletta, Ken, *Backstory: Inside the Business of News*, Penguin Group, 2003.

Bauerlein, Mark, *The Dumbest Generation: How the Digital Age Stupefies Young Americans and Jeopardizes Our Future (or Don't Trust Anyone Under 30)*, New York: Penguin Group [USA] Inc., 2008.

Bivins, Thomas H., *Mixed Media: Moral Distinctions in Advertising, Public Relations and Journalism*, Mahwah, N.J.: Lawrence Erlbaum Associates, 2004.

Black, Jay, *Mixed News*, Mahwah, NJ: L. Erlbaum Associates, 1997.

Black, Jay, and Bryant, Jennings, *Introduction to Media Communications, 4th ed.*, Madison: Brown & Benchmark, 1995.

Bok, Sissela, *Lying: Moral Choice in Public and Private Life*, New York: Vintage Books, 1999.

Brooks, Brian, and Missouri Group, *News Reporting and Writing*, 8th ed., Boston: Bedford/St. Martin's, 2005.

Bugeja, Michael, *Living Ethics across Media Platforms*, New York: Oxford University Press, 2007.

Christians, Clifford, Fackler, Mark, Brittain, Kathy McKee, Kreschel, Peggy J., and Woods, Robert H.., *Media Ethics: Cases and Moral Reasoning*, 8th ed., Reading, Mass.: Addison-Wesley, 2008.

Cooper, Stephen D., *Watching the Watchdog: Bloggers as the Fifth Estate*, Spokane: Marquette Books, 2006

Day, Louis A., *Ethics in Media Communications: Cases & Controversies*, 5th ed., Belmont, Calif.: Wadsworth Publishing Co., 2006.

Ess, Charles, *Digital Media Ethics*, Cambridge: Polity, 2009.

Foreman, Gene, *The Ethical Journalist: Making Responsible Decisions in the Pursuit of News*, Malden, Mass.: Wiley-Blackwell, 2010.

Friend, Cecilia, and Singer, Jane B., *Online Journalism Ethics: Traditions and Transitions*, Armonk, N.Y.: M.E. Sharpe, 2007.

Gordon, A. David, Kittross, John M., Reuss, Carol and Merrill, John C., *Controversies in Media Ethics*, 2d ed., White Plains, N.Y.: Longman, 1999.

Harcup, Tony, *Journalism: Principles & Practice*, 2nd ed., Los Angeles: SAGE publications, 2009.

Hirst, Martin, and Patching, Roger, *Journalism Ethics: Arguments and Cases*, 2nd edition, New York: Oxford University Press, 2007.

Journal of Mass Media Ethics, published quarterly by Routledge, Taylor & Francis Group, Philadelphia.

Knowlton, Steven R., *Moral Reasoning for Journalists: Cases and Commentary*, Westport, Conn.: Praeger Publishers, 1997.

Kovach, Bill, and Rosenstiel, Tom, *Warp Speed: America in the Age of the Mixed Media Culture*, Manassas, Va.: Century Press, 1999.

Kovach, Bill, and Rosenstiel, Tom, *The Elements of Journalism: What Newspeople Should Know and the Public Should Expect*, New York: Three Rivers Press, 2001.

Kovach, Bill, and Rosenstiel, Tom, *Blur: How to Know What's True in the Age of Information Overload*, New York: Bloomsbury USA, 2010.

Kurtz, Howard, *Reality Show: Inside the Last Great Television News War*, New York: Free Press, 2007.

Lester, Paul Martin, *Images that Injure: Pictorial Stereotypes in the Media*, Westport, Conn.: Praeger Publishers, 1996.

Malcolm, Janet, *The Journalist and the Murderer*, New York: Alfred A. Knopf, 1990.

McChesney, Robert W., *Rich Media, Poor Democracy: Communication Politics in Dubious Times*, New York: The New Press, 1999.

McGowan, William, *Coloring the News: How Crusading for Diversity Has Corrupted American Journalism*, San Francisco: Encounter Books, 2001.

Mencher, Melvin, *News Reporting and Writing*, 9th ed., Boston: McGraw-Hill, 2002.

Merrill, John C., *Journalism Ethics: Philosophical Foundations for Mass Media*, New York: Carol Publishing Group, 1997.

Meyer, Philip, *The Vanishing Newspaper: Saving Journalism in the Information Age*, Columbia: Mo.: University of Missouri Press, 2004.

Overholser, Geneva, and Jamieson, Kathleen Hall, *Institutions of American Democracy: The Press*, Oxford: Oxford University Press, 2005.

Patterson, Philip, and Wilkins, Lee, *Media Ethics: Issues and Cases*, 6th ed., New York: McGraw-Hill, 2008.

Plaisance, Patrick, *Media Ethics: Key Principles for Responsible Practice*, Los Angeles: SAGE publications, 2009.

Roberts, Gene, and Klibanoff, Hank, *The Race Beat: The Press, the Civil Rights Strugggle and the Awakening of a Nation*, New York: Alfred A. Knopf, 2006.

Seib, Philip, *The Al Jazeera Effect: How the New Global Media Are Reshaping World Politics*, Dulles, Va.: Potomac Press, 2008.

Ward, Stephen J. A., *The Invention of Journalism Ethics: The Path to Objectivity and Beyond*, Montreal: McGill-Queen's University Press, 2005.

Ward, Stephen J. A. and Wasserman, Herman, *Media Ethics Beyond Borders: A Global Perspective*, New York: Routledge, 2010.

Willis, Jim, *The Mind of a Journalist: How Reporters View Themselves, Their World and Their Craft*, Los Angeles: SAGE publications, 2010.

Index

Practical Books for Journalists

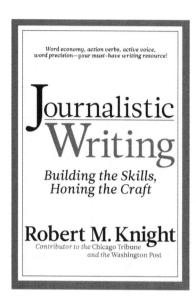
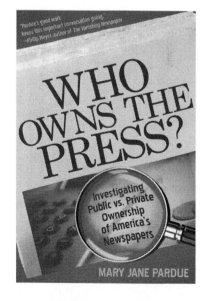